THE TUNNELS OF CU CHI

"A striking viewpoint of a neglected but crucial aspect of the war . . . Full of humanity . . . A wonderfully rounded history."

—*Publishers Weekly*

"Intriguing."

—*New York Post*

"An important contribution to the literature on the Vietnam War . . . an exciting story . . . required reading for anyone who wants to understand the American experience in Vietnam."

—*Kirkus Reviews*

"A claustrophobic but fascinating tale of a little-known campaign of the Vietnam War . . . This book is fraught with moments of heroism. The authors interviewed many of those who fought on both sides, and the individual stories convey fear and suspense."

—*The Wall Street Journal*

"Comprehensive, readable, and consistently absorbing . . . a fascinating full-scale profile."

—*Booklist*

THE TUNNELS OF CU CHI

A Harrowing Account of America's "Tunnel Rats" in the Underground Battlefields of Vietnam

Tom Mangold and John Penycate

PRESIDIO PRESS

BALLANTINE BOOKS • NEW YORK

2005 Presidio Press Mass Market Edition

Published in the United States by Presidio Press, an imprint of The Random House Publishing Group, a division of Random House, Inc., New York.

PRESIDIO PRESS and colophon are trademarks of Random House, Inc.

Originally published in hardcover in the United States by Random House, an imprint of The Random House Publishing Group, a division of Random House, Inc., in 1985.

ISBN 978-0-89141-869-6

Printed in the United States of America

www.presidiopress.com

ACKNOWLEDGMENTS

Our grateful thanks are owed to scores of people who have generously given their time, documents, and photographs, which contributed so much to this book. First and foremost are those in Vietnam and the United States whom we interviewed, and whose names and stories appear.

In addition, we wish to thank:

In Hanoi, Vo Dong Giang, Deputy Minister of Foreign Affairs of the Socialist Republic of Vietnam; in Ho Chi Minh City, Colonel Nguyen Phuong Nam of the People's Army; interpreters Tran Van Viet and Nguyen Chinh.

In Washington, D.C.: Robert Fink, whose brilliant and resourceful research uncovered people and records we were sure were untraceable; Bettie Sprigg of the Defense Information Directorate at the Pentagon; Wanda Radcliffe, of the Washington National Records Center; the staff of the U.S. Army Center for Military History; Catherine Morrison, for her kindness and help.

Elsewhere in the United States: Joyce Wiesner of the U.S. Army Records Center; the public affairs officers and librarians of the Command and General Staff College, Fort Leavenworth, Kansas; the Army War College, Carlisle Barracks, Pennsylvania; the Office of the Chief of Engineers, Fort Belvoir, Virginia; Schofield Barracks and Fort Shafter, Hawaii; Fort Riley, Kansas; Fort Carson, Colorado; and Fort McClellan, Alabama. We especially value the time given us by retired generals Fred C. Weyand, Ellis W. Williamson, William E. Depuy, Richard T. Knowles, and Harley J. Mooney.

In Sydney, researcher Chris Masters uncovered the role of the Australian army.

In Paris, the late Wilfred Burchett—one of the only English-speaking Westerners to spend time with the Viet Cong during the war—was generous with his advice and written material; he died in September 1983.

In London, we were appreciative of the help of Sir Robert Thompson KCB CMG DSO MC, former adviser to the government of South Vietnam; and of Colonel Robert Scott

L/RAMC, Professor of Military Surgery at the Royal Army Medical College. The diplomats at the Embassy of Vietnam in London (and its delegation to the United Nations in New York) were unfailingly helpful. So, too, were fellow journalists and Southeast Asia specialists William Shawcross and Chris Mullin.

We owe a special debt to our Vietnamese translator in England, Van Minh Tran; and to the loyal typist of the manuscript, Heather Laughton. The book's very existence results from the professional skills and dedication of our literary agent, Jacqueline Korn of David Higham Associates; and our editors, Robert Loomis of Random House, and Ion Trewin of Hodder & Stoughton. Christopher Capron, former Head of Current Affairs Programmes at BBC Television, kindly allowed this book to be written, and gave it his encouragement.

T.C.M.
J.V.G.P.

For Sarah, Abigail, Jessica, and Lucian—
and all those still young enough to learn.

T.C.M.

For Eve,

J.V.G.P.

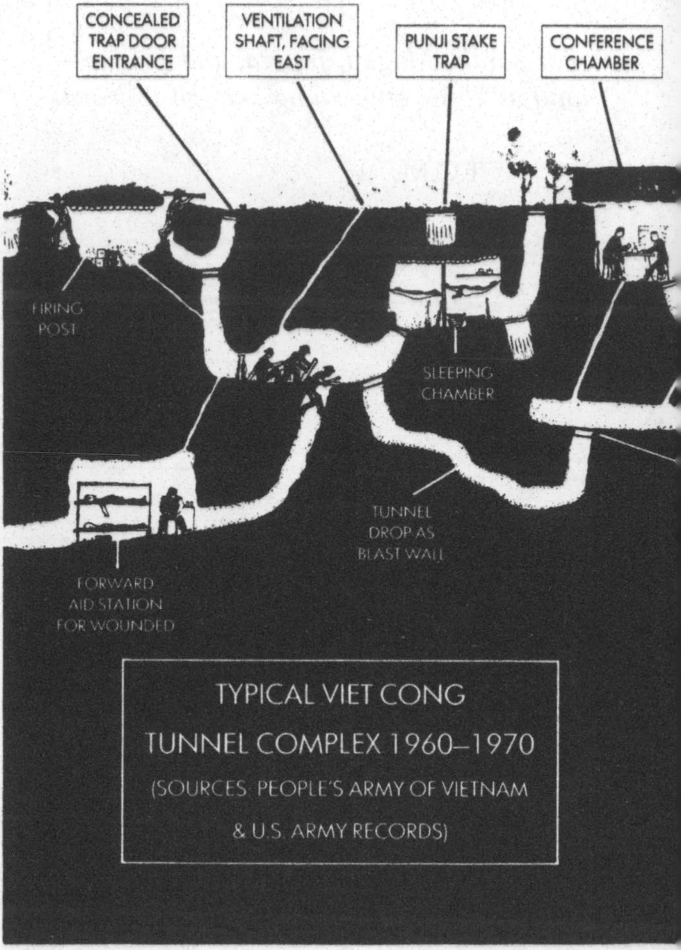
CONCEALED TRAP DOOR ENTRANCE
VENTILATION SHAFT, FACING EAST
PUNJI STAKE TRAP
CONFERENCE CHAMBER
FIRING POST
SLEEPING CHAMBER
TUNNEL DROP AS BLAST WALL
FORWARD AID STATION FOR WOUNDED
TYPICAL VIET CONG
TUNNEL COMPLEX 1960–1970
(SOURCES: PEOPLE'S ARMY OF VIETNAM
& U.S. ARMY RECORDS)

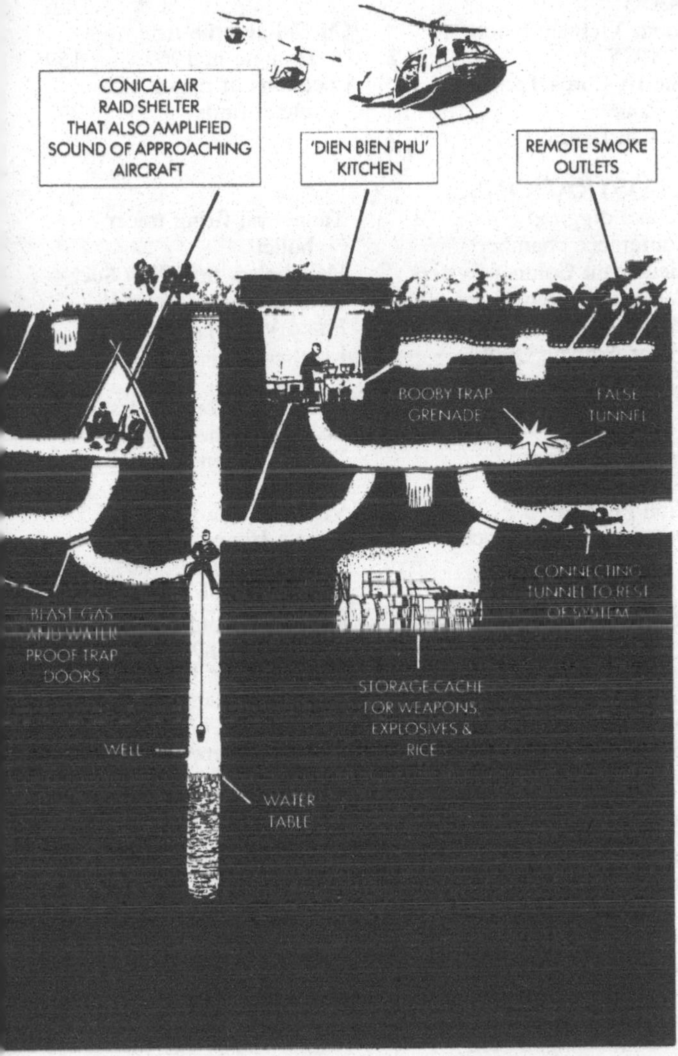

CONICAL AIR RAID SHELTER THAT ALSO AMPLIFIED SOUND OF APPROACHING AIRCRAFT
'DIEN BIEN PHU' KITCHEN
REMOTE SMOKE OUTLETS
BOOBY TRAP GRENADE
FALSE TUNNEL
CONNECTING TUNNEL TO REST OF SYSTEM
BLAST GAS AND WATER PROOF TRAP DOORS
STORAGE CACHE FOR WEAPONS, EXPLOSIVES & RICE
WELL
WATER TABLE

MAPS AND ILLUSTRATIONS

MAPS:

ILLUSTRATIONS:

ACKNOWLEDGMENTS:

1. Duong Thanh Phong, Ho Chi Minh City
2. AP Photos
3. Tom Mangold and John Penycate
4. U.S. Army
5. Colonel Jim Leonard
6. Arnold Gutierrez
7. Black Star
8. Jack Flowers
9. Major Randy Ellis
10. Pedro Rejo-Ruiz
11. Major Denis Ayoub

"THE MOTHER—THE NATIVE LAND"

by Duong Huong Ly

When she dug the tunnels, her hair was still brown.
Today her head is white as snow.
Under the reach of the guns she digs and digs.
At night the cries of the partridge record the past.
Twenty years, always the land is at war.
The partridge in the night cries out the love of the native land.
The mother, she digs her galleries, defenses,
Protecting each step of her children.
Immeasurable is our native land.
The enemy must drive his probes in everywhere.
Your unfathomable entrails, Mother,
Hide whole divisions under this land.
The dark tunnels make their own light.
The Yankees have captured her.
Under the vengeful blows she says not a word.
They open their eyes wide but are blind.
Cruelly beaten, the mother collapses.
Her body is no more than injuries and wounds
Her white hair is like snow.
Night after night
The noise of picks shakes the bosom of the earth.
Columns, divisions, rise up from it.
The enemy, seized by panic, sees only
Hostile positions around him.
Immeasurable is our native land.
Your entrails, Mother, are unfathomable.

FOREWORD

In 1968 one of the authors covered the war in Vietnam for three months for BBC Television News. Ten years later we were, together, the first BBC journalists to be granted visas by the newly victorious Communist government of the Socialist Republic of Vietnam to visit Hanoi and Ho Chi Minh City (formerly Saigon) to film a special report for *Panorama*. It was on this visit that we were introduced to Captain Nguyen Thanh Linh, who had commanded the guerrillas of Cu Chi district in the tunnels. At the former military headquarters at Phu My Hung, our first introduction to the tunnels and some of the men who fought in them took place.

Subsequently we were given permission to return to Vietnam—not as journalists but as authors—to study the tunnels and the tunnel war in greater detail. The Foreign Ministry in Hanoi not only cleared us to visit the tunnels of Cu Chi whenever we wished, but gave us unusual access to senior commanders in the People's Army who had formerly served with the Communist forces in South Vietnam.

We were invited for several briefings at the headquarters of Military Region VII in Ho Chi Minh City, which covers Cu Chi district. We met officers who had never spoken to Western visitors before, and we were allowed unlimited time with Colonel Nguyen Quang Minh, formerly a staff officer in the People's Liberation Army (as all Communist forces fighting in the South were called) and today the chief military historian of Military Region VII. (The official Communist history of the war is still in preparation.) At further briefings in Cu Chi town, Song Be, Tay Ninh, and other regional headquarters, People's Army officers quoted at length from a still-secret account of the war called "Summary Report on Experiences in the Anti-U.S. Struggle for National Salvation on the Battlefield in Eastern South Vietnam and the Southern Part of Central Vietnam (Zone B_2)."

Original maps of the tunnel system and drawings and diagrams of the construction processes were also supplied in Ho Chi Minh City by Military Region VII.

In the villages and hamlets of Cu Chi and adjoining districts we met numerous former tunnel fighters—some still in uniform, many now back on the land as farmers. Other important civilians we interviewed were located and brought to meet us in Ho Chi Minh City. We met the city's party chairman, Mai Chi Tho, brother of Le Duc Tho, who signed the cease-fire agreement with the United States for North Vietnam. Mai Chi Tho was responsible for the political direction of the war in the Saigon area, and reported personally to the Communist headquarters in South Vietnam.

All the interviews were made on the basis of full attribution. Each was tape-recorded, and later translated and transcribed in London.

Surprisingly, there were greater difficulties in locating the relevant American veterans. The character of those who fought in tunnels precludes clubbiness or fondness for joining veterans' associations. Many of these lonely men found life after service discharge an anticlimax. Restless by nature, many had changed jobs leaving little trace. Few stayed in touch with their former comrades. Of the GI tunnel fighters who survived—probably one of the most exclusive ex-servicemen's groups in the world—only a few dozen could be found after extensive inquiries, and of these, a small number were still too traumatized by their experiences to tell their stories for publication. Most, however, agreed to meet us and discuss for the first time since Vietnam their combat experiences in the tunnels.

This is a story about heroes on both sides.

CONTENTS

1

War Underground

HE HEARD THE tracks of the armored personnel carriers long before the malignant clouds of dust came into view. Nam Thuan lay very still, trying to count the number, but in his eyes and ears was only the fusion of squeaky steel belts and the approaching halo of dirt as the American armor moved busily out of the early morning sun and straight toward him.

As Communist party secretary of Phu My Hung village with its six small hamlets, Nam Thuan was automatically political commissar of the village defense force, a small unit already much depleted by action and promotions to the regional fighting forces. His small platoon that morning comprised a good deputy commander and a couple of village farm boys. His orders had been simple enough: He was to delay any American thrust on Phu My Hung by luring the enemy into engagement. He would destroy them if possible; if not, his diversionary battle would allow ample time for the village to be evacuated and the arms and guerrillas to be hidden.

It was August 1968; the war against the Americans was three years old. The great Tet offensive seemed to have taken many lives, yet South Vietnam had still not been reunited with the North. If anything, Thuan thought, the Americans seemed

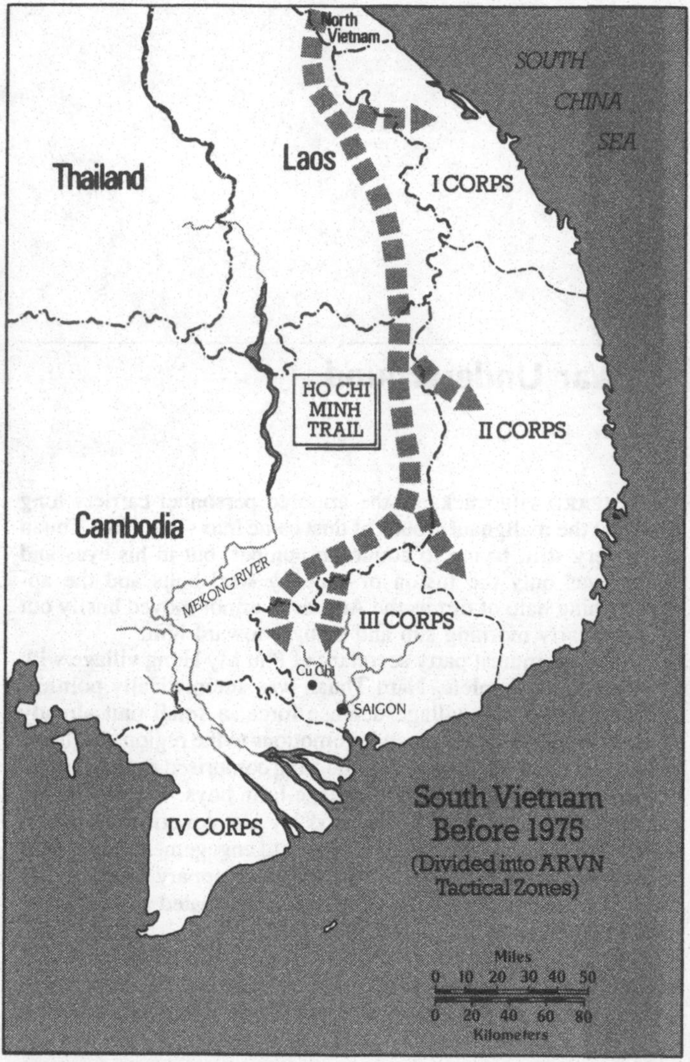
North Vietnam
SOUTH CHINA SEA
Laos
Thailand
I CORPS
HO CHI MINH TRAIL
II CORPS
Cambodia
MEKONG RIVER
III CORPS
Cu Chi
SAIGON
IV CORPS
South Vietnam Before 1975
(Divided into ARVN Tactical Zones)
Miles
0 10 20 30 40 50
0 20 40 60 80
Kilometers

more confident and more powerful than ever. But at least they were predictable—it was a necessary consolation as the small armored column rattled nearer; the Americans always came when expected, came noisily, and came in strength.

He counted thirteen M-113 carriers. It was a larger force than he had expected. Thuan needed to move quickly if he was to draw the column toward him and toward the tunnels. To fight with he had just two remote-controlled mines which he would detonate, and a boxful of captured American M-26 grenades. In the confusion, he would retreat and escape down the tunnel, but not so quickly that the Americans would not see him.

Things went wrong from the beginning. He detonated the first DH-10 mine prematurely and it exploded harmlessly just ahead of the lead American APC. The second mine failed to go off. The column was still too far away for Thuan to hurl the grenades. He stood up, deliberately breaking cover, and began to run awkwardly toward the tunnel entrance—its position marked by the open trapdoor—hugging the box of grenades. The lead APC spotted him and changed course to follow. Thuan wondered whether the Americans would now fire the turret-mounted machine gun; even if they did, it was improbable that a bumping gun would hit a small running target. Hands reached out of the open tunnel trapdoor to take the box of grenades. Thuan vaulted into the shaft and closed the door above his head. Blinded by the sudden change from sunlight to darkness, Thuan remained still for a few moments, crouching in the three-foot-deep shaft, gathering breath, waiting for images to return to his retinas. At the bottom of the shaft in which he stood and almost at a right angle to it began a sixty-foot communication tunnel. Thuan wriggled easily into its secure embrace. He realized he could no longer hear the noisy tracks of the APCs. Control of the battle had now passed from his hands to those of an American above ground. If the carriers passed overhead it would be impossible to rechallenge them before they reached Phu My Hung. He had been ordered not to allow that to happen.

For a few moments Thuan considered his environment. He had just entered the shaft that connected with the communication tunnel. At the end of the communication tunnel was a second shaft going down another three feet and at the end of that was a second communication tunnel. If he crawled along that, he would eventually reach a similar shaft and tunnel system leading up and out. However, the exit point for *this* system was some 120 feet away from the place where the Americans had seen him. It was crucial to his plan that they never discover the second exit. It was only sparsely camouflaged, but he had his own man hidden there who could tell him with minimum delay what the Americans were doing above ground while Thuan was below.

The tunnel was still cool from the evening air of the night before. Thuan crawled carefully into a small alcove dug some four feet into the first communication tunnel. As he hunched inside, he heard a muffled explosion followed by a blast, and a sudden beam of dust-filled sunlight pierced the shaft. The Americans had hit the tunnel trapdoor, blowing it clean away. It was what he had prayed for. The column was bound to stop while the tunnel system was fully explored and then destroyed by the Americans. As the dust and debris stung his eyes, Thuan squinted through the gloom and picked up his AK-47 automatic rifle, hugged it to his chest, and waited quietly in the alcove.

He waited over an hour. When he heard the first American helicopter he knew there would be no attempt to explode the tunnel without exploration. As the machine clapped and whirred its noisy way to the ground, Thuan assumed that the Americans had flown in their special tunnel soldiers, trained to fight in the honeycomb of underground tunnels and caverns that spread beneath the protective clay of the district of Cu Chi.

Thuan's observer, secreted above ground in the second hidden tunnel exit, had sent a messenger through the tunnels to Thuan in the alcove. The message was wholly predictable. The Americans had indeed brought more men by helicopter. They were small. They were tunnel soldiers.

The first GI did not even approach the open tunnel entrance for another hour. Earlier, Thuan had heard some conversation above his hiding hole, but nothing for about thirty minutes. Whatever happened, only one American could come in at a time. Both the first entrance shaft and the second long communication tunnel were only just wide enough for one thin man. The tunnel soldiers were thin; they fought well, but unlike Nam Thuan and his small village platoon of Communist guerrillas, they had not spent years inside the tunnels of Cu Chi;

they had not fought many battles in their dank blackness.

Thuan could not conceive of failure. He had already been awarded one Victory Medal third class and one Victory Medal second class. He was about to earn another. Small even by Vietnamese standards, naturally slender, Thuan had never known peace in his land. His father had fought the French from similar tunnel complexes in Cu Chi when Thuan was still a child. Thuan had been allowed occasional tunnel sorties, playing soldiers with his friends. The enemy had been other village boys, ludicrously made up to look like the French soldiers, with charcoal mustaches and charcoaled arms, in an attempt to ape the perpetual wonder of hirsute Westerners.

As he grew up, it was the Americans who took the place of the French, and their hairy arms and large frames were no joke to the handful of village children who had been selected by the Communist party to receive a full education. He soon hated the Americans. A friend from Hanoi had told him the Americans called the village fighters Viet Cong, to him an insulting and derogatory term. Now, at thirty-three and still unmarried, Thuan was waiting for the call to join the regular soldiers, but the party had deliberately kept him as a village commander of the part-time self-defense force. He had fought a brave war. He was cunning and ruthless and, above all, he was one of the few cadres who knew the geography of all the eight miles of underground tunnels that the villagers had built in the area. Sometimes he was the only man who could guide the soldiers from Hanoi along the tunnels on their secret journeys through Cu Chi; the men from the North marveled at being able to travel safely under the Americans' noses.

A small earth-fall from the exposed tunnel entrance warned Thuan that the first American tunnel soldier was descending. He had purposely ordered that the first shaft be dug just over three feet deep; it meant the American would have to descend feet first and then wriggle awkwardly into the long communication tunnel where Thuan waited, hidden in an alcove. In the past, as a GI's feet had touched the bottom, Thuan had stabbed the soldier in the groin with his bayonet. This time, as the green-and-black jungle boots descended, Thuan leaned out of his alcove and, using the light from the tunnel entrance, shot the soldier twice in the lower body.

Above ground, the Americans were now in trouble. They

could not drop grenades down the shaft because their mortally wounded comrade jammed the hole—anyway, he might still be alive. Slumped in the narrow shaft, he prevented other soldiers from making their way down to chase Thuan. He guessed it would take the Americans at least thirty minutes to get the ropes slipped under the dying man's arms and then haul him out. The Americans' concern for their dead and wounded remained a source of bewilderment and relief to the Communist soldiers. Anything that delayed the battle inevitably favored the weaker side and allowed reloading, regrouping and rethinking.

Once the American's body had been removed from the shaft, Thuan anticipated that his comrades would probably drop a grenade or two down the hole, wait for the smoke to clear, then climb into the shaft and crawl quickly into the first communication tunnel, firing ahead with their pistols. They would be smarter this time and they would be angrier. He would not wait where he was.

His next fighting position was the second shaft, some four feet deep, which connected the first communication tunnel with the second lower one. There was a trapdoor at the top of the second shaft, but Thuan had to remove it for his next operation to succeed. He prayed the Americans would not be using gas at this early stage to flush him out. If they did not, and he was very lucky, the Americans would follow him, using flashlights. Thuan hid in the second shaft, its trapdoor off. He crouched low enough to be invisible to the Americans as they groped their way along the communication tunnel toward him. And yes, they were using flashlights. They might as well have been using loudspeakers to announce their intentions.

The tunnel soldiers had not thrown grenades but they had fired their pistols in volleys to clear the tunnel ahead. From his crouching position in the shaft at the end of this tunnel, Thuan could look up and feel sharp splinters of clay falling on his face as the bullets struck the end of the tunnel above the open shaft. The noise of the firing was deafening. Now the tunnel soldiers were slowly advancing. As soon as their flashlights saw an open shaft entrance ahead, they would roll a grenade down it and Thuan would be blown to pieces. The timing was now critical. He waited for a pause in the pistol volleys and then popped his head and shoulders out of the shaft. He saw at least two flashlights, they blinded him. As a foreign voice shouted, he fired the first clip from his AK-47, loaded the second by touch, and fired that, too. The tunnel exploded in a roar of noise, orange light, and screams of the wounded. He ducked back into the shaft, picking up the trapdoor from the bottom and replacing it above his head. He wriggled down the shaft and slipped along the second communication tunnel far enough for safety should the Americans be able to remove the trapdoor and throw grenades down after him. He lay breathless and sweating on the earth.

From his hiding place above ground at the top of the secret shaft, about 120 feet away from the American position, Thuan's observer watched as the Americans slowly brought out their dead and wounded from Thuan's attack. Three helicopters arrived for the victims. Thuan carefully noted all the information the messenger brought him from above ground. It gave him the basic material to make his next plan for below ground. Thuan's deputy was convinced that now, surely, the Americans would dynamite the tunnel. Thuan was not so sure. It was four in the afternoon, and the Americans would want to leave, spend the night in Dong Zu base, next to Cu Chi town, and return by helicopter at first light. They still had not discovered the second secret tunnel entrance; they had lost surprise; they had lost men. They might hope there was a tunnel complex large enough to be worth exploring for documents or Communist military equipment. Thuan still had his box of grenades and a perfect escape route behind him. He gambled on another battle.

That night Thuan developed a mild fever and went to a small sleeping hole inside the tunnel. Just large enough for one man but with the luxury of a specially dug air ventilation hole leading in from the surface three feet above, the hole was also used for the wounded before they could be taken by tunnel on the longer trip to the underground tunnel hospital at Phu My Hung. Indeed, there were still bloodstained bandages in the hole. The guerrillas had been unable to burn them or bury them since the last battle. The incessant heavily armored sweeps mounted by the 25th Division from their huge fortress next to Cu Chi town had kept the Communist defense forces pinned inside their tunnels for weeks on end. Sometimes there had been surprise raids by the tunnel soldiers; sometimes there had been many deaths. As Thuan sweated his way through the night, he assumed the new tunnel soldiers would be more careful and cautious than the last squad. Success would depend on the Americans' not knowing the layout of the system, and anticipating that the Communists had now fled.

This time, he would allow the Americans to crawl forward without any impedance and let them travel much farther than they had gone before. Their journey would take them down the first shaft and along the first communication tunnel, then down the second shaft (scene of the previous day's attack) and along the second, or bottom, communication tunnel. They would then reach a third shaft, one that led *up*. The tunnel soldiers would know what Nam Thuan knew, that this was the most dangerous and critical moment of any tunnel exploration. Thuan would be waiting for them.

He called one of the village boys and ordered him to fill a bag with earth. Then he checked and rechecked his grenades. The American ones were infinitely superior to the homemade ones or even the grenades the Chinese had sent, but tunnels had a way of destroying sensitive mechanisms. In the kind of war that Nam Thuan fought in the tunnels, there were only first chances—never seconds.

The Americans came, as they always seemed to, shortly after eight in the morning. A team crawled with exaggerated care through the tunnel system that had seen such havoc the day before. They moved by inches, looking for tunnel booby traps, but Thuan had dismantled everything—he wanted the soldiers dead, not saved through their own vigilance. He waited until the first dim hint of light announced they were now on their way along the second, the lower, communication tunnel. The leader would find himself facing the shaft at the end of the tunnel. He would shine his flashlight up. He might even have time to see the grenade that would fall to end his life.

In the five seconds before the grenade exploded in the middle of the Americans—Thuan never knew how many there were—he had time to slap the trapdoor shut and heave the heavy bag of earth on top and himself on top of the bag. The explosion just managed to lift the trapdoor with its extra weight. Afterward there was complete silence.

Before American soldiers later destroyed the tunnel with Bangalore torpedoes—chains of explosives linked by detonating cord—Thuan's men had time to retrieve four working pistols, all .38s, and two broken flashlights left by the Americans. His platoon escaped from the secret exit. In fact, the explosions destroyed only some seventy feet of the tunnel complex, and the system was usable again within a few weeks.

Fourteen months later, Nam Thuan was invited to join the regular forces as an officer. He became fully responsible for the defense of the six hamlets of Phu An village. Three years later, in November 1973, the Americans were gone and the war was being fought only by the South Vietnamese army; Thuan was a member of the district party committee when the guerrilla forces of Cu Chi, strengthened by regular troops from North Vietman, went on the offensive for the first time in five years. They wiped out forty-seven South Vietnamese military posts in one month alone. Two years later, on 28 March 1975, Thuan was with the forces who raised the flag of the Communist National Liberation Front over the town of Cu Chi. He is now a major in the People's Army of Vietnam.

Sergeant Arnold Gutierrez, thirty-eight years old, five feet six inches tall, weight 125 pounds, sat in the undergrowth eating his C-rations and cursing his luck. He had been in and out of the service for decades—joined the marines in '45, did a spell in the New Mexico National Guard, did a bit more in the Marine Corps reserves, joined the army in '62, made sergeant within two years, and staff sergeant just in time to make it to Vietnam and real action. It was April 1966. There was still no action. Instead he was with a unit of grunts, poking around looking for holes in the ground. With a curious mixture of restlessness and deviousness he had managed to maintain some control over his military career—the ultimate ambition of nearly every professional soldier. He knew he probably would not rise in rank much during this war, but at least he would see some action, he would win a couple of Purple Hearts, and he would find out how good a soldier he really was. But hole hunting—that was for beagles.

Nothing in training with the 25th ("Tropic Lightning") Division in Hawaii had prepared him for this kind of work. He had shone at all the gung ho jungle-warfare training courses. He was immensely sinewy and strong; with his New Mexican background, he tolerated the heat and humidity without complaint. But in Hawaii they had trained for the kind of war the

GIs had fought in Korea—human waves of screaming Chinese. No one had said anything about holes in the ground. When the 25th had finally arrived in Cu Chi, it seemed to have set up its base camp on a former peanut plantation that was either directly over or pretty damn near some weird kind of underground city. With increasing embarrassment, the 25th had been unable to secure its own perimeter. Now they needed special little guys to go down the tunnels and dig Charlie out. It was this that had brought Arnie Gutierrez into the jungle; NCO in charge of A company of the 4th Battalion of the 23rd Mechanized Infantry.

It had been a bad day so far and it was still only eleven-thirty in the morning. They had been looking for Viet Cong tunnels, which were about as easy to find as truffles in a Kansas cornfield. Tunnel entrances were wonderfully camouflaged, and if you did get too close, snipers usually hit your point man, there would be panic, and you still did not find the entrance. If you were lucky enough to be around on the rare moments that an entrance was exposed, some officer would call your name, and with that sweet and sour mixture of anticipation and fear, you would prepare to crawl in. Holes were hot (active) or cold (empty). Arnie Gutierrez had never had a hot hole yet.

Today's patrol had been fruitless, and the man chewed their rations silently. It was that time of day when you didn't believe it could get hotter; the very oxygen in the air seemed to fry. Some of the larger men took it very hard. Skinny runts like Gutierrez suffered far less. But tempers always ran parallel with the heat of the day, and Gutierrez could feel his rising. His SP4, sitting just ten feet away, had been staring at him for some time. It was beginning to unnerve the sergeant, when suddenly the corporal spoke softly: "Don't move one single inch, Sarge." Gutierrez froze. It was either a snake or a booby trap, and he prayed it was a snake. The corporal pointed a finger and said: "You're sitting on a bamboo stake that's rigged. It's maybe rigged to explosives or to a mine. Look to your right."

Gutierrez swung his head round as if it were on a well-oiled ball race and had no relationship with his shoulders or spine. The piece of bamboo was obviously part of the booby trap. The bad news was he had not spotted it when he sat down; the good news was that if he was not sitting on a pressure-detonated mine, then he might survive. "We're bound to be near a tunnel entrance," the corporal said unnecessarily, as he inched toward Gutierrez to examine the bamboo stake. "They always have these things to protect the entrance and keep us away." The SP4 carefully explored the area around Gutierrez and then told the sweat-soaked NCO it was safe to get up. The bamboo stake was not wired but *was* the trigger for a mine directly beneath it. The two men told their squad to leave the area, then dug themselves a small trench hole with their bayonets. They hid inside it and the corporal tossed a grenade at the bamboo stake. The mine detonated with a roar and, as an added bonus, exposed the entrance to an underground tunnel. The corporal went back to his unfinished C-rations.

It was now long enough into Arnie Gutierrez's mercifully short career as a tunnel soldier for him to have pondered the harder realities of tunnel work. He pretended to be the hunter, but in truth he knew he was the hunted. Almost nothing worked to his advantage in those holes, with their appalling smells, except that sometimes, in the heat of the day, they were still cool and dank from the night. Otherwise they generated claustrophobia, fear and physical fatigue. All this, and he had not even met a VC in a tunnel yet; there had not been one single firefight. Yet one small part of him, a part he feared, produced enough adrenaline for him to want to go down there; that little unquenchable flame, fed by curiosity and an instinct more primitive than he cared to admit, now warmed him for action.

He took his personal .22 pistol, his flashlight, some wire and rope, a small stick, and a bayonet. He left his helmet and fatigue top behind, and wore only a green T-shirt, boots and trousers. The mine had blown away a large jagged opening, revealing no less than three separate small tunnel entrances, each one just large enough to take one thin man. For no reason at all he chose the right-hand tunnel. The coward in him kept repeating that Charlie would be long gone with all that mine-blowing outside; with luck it would be a short trip. Even so, the tunnel was bound to be booby-trapped. He would have to use the flashlight to spot the worst danger—old GI communications wire used by Charlie to act as a tripwire that set off a booby-trapped grenade. A grenade exploding in a tunnel on top of a human being did unspeakable things. All the blast was concentrated and bounced off the tunnel walls. You could put a man inside a handbag after one of those went off.

The tunnel swung in a slow arc to the right. The air was good, and there was no smell of body or excrement. As long as the tunnel bent round, Charlie should not be able to see the flashlight at too great a distance. There were no booby traps on the ground or the roof, and Gutierrez stuck to his own golden rule in tunnel crawling. He had figured out that the VC had learned that impatient Americans always took the shortest distance between two points—and consequently the VC tended to wire booby traps at places where an American soldier would be tempted to take a short cut. Gutierrez's golden rule was fo stay with one side of the tunnel *all the way*, never cross over, never walk across a chamber if he found one, but hug the wall and try to finish up where he started.

As he inched through the tunnel, and the familiar fear gripped his sphincter muscle, and earth and sweat began to fill his eyes, he stopped for a moment to apply golden rule number two—and in doing so spent two minutes in saving his life. The tunnel was beginning to straighten out. He had to use his flashlight to search for booby traps, but the light was a perfect target if Charlie was up there. Gutierrez took the small stick and some wire, tied his flashlight to the stick, and began holding the light in his left hand as far above his left ear as the low tunnel roof allowed. He sheathed his knife, with which he had been delicately probing suspicious-looking roots that stuck through the earth, and unholstered the little .22 and placed it in his right hand. There could be no more uncomfortable, or difficult way of traversing a tunnel, but it was the only way that made sense. The sergeant cursed at not having brought his homemade knee pads, as he saw blood coming from the knee. He began to sense that he had gone almost far enough without a backup, who would have carried the TR-12 radio. He decided to give the tunnel one more bend, look for a lay-by in which he could turn around, and then return.

He actually saw the VC firing at him. He saw his face, saw the flash of the gun; the noise defied belief, and as it exploded around his skull, he was convinced he had been shot in the head. Stunned and deafened, he dropped the flashlight, fell, and fired blindly at where the face had been. He lay coughing in the acrid gun smoke, slowly realizing he was not only alive but unhurt. Why hadn't Charlie delivered the coup de grâce?

Still deafened, he saw his flashlight lying on the ground and still alight. He waited, prone, a little longer, then gingerly edged toward the flashlight and picked it up. There was no more firing. Through the settling dust he could just see a figure lying about twenty yards away. If there had been a second VC, Gutierrez would be dead by now, so that was no problem, but maybe the second VC had fled, leaving his fallen comrade booby-trapped? Maybe the figure lying on the ground was not dead but just waiting. Gutierrez tried to work out how much time had passed between the shooting and now. His options were too limited to worry about. He could only move forward or move arse-end out. He began to crawl forward. The twenty yards took forever.

His adversary had been shot in the head. The bullet had made a small hole in the temple and the wound had stopped bleeding. The man was still breathing. Gutierrez took the wire he had brought and carefully wrapped it round the muzzle of the AK-47. If the gun was booby-trapped, this was the only way to find out. Gutierrez then holstered his .22 and began to back out of the tunnel, playing the wire out in front of himself, making sure the gun was never jerked. They were already coming in to help him as he appeared, butt first, round a corner. He hissed at his corporal to back out, too, and one by one they reached the light and the air. Only then did Gutierrez pull the wire—there was no booby-trap explosion—and drag out the AK-47 as well.

He went back in carrying a rope, with an additional rope tied to his ankle in case they had to drag him out, too. Inch by inch he crawled back to where the wounded VC still lay. If the AK-47 had not been booby-trapped it was unlikely the body had been. Nevertheless, Gutierrez gently explored it for any telltale wires before tying the rope around the man's neck. He was not going to take the risk of lifting the body to tie the rope under the VC's armpits. Once again, Gutierrez backed out of the tunnel, playing the rope out in front of him. Once out, he had the squad pull the VC out. When the body emerged from the hole, the man was already dead.

For the last time, Gutierrez went into the tunnel complex. Nobody knew what was in there. They discovered they had killed a solitary guard, posted there to allow wounded VC from some earlier battle to be carried away from the small underground hospital at the end of the communication tunnel. Gutierrez's squad eventually found two chambers, with soiled clothes and bloody bandages inside. How and where the inhabitants had escaped was, as ever, the mystery. Gutierrez was now past caring. It was dusk and time to return to the comparative safety of the base.

Gutierrez sat silently inside the APC as they bumped and bounced their way back to Cu Chi. Everything he had learned about fighting seemed to have no relevance to what he had been doing today. Every infantry course, all the technology, the backup artillery and air support, the choppers that could fly half a division into and out of the battlefield within a few hours—what did any of this have to do with any enemy you never saw alive, who existed in holes in the ground, and against whom only a man's brute strength and luck seemed to prevail?

They had told him in Hawaii and during special training in Alaska that this was a war against only a handful of Communist terrorists. Yet wherever his unit traveled, the turf seemed to belong to the enemy. Even the American fortress at Cu Chi was not safe. How could this be, when it was so close to Saigon itself? Just how far away were they, anyway? "Only twenty miles," said his corporal, "and the tunnels stretch right up to the edge of the city."

2

Cu Chi District

THE UNDERGROUND TUNNELS of Cu Chi were the most complex part of a network that—at the height of the Vietnam War in the mid sixties—stretched from the gates of Saigon to the border with Cambodia (today, Ho Chi Minh City and Kampuchea). There were hundreds of kilometers of tunnels connecting villages, districts, and even provinces. They held living areas, storage depots, ordnance factories, hospitals, headquarters, and almost every other facility that was necessary to the pursuit of the war by South Vietnam's Communists and that could be accommodated below ground. General William Westmoreland, who commanded the American forces in Vietnam from 1964 to 1968, said in his memoirs: "No one has ever demonstrated more ability to hide his installations than the Viet Cong; they were human moles."

No single military engineer designed this vast labyrinth, nor—despite Vo Nguyen Giap's overall generalship in Hanoi—did any one commander order it to be built. The tunnels evolved as the natural response of a poorly equipped and mainly local guerrilla army to mid-twentieth-century technological warfare. Aircraft, bombs, artillery, and chemicals obliged the Viet Cong to live and fight underground. Ironically, by becoming an army

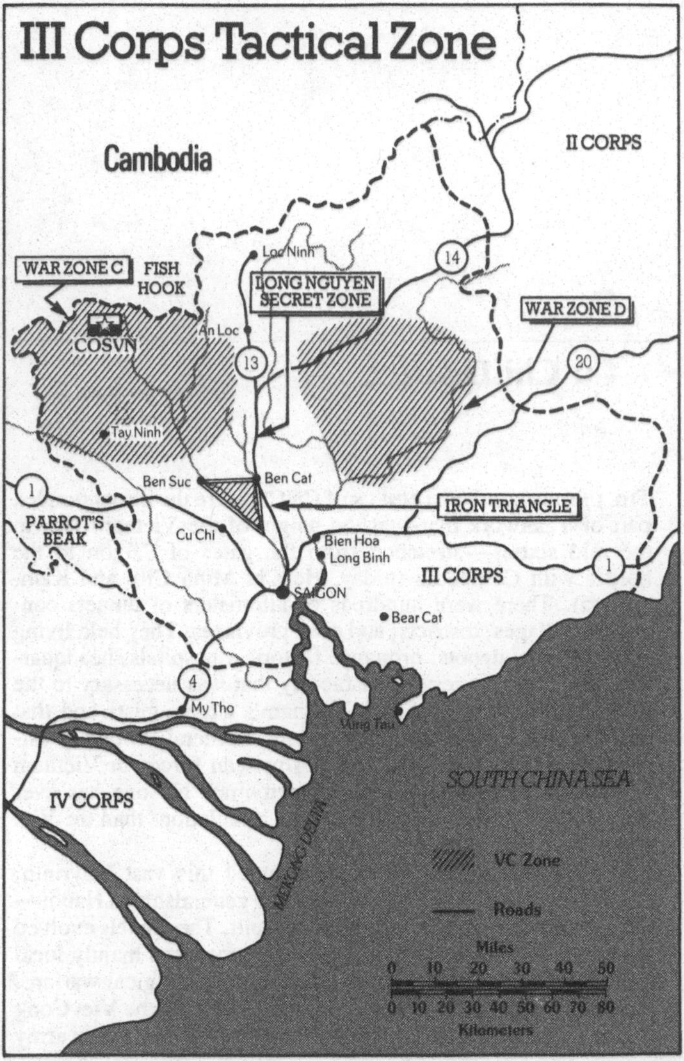
III Corps Tactical Zone
Cambodia
II CORPS
WAR ZONE C
FISH HOOK
COSVN
Loc Ninh
LONG NGUYEN SECRET ZONE
14
WAR ZONE D
An Loc
13
20
Tay Ninh
Ben Suc
Ben Cat
IRON TRIANGLE
1
PARROT'S BEAK
Cu Chi
Bien Hoa
Long Binh
III CORPS
1
SAIGON
Bear Cat
4
My Tho
Vung Tau
SOUTH CHINA SEA
IV CORPS
MEKONG DELTA
VC Zone
Roads
Miles
0 10 20 30 40 50
0 10 20 30 40 50 60 70 80
Kilometers

of moles pitched against armies winged into battle by helicopter, the Viet Cong guerrillas, and later the North Vietnamese army, protracted the war to the point of persuading the United States that it was unwinnable. And once America began disengaging itself from Vietnam, complete victory for the Communists moved irresistibly nearer.

The district of Cu Chi, in what was South Vietnam, became the most bombed, shelled, gassed, defoliated, and generally devastated area in the history of warfare. For years, most of Cu Chi suffered the fate of being a "free strike zone." That meant that random artillery fire, known as "harassment and interdiction," rained upon it by night; bomber pilots were encouraged to offload unused explosives and napalm over Cu Chi before returning to base.

The area has since been glorified in the accounts of the Communist victors with honorific titles, such as Iron Land, or Land of Fire. Nearly every village or hamlet is a "heroic village" or enjoys some other decoration or citation. The area is dotted with the graves of fallen "heroes" of both sexes, grouped around memorial obelisks engraved "The Nation Remembers." In independent Vietnam's short history the name of Cu Chi already carries the mystique and historical resonance of Agincourt and Bunker Hill. The Vietnamese fought for thirty years throughout the thousand-mile length of their country to finish with the unified territory they now have. But the war in Cu Chi has come to epitomize the horror, the heroism, and the endurance of the Vietnamese struggle for Ho Chi Minh's dream of freedom and independence.

Cu Chi district, administered from the small market town of the same name, is today part of greater Ho Chi Minh City, which lies to the southeast; formerly called Saigon, it was the capital of the Republic of Vietnam—South Vietnam—which existed from 1954 to 1975. To its south lies the delta of the Mekong River, the rice bowl of Southeast Asia, a region of paddyfields, swamps, and canals. To Saigon's north are the foothills of the central highlands, which stretch back up the spine of Vietnam past the 1954 demarcation line (known as the demilitarized zone, or DMZ) and into what, until 1975, was called North Vietnam. The hills are steep, rugged, covered in deep jungle, infertile, and thinly populated with native tribes. Between the delta and the mountains lies the plain, known as the piedmont, or Mekong terrace. It runs northwest from Saigon to the Cambodian border like a huge slice of cake with its apex in the former capital. At the narrow end of this triangle is Cu Chi.

Less fertile than the delta, but heavily settled and cultivated, Cu Chi district is a network of villages astride Route 1, the road that links Saigon with Phnom Penh (in what was Cambodia) and with Tay Ninh, the adjoining border province. Cu Chi district is bordered to the north by the Saigon River. Just across it is a district that takes its name from the largest town, Ben Cat. This area, like Cu Chi, was to earn a fearsome reputation as a Viet Cong stronghold. "The Commies always seem to have an Iron Triangle," wrote Melvin Walthall, historian of the U.S. 25th Infantry Division, referring to the area in Korea that was given that name in 1951. Ben Cat district—plus neighboring overlaps—became Vietnam's Iron Triangle. Beyond it to the north is the town of Loc Ninh, which for years was wholly controlled by the Viet Cong. Cu Chi and the Iron Triangle lay between it and the South Vietnamese capital—in the words of an American general, "a dagger pointing at Saigon."

The strategic significance of this part of South Vietnam is self-evident: It straddled the main land and river routes into Saigon. During the war these were the Viet Cong's supply routes from Cambodia, where the Ho Chi Minh trail from North Vietnam ended. Secondly, Cu Chi district covers the only sizeable territory in South Vietnam across which troops and vehicles can move easily, even in the monsoon rains that fall on the area in the summer months every year. The significance of this was not lost upon any of the warring parties and nations that engulfed Vietnam in conflict for thirty years, and the area was to be dotted with the military bases and headquarters of them all. It was called the III Corps Tactical Zone by the South Vietnamese army, which divided the South into four zones. The Viet Cong, on the other hand, called the whole area surrounding Saigon their Military Region IV.

Mai Chi Tho fought the war from its headquarters. The brother of Hanoi Politburo member Le Duc Tho, today he runs Ho Chi Minh City as party chairman. But in 1965 he was the political commissar of the Viet Cong in the Saigon area, and was based in the Cu Chi tunnels. He remembered: "Cu Chi was a springboard for attacking Saigon, the enemy's brain center. It was like a thorn stabbing in the eye. The enemy had to find some way of sweeping Cu Chi and Ben Cat districts clean; the fight was a fierce one. We used the area for infiltrating Saigon—intelligence agents, party cadres, sabotage teams. The Tet offensive of 1968 [on Saigon and other towns] was prepared—the necessary troops and supplies assembled—in the Cu Chi tunnels. The Americans appreciated the area's importance because it constantly threatened the security of Saigon, of their own headquarters. If they could not solve the problem of the tunnels of Cu Chi, how could they deal with the problem of Vietnam?"

The people of Cu Chi had such a reputation for secret revolutionary activity and resistance that Ngo Dinh Diem, the former imperial mandarin who was the first president of South Vietnam, from 1955 till his murder in 1963, abolished the district administration. New provinces were created in 1956, and towns and villages were renamed to wipe out the memory of the anti-French insurgency. Cu Chi was divided between the provinces of Hau Nghia in the south and Binh Duong to the north. The Vietnamese Communists, however, continued to use the old names and base their regional, district, and village organizations, civil and military, upon the old forms. The United States Army found place-names a headache, and so adapted some and made up others. They described as the "Ho Bo woods" the two critical Cu Chi villages of An Nhon Tay and Phu My Hung (the latter the Viet Cong's Saigon area command post). They invented names like War Zone C, the Trapezoid, and the Long Nguyen Secret Zone for the tunnel-riddled VC base areas that they came to regard with well-deserved caution. Since the Communist victory in 1975 there has been more redrawing of provinces and districts and renaming of towns and villages. Place-names in this book are those most commonly used during the war.

Cu Chi used to be a green area of intensive agriculture, especially rice paddies, orchards, nut trees, and rubber plantations. The people kept a few chickens and pigs, and water buffalo dragged plows or wallowed in the irrigation canals between the fields. At work, the peasants wore black silken pajamas and wide conical hats. The huge Fil Hol rubber plantation used to lie to the north of Cu Chi town along the Saigon River, facing the Iron Triangle. Its French management abandoned it during the anticolonial agitation of the late forties, but its orderly lines of rubber trees became a Viet Cong sanctuary. Further north, near Dau Tieng in Tay Ninh province, was the Michelin rubber plantation. It continued production throughout the war. Some French planters dutifully paid taxes to both the Saigon government and the unofficial nocturnal government of the Viet Cong. Because the French were still there, the American army left the Michelin plantation alone. The VC took full advantage of its immunity and located base camps in the vicinity. Where cultivation ceased, wild vegetation began: either bamboo thickets or dense jungle. But at the height of the Vietnam War, Cu Chi had been turned into a barren chemical desert, pitted with cavernous bomb craters, denuded of trees, where the air itself was noxious with gas. The Americans called it a white area, for surveillance from the air was so easy. On their military maps, over what had been villages and plantations, they printed—repeatedly and brutally—the word "destroyed." Nevertheless, it stayed a battlefield. Viet Cong guerrillas remained in the area for most of the war in the tunnel system.

Both guerrilla warfare and the military use of tunnels in Vietnam preceded the American involvement. There was a historical background to the tunnel war.

The tunnels in Cu Chi were originally dug as hiding places for the Viet Minh, the nationalist guerrillas who fought the colonial power, France, in the 1940s and 1950s. As with their successors, the Viet Cong, Communists dominated the independence movement. Ho Chi Minh was its undisputed leader. Until his death in 1969, "Uncle Ho" personified his people's tenacious pursuit of independence and unity. His shrewd and open face with the wispy white beard now stares down from almost every Vietnamese wall: the founder of the state, Vietnam's Lenin or George Washington, depending on one's point of view.

In 1940, the collaborationist French colonists allowed the Imperial Japanese Army access to Vietnam's ports and other facilities for their expansionist war. In 1945, when Japan surrendered, Ho Chi Minh seized power in Hanoi and proclaimed Vietnam's independence. The victorious allies of World War II disagreed about the old colonial empires. President Franklin Roosevelt had wanted the former subject peoples of Asia to have independence in the postwar world. France, Britain, and

Holland, however, saw the repossession of their imperial territories as legal and correct. After Roosevelt's death in 1945, American policy changed. Ho Chi Minh's tenure of power in Hanoi led to negotiations with France, which broke down, and a nine-year war of independence resulted. British troops landed in Saigon in September 1945 to help reestablish French authority; to maintain order, they delayed disarming the surrendered Japanese soldiery.

But history had turned the corner in Asia. Europeans had recently been defeated by the Japanese; Singapore's surrender was the symbol of the end of the white man's empire in the East. Ho Chi Minh had temporarily held power in Hanoi. From then on Vietnam's nationalists were unyielding. To wage guerrilla war against the arriving French army, nationalists of different political hues coalesced to form the Viet Minh League.

The tunnels were dug for the Viet Minh—for communication from one hamlet to another so that guerrillas could evade French army sweeps or spotter planes. Major Nguyen Quot, a short, wiry, cadaverous officer, who spent the best part of ten years living in Cu Chi's tunnels, explained their origin. "The tunnels were started in areas temporarily occupied by the enemy. The revolutionary forces were small. It would have been impossible to conserve our forces if we had fought in the open. We had to be in a position to choose the time, the place, and the target of an attack. By 1948 we had already dug a tunnel system: Each family, each hamlet, had a tunnel communicating it with others."

In October 1949, Mao Zedong's Communist victory in neighboring China's civil war gave General Vo Nguyen Giap a safe sanctuary for the training of Viet Minh forces, rearmed with American artillery captured from the defeated Chinese nationalists. Despite Vietnam's historic antipathy toward China (which has resurfaced in recent years), the Chinese Communists were pleased to assist their fellow revolutionaries; China would be supplying arms and equipment to North Vietnam in the sixties and early seventies.

But in Vietnam in 1949, the French were suffering military reverses, and Viet Minh control spread across most of the countryside. In June 1950, Communist North Korea invaded its southern neighbor and drew the United States and its allies into an Asian anti-Communist war. At the same time America, concerned by Soviet and Chinese recognition of Ho Chi Minh's rebel government, began pouring military and economic aid into France's Vietnam struggle. When the Korean War ceased in 1953, Communist aid to the Viet Minh was stepped up. France made the fatal error of trying for a set-piece confrontation with the Viet Minh in a remote northern valley, Dien Bien Phu. Giap's men besieged and finally overran the French fortress, and thereby terminated France's involvement in his country. During the siege, the Viet Minh approached the perimeter in tunnels, and burrowed underneath the French defenses. Professional soldiers, including the legendary Foreign Legion, had been defeated by an Asian guerrilla army—a lesson for the future that few Americans heeded.

With the cease-fire in 1954 came the agreement between the world powers and Viet Minh at Geneva: Provisionally, Vietnam was divided into two halves at the 17th parallel. Ho Chi Minh was able to consolidate his Communist rule in the northern half, while in the South an independent republic was set up with generous American aid, based on Saigon; the Catholic Ngo Dinh Diem became its first president. Under the Geneva agreement, nationwide elections were to take place in 1956. Meanwhile, active Viet Minh soldiers and organizers were to "regroup" in North Vietnam. About 90,000 men and women active in fighting the French traveled north, assuming they would return home with the inevitable victory of Ho Chi Minh and his Lao Dong (Workers', in fact, Communist) party in the 1956 election. Thousands of active Viet Minh, however, were instructed to stay behind, continue political activity, and store their weapons in secret caches for possible future use.

At the same time, nearly a million Roman Catholic Vietnamese from North Vietnam took the opportunity offered by the armistice to relocate in the South. Many of the northern Catholics, who settled around Saigon, became government officials or army officers (which often amounted to the same thing). Air Marshal Nguyen Cao Ky, for example, who ran South Vietnam's air force, became president and (from 1967 to 1975) deputy to President Nguyen Van Thieu, was of northern origin. Most of the Communist cadres, or organizers, who came south down the Ho Chi Minh trail through Laos were southerners by birth. Le Duc Tho, who was to negotiate American troop withdrawal with Henry Kissinger in Paris, was a southerner. Leaders of the South Vietnamese National Liberation Front, such as Nguyen Huu Tho, are today ministers in the Hanoi government.

America always made a distinction between the southern guerrillas and the North Vietnamese army, which, it said, was "invading" South Vietnam, the victim of "aggression." Nationalist Vietnamese saw it differently: The social revolution that was complete in the North was incomplete in the South, where only massive American help propped up what the Communists referred to as a "puppet" government.

The elections of 1956 did not take place, and Ho Chi Minh was cheated of his goal of a unified Vietnam. Diem argued that so tight was Ho Chi Minh's hold on power in Hanoi that elections in the North could not be free and fair. He was probably right, but his deeper fear—that Ho Chi Minh would have won decisively in the countryside of the South also—was almost certainly equally well-founded. As American money and equipment and military advisers arrived in Saigon, Diem set about establishing his regime along strong and uncompromising lines. In brief, he allowed his brother Ngo Dinh Nhu, who ran the state security apparatus, to create a police state with a view to rooting out and liquidating all opposition. And opposition meant, in Nhu's eyes, not only armed gangs and armed religious sects but also those who had organized and fought for the Communist-led Viet Minh against the French. Cu Chi had always been a hotbed of revolutionary activity, and Nhu's police descended on the area with ferocity. Today, people estimate that three-quarters of the Viet Minh who remained in Cu Chi were apprehended. Some were imprisoned, usually after torture, and held in horrific conditions; others were publicly guillotined, in the French colonial manner.

In December 1958, several hundred suspected Communists or dissidents were poisoned to death with dosed bread at a prison camp at Phu Loi, a few miles to the east of Cu Chi across the Saigon River. This massacre generated a new mood of militancy; the famous Viet Cong Phu Loi battalion would be named after the event. Under Law 10/59 (the month of its enactment), President Diem specifically outlawed former Viet Minh fighters. Resistance to Diem increased. At the village of Phuoc Hiep, just north of Cu Chi town, is a memorial to marchers in a demonstration in April 1961, gunned down by members of the Army of the Republic of Vietnam (normally written ARVN and pronounced "Arvin" by the Americans). They had established a paratroop training school in the nearby Cu Chi village of Trung Lap.

At long last, in 1960, the Communists lifted the ban on armed resistance; the National Liberation Front (NLF), a Communist-dominated coalition of antigovernment groups, was formed to supervise the resumption of guerrilla war in the South. Coordinated armed attacks began on army and police posts, and for the first time the essential weakness of the Diem regime was exposed. Army posts were either easily overrun or sufficiently intimidated by demonstrators or persuaded by the threats and blandishments of villagers so that all the weapons were surrendered. To the exasperation of their American advisers, the ARVN units deliberately avoided enemy contact and the consequent casualties. One by one the villages of Cu Chi and adjoining districts disarmed local ARVN detachments and effectively cut themselves off from government control. The arms acquired by this means were the first and only weapons many nascent Viet Cong units had; enterprising villagers set about making copies, founding the huge cottage ordnance industry in the tunnels that would last until the late sixties, when newer guns came south from Hanoi.

With the resumption of guerrilla warfare the old redoubts of the Viet Minh had to be reactivated. The French had used aircraft to spot and bomb the Vietnamese fighters; Diem's army was increasingly transported by American helicopters. In villages all over Cu Chi, Tay Ninh, the Iron Triangle, and wherever possible, old tunnel networks were repaired, and a great program of tunnel-digging began. "When we got orders to set up a secure base here," related one Cu Chi survivor of that period, ex-guerrilla Ba Huyet, "the first thing we did was to start digging thirty kilometers of underground tunnels. It was in 1960. Not only was this one of our closest outposts to Saigon, but it was our advanced command post throughout the war. The Americans were sure something was going on here, but they were not sure what." Tunnel veteran Major Nguyen Quot estimated that forty-eight kilometers of tunnel excavated during the war against the French had grown to two hundred kilometers by the time the American army arrived in 1965. After 1961, hitherto piecemeal local digging was connected up to form an integrated network. The Americans would nickname it the little IRT, after part of the New York City subway system.

Diem's reaction to the guerrilla offensive was to seek the best available advice on rural pacification. He hired as an adviser Sir Robert Thompson, architect of Britain's successful "strategic hamlet" policy to overcome the Chinese Communist-led insurgency in Malaya (as it then was). Acting on his advice, the ARVN began concentrating the rural population into special encampments fortified by government troops. Ngo Dinh Nhu himself supervised the inauguration of the first strategic hamlet in Cu Chi district in 1961. Most of the population was rehoused in this compulsory fashion, to separate them from the guerrillas; the exceptions were the villages in the Ho Bo woods, which remained "liberated" and under Viet Cong control. On 3 February 1963, the ARVN launched Operation Sunrise into the adjoining district of Ben Cat. The Viet Cong avoided contact, and the peasants were herded into a new showpiece strategic hamlet at Ben Thuong. In fact, the Viet Cong usually remained in the countryside, hidden in the tunnel system, when their families were displaced into "agrovilles." Supplying the guerrillas with the strictly rationed rice and other food became an elaborate operation of smuggling and concealment, ruthlessly punished when detected. Meanwhile, propaganda was created to distance the villagers from the guerrillas. The disparaging name Viet Cong (Vietnamese Communist) was coined to describe all those South Vietnamese groups that opposed President Diem and to give them an image of ruthless and fanatical cruelty. (The names Viet Cong, VC, and Charlie—short for Victor Charlie—have survived the war and are now used without any pejorative overtone.) The Viet Cong could be murderous, in that they saw themselves as at war, and executed appointed officials and sympathizers of the government, such as the district chief of Cu Chi. However, the peasants did not in the main have to be terrorized into acquiescence by such tactics. The Viet Cong were themselves villagers, or their sons and daughters, and operated most of the time with the consent and assistance of the people among whom they lived.

President John F. Kennedy took office in 1961, and found that his administration's resolve in confronting Communism was on the line in Southeast Asia. Anxious to avoid the slur of being "soft" on Communism, he was embarrassed by early upsets like the Bay of Pigs fiasco in Cuba. After his unhappy summit with Nikita Khrushchev in Vienna, Kennedy said, "Now we have a problem making our power credible, and Vietnam is the place." The internal threat to Diem's regime was perceived as the tide of Communism engulfing Asia; South Vietnam, said Kennedy, was "a proving ground for democracy." Both he and his successor, Lyndon Johnson, were confident that American military might would reverse Communist successes. Gradually, its presence in Vietnam was stepped up: U.S. advisers to the ARVN were increased to 12,000 by mid-1962. Earlier that year American Military Assistance Command Vietnam (MACV, pronounced "Macvee") was set up in Saigon. Kennedy was consciously edging his country into what French president Charles de Gaulle had warned him would be "a bottomless military and political swamp."

The strategic hamlet program progressively decayed and collapsed. The peasants returned to their native villages and the ARVN was unable to restrain them. In August 1963 the Viet Cong even overran the showpiece hamlet of Ben Thuong near Ben Cat. ARVN military disasters multiplied, despite superior equipment, aircraft, and American advisers. Of particular psychological impact in South Vietnam was the destruction by the Viet Cong Phu Loi battalion of the elite ARVN unit, the Black Tiger (or Panther) battalion. It was at Duong Long, about a mile north of the village of Ben Suc, on 31 December 1963. The Black Tigers were notorious for their cruelty, rape, and looting, and were alleged to have eaten the livers of dead Viet Cong.

A few weeks before Kennedy was assassinated, in November 1963, President Diem was murdered during a coup staged with Washington's consent. This followed city-based agitation by Buddhists, long offended by Catholic domination, and led to a bewildering series of military juntas in Saigon. Viet Cong activity was, by 1964, augmented by practical help from North Vietnam. The militants who had gone north after 1954 had filtered home, trained and motivated for political action and guerrilla war. With them came the first North Vietnamese soldiers to fight alongside the Viet Cong under the command of the Communists' southern headquarters, the Central Office for South Vietnam (COSVN).

Shortly before American soldiers arrived in force in 1965,

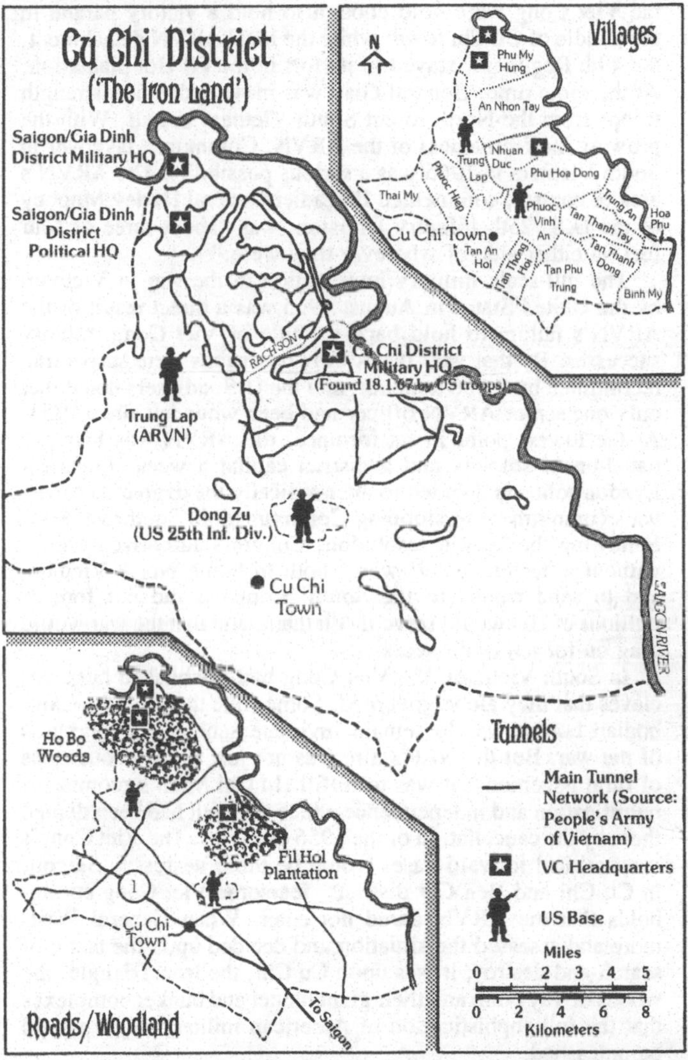
Cu Chi District
('The Iron Land')
Saigon/Gia Dinh District Military HQ
Saigon/Gia Dinh District Political HQ
RACH SON
Cu Chi District Military HQ (Found 18.1.67 by US troops)
Trung Lap (ARVN)
Dong Zu (US 25th Inf. Div.)
Cu Chi Town
SAIGON RIVER
Villages
N
Phu My Hung
An Nhon Tay
Trung Lap
Nhuan Duc
Phu Hoa Dong
Thai My
Phuoc Hiep
Phuoc Vinh An
Trung An
Hoa Phu
Tan Thanh Tay
Cu Chi Town
Tan An Hoi
Tan Thong Hoi
Tan Phu Trung
Tan Thanh Dong
Binh My
Ho Bo Woods
Fil Hol Plantation
1
Cu Chi Town
To Saigon
Roads/Woodland
Tunnels
Main Tunnel Network (Source: People's Army of Vietnam)
VC Headquarters
US Base
Miles
0 1 2 3 4 5
0 2 4 6 8
Kilometers

the Viet Cong were bold enough to hold a victory parade in the middle of Cu Chi town, while the local ARVN detachment, the 49th Regiment, stayed in its fort in the Fil Hol plantation. At the same time, General Giap was moving division-strength troops from the North to cut South Vietnam in half. With the growing ineffectiveness of the ARVN, Communist takeover in South Vietnam in 1965 was a serious possibility. The ARVN's area of control, commented Brigadier General Harley Mooney of the U.S. 25th Infantry Division, was "about three or four feet on either side of wherever they were."

The full-scale military intervention in the war in Vietnam by the United States in August 1965 was a direct result of the ARVN's failure to hold back the tide of Viet Cong military successes. By that year the ARVN desertions were surpassing recruitment by 2,000 a month, and the U.S. advisers noted that only one senior ARVN officer had been wounded since 1954. At the lowest point in its fortunes, the ARVN was losing a battalion of soldiers and a district capital a week. President Lyndon Johnson decided to alter radically the degree of America's commitment to stopping Communism in Southeast Asia. Following the Tonkin resolution, Congress authorized him—without a declaration of war—both to bomb North Vietnam and to send troops to the South; Congress did not foresee millions of GIs would serve in Vietnam, and that the war would drag on for ten more years.

In South Vietnam, the Viet Cong had established huge enclaves that they alone governed. Some, like those on the Cambodian border, would remain inviolate sanctuaries for much of the war. But the NLF's aim was not just to carve out areas of rural hegemony; it was to fulfill Ho Chi Minh's promise of reunification and independence which they felt had been denied them by the cancellation of the 1956 elections. The Viet Cong's most critical forward bases would be those nearest to Saigon, in Cu Chi and Ben Cat districts, fearsome Viet Cong strongholds that the ARVN dared not enter. When General Westmoreland assessed the situation and decided upon the tactic of search-and-destroy, it was upon Cu Chi, the Iron Triangle, the woods of Tay Ninh and their giant tunnel and bunker complexes that the full sophistication of American military might would be unleashed.

The first sizable American units to reach Vietnam were

the marines. Their initial task was to defend coastal enclaves and airstrips. Large units of the army soon followed and halted the downhill slide caused by the collapsing ARVN. In mid-1965, General Giap tried to cut South Vietnam in two along a line from Pleiku in the central highlands to the coast. This threat was averted in October by the bloody confrontation in the Ia Drang valley between three North Vietnamese regiments and the 1st Air Cavalry Division, helicoptered into battle. This event established the pattern that would be one of General Westmoreland's proudest boasts, that the United States Army never lost a battle in Vietnam. Faced with such overwhelming firepower, including air support, the Communists were obliged to fight a different sort of war—harrying their enemies at times and places of their own choosing and otherwise avoiding contact by concealment. Only when the Americans had left Vietnam did the Communists again wage a conventional war of movement—eventually with success.

By the end of 1965, the ground war in South Vietnam was the main focus of American strategy. The bombing of North Vietnam was having little effect, nor was diplomatic pressure on Hanoi. The policy of nation-building, developing schemes such as irrigation, to ingratiate the Saigon regime with the peasants, could not undo historic xenophobic attitudes. The only place where America could be seen to be succeeding was in killing the Viet Cong by the use of its unmatched military technology and the size of its units. A war of attrition was the result, one that measured its success by counting the enemy dead.

General Westmoreland, who had headed American Military Assistance Command, Vietnam, since 1964, saw numbers as the solution to the deteriorating situation in the South. American commitment grew throughout 1965, and whole divisions of over 20,000 men each found themselves crossing the Pacific. Westmoreland's first concern was to protect Saigon; his second to "pacify" the countryside. He decided, therefore, to ring Saigon with huge base camps that would, in time, become almost permanent in character. The sites chosen were, not surprisingly, close to areas of Viet Cong domination and intense activity. At Di An, south of the Iron Triangle, would be the headquarters of the 1st Infantry Division, the "Big Red One." The Hawaii-based 25th (Tropic Lightning) Division would be based beside Cu Chi town. And there were many others. Before establishing these camps, there had to be sweep operations to secure the areas.

Large military operations had to await the dry season. In January 1966, Operation Crimp was the first sweep by American and allied troops into the Viet Cong strongholds of the Ho Bo woods and other parts of Cu Chi district. This was to "clear and secure" the area adjoining the planned new base camp. Before the operation began, artillery fire was rained on the area, and there were softening-up raids by B-52 bombers. B-52s had been built for strategic, or nuclear, attack, but from 1965 on, over a hundred were adapted to carry dozens of 750-pound conventional bombs. They flew from bases on the island of Guam and in northern Thailand. B-52 raids were called up at twenty-four hours' notice, and targeted by controllers on the ground in Vietnam. The planes were almost inaudible to their targets because they flew so high. The thirty-ton load of high explosive would leave a mile-long swath of destruction and deep craters.

After the bombing came the GIs and their allies. On 7 January 1966 over 8,000 soldiers of the 1st Infantry Division, the 173rd Airborne Brigade, and the Royal Australian Regiment were airlifted from Phu Loi to Cu Chi district, and straight into trouble.

3

Operation Crimp

AS THE SUN rose on another cloudless day that promised only the inevitable invasion of heat by breakfast time, the U.S. Air Force C-130 transport aircraft coughed noisily into life and lumbered awkwardly down the runway at Phuoc Vinh. It was Friday, 7 January 1966, and the 1st Battalion of the 28th Infantry, part of the 3rd Brigade of the U.S. 1st Infantry Division, the Big Red One, was being airlifted to Phu Loi in preparation for the start of the largest American operation yet in Vietnam—Operation Crimp.

The Christmas pause in the bombing raids against North Vietnam ordered by President Johnson was two weeks old—his public gesture to lure the Communists to the negotiating table would end in failure three weeks later. In the South, General Westmoreland's Operation Crimp was intended to teach the Communists a lesson they would never forget. With full armed might—helicopters, tanks, armored personnel carriers, and no fewer than 8,000 fighting men—he was going to solve the problem of Cu Chi.

A recently declassified U.S. Army report reveals that Crimp was to be "a massive attack . . . to strike at the very heart of the Viet Cong machine in South Vietnam at the notorious Ho

Bo woods just west of the fabled Iron Triangle itself." This no-nonsense offensive was planned to destroy the long-time Communist redoubt by finding and eliminating the politico-military headquarters of the entire Viet Cong Military Region IV.

No World War II scenario could have been more apt. After playing cat-and-mouse with the ARVN troops for several years, the Viet Cong had it coming to them. Now the dogs of war were about to be unleashed.

From Phu Loi, the GIs of the 1st Battalion, 28th Infantry, were to be flown by helicopter directly to Landing Zone Jack, following on the heels of the 1st Battalion of the 16th Infantry. The location was almost on top of the Ho Bo woods. Long before the sun had flattened the dawn blue of the sky into an opaque glare, Operation Crimp had begun.

At Phu My Hung, on the banks of the Saigon River and within the Ho Bo woods area, Lieutenant, later Captain, Nguyen Thanh Linh of the Viet Cong's 7th Cu Chi Battalion sat deep inside the tunnels reading and rereading the long handwritten reports he had already drafted to his regional commander about the forthcoming American operation. Linh had command of a VC battalion of under 300 men. "We knew they were coming," he said. "It followed basic military principles. They'd bombed, shelled, taken reconnaissance photographs. All this was unusual enough to make it clear there would be a big operation."

Linh's battalion was one small unit within the local Communist defense force of at most some 1,000 men. Its mission was the defense of the all-important Phu My Hung tunnel complex, one of the largest in the entire Cu Chi district. Linh's soldiers were scarcely battle-hardened veterans. Most were teenagers or younger. Linh had, paradoxically, argued against being given command of too many men to defend the tunnels. "The more men I had, the more casualties I would receive," he explained. "Fighting from the tunnels was an advantage if I did not have too many men. Often one or two riflemen would be enough, five or six rifles would be sufficient. In this kind of war one should attack numerous enemy troops with only a few men."

Linh's major problem was to stimulate his youngsters into facing and fighting the Americans. Small unit attacks on the

South Vietnamese soldiers, random guerrilla assaults, all this was one thing. But facing a superpower that had put rockets in space and had the capacity to destroy the world was another. Besides, Americans were very tall, some were tall *and* black. They even had hair on their arms.

In his role as cadre, Linh fielded some awkward questions from his boy soldiers. Would a bullet fired from an old carbine kill a big American? Would it kill a black the same as a white? "I reassured them their bullets would kill if they struck the right spot, and I warned them that American bullets would kill them just as easily. Four days later, the Americans came. We watched with heavy hearts the helicopters endlessly landing men."

As the 1st Battalion, 28th Infantry, settled down on the landing zone, the men could see that their colleagues from the 1st Battalion, 16th Infantry, were already in trouble and taking fire from the north corner edge of the landing zone. Battalion commander Lieutenant Colonel Robert Haldane could see his men were growing increasingly apprehensive, particularly when they saw their comrades from the lead battalion being hit by enemy bullets and grenades. Captain Terry Christy, in command of B Company, knew he had to move his men off that landing zone and into the tree line quickly. He yelled at his platoon leaders and NCOs and moved all his men within minutes. But the enemy had suddenly and mysteriously disappeared. A few meters inside the tree line at the edge of a rubber plantation, Christy's men stumbled across a large trench. It was the first sign of a most elaborate underground fortification. Haldane did not have time to check the complex. He remained puzzled. How could the Viet Cong, who had been firing on the 1st Battalion, have fled undetected through the relatively open rubber trees? Haldane knew his unit was to operate here for several weeks, before handing the area over to the newly arrived U.S. 25th Infantry Division, and he did not want an enemy that simply melted away every time he advanced.

As the battalion moved forward with three companies, cache after cache of rice, salt, and other foodstuffs was turned up, perhaps enough to feed an enemy regiment. A large minefield was found across the wooded north end of the area, indicating the enemy had planned the area to be a permanent military complex. During the next two days of Crimp as the huge sweeps continued, soldiers began reporting foxholes, trenches, mines, caves, right across the 1st Battalion's 1,500-meter front. The men were slowly approaching the Saigon River; there was ample evidence of VC base activity, but something was still wrong. Battle was simply not being joined. There were no running fights, no shouts, nobody was surrendering—yet GI after GI was being hit by Viet Cong sniper fire. Haldane watched anxiously as his men's morale began to ebb; he prayed they would soon pin the enemy against the river and extract their revenge for their own mounting losses. But when, on Monday 10 January, his battalion finally reached the wide expanse of rice paddies that linked the dry ground to the wide, sluggish Saigon River, his soldiers had seen only two fleeting glimpses of the enemy running through the jungle.

Haldane spent half the day by the river. Then, late in the afternoon, the communications net began to reveal that the 173rd Airborne, and the Australians to the north, had at last made contact with the Viet Cong—in tunnels. On Tuesday morning at first light, Haldane's battalion began to retrace its steps. It was beginning to dawn on the commander what had happened. He had actually walked over the enemy. He began a detailed search for tunnel entrances. But nothing was obvious to the eye. A few GIs, very reluctantly, lowered themselves into a trench, explored it, and discovered an air-raid shelter large enough to house several men. But no tunnels. The men, now hot, tired, and nervous at their inability to fight the kind of infantry war they had been taught to fight, waited for further instructions. Platoon Sergeant Stewart Green, a slim, wiry 130-pound NCO, hunched down to relax. Suddenly he leaped up cursing. The country was full of scorpions, huge fire ants, and snakes, and he had just been bitten on his backside, or at least assumed he had. But as he searched the dead leaves on the ground with his rufle butt, ready to crush his tormentor, he discovered the bite had come from a nail. A further, gingerly conducted search disclosed a small wooden trapdoor, perforated with air holes and with beveled sides that prevented it from falling into the tunnel below. The first tunnel had been found.

Haldane ran almost gratefully toward it, but as he stood at the entrance he realized that there were no training manuals to tell him precisely what to do next. When the battalion had trained for combat back at Fort Riley in Kansas, the program had not included instruction in tunnel warfare. The lessons of the stunning Viet Minh victory at Dien Bien Phu, if studied, had not been digested. Neither the Americans nor the Australians had any experience of dealing with what to them was a new phenomenon. But they were relatively unconcerned; the famous OJT principle (On-the-Job Training) would somehow see them through. But in January 1966, muddling through, adapting, applying combat empiricism, would not be enough to wipe out the Communist presence in the "liberated zones" of Cu Chi district.

Stewart Green volunteered to explore the tunnel he had uncovered with his behind. He leaped in and, with Haldane's encouragement, others joined the platoon sergeant to explore the black depths. The men penetrated a short distance and found hospital supplies, which were brought up and handed to the unit's S-2 (intelligence officer), Captain Marvin Kennedy. As Kennedy was analyzing the packages in detail he suddenly heard shouts; he turned and was astonished to see the tunnel explorers shoot out of the tunnel hole in breathless haste. Stewart Green was last out, sweating and covered in dirt. He told Kennedy that they had found a side passage from the main tunnel and had suddenly stumbled on some thirty Viet Cong soldiers, whom he could see in the dim light of a candle one of them was holding, which the Communists had rapidly extinguished as the GIs blundered near to them. Captain Kennedy, delighted that he had some thirty enemy trapped under his very feet, called a Vietnamese interpreter and ordered him to return to the tunnel with the unfortunate Stewart Green and order the enemy to surrender. The two men reluctantly went back down. Their mission lasted all of a few minutes and they returned embarrassed and empty-handed. Green explained to Captain Kennedy that the interpreter had actually refused to talk to the enemy. The captain quizzed the interpreter, who balefully informed the American officer that he had to "hold his breath" in the tunnel because "there was no air" and he would have "died if he had started to talk." From a military rather than a medical point of view, that last statement might have been extremely accurate. In the event, the VC escaped.

Sensing the overpowering reluctance to investigate the tunnels that had descended on his men and their ARVN interpreter, Lieutenant Colonel Haldane decided to smoke the enemy out, and ordered a lightweight gasoline-powered blower to be brought to the tunnel entrance. Several red smoke grenades were dropped into the hole and blown through the tunnel. Within a few minutes the GIs were astonished to see red smoke emerging from numerous exit points all over the ground. However, the smoke made no impact on the enemy, so the battalion commander ordered CS, a nonlethal riot-control gas, to be pumped through the tunnel. Once again this brought no result. So finally, Stewart Green was prevailed upon to make his third and last trip into the hole, accompanied this time by a demolitions expert. The men placed charges on each side of the main and secondary tunnels, and crawled quickly back to the surface. The earth exploded and with grim satisfaction Haldane moved his unit on to catch up with the 2nd Battalion.

It had been exactly two days earlier and a few miles away at Phu My Hung that Lieutenant Nguyen Thanh Linh made *his* first contact with the Americans on the sweep. He had thought his tactics through very carefully. Everything depended on the tunnels. But did the Americans know about them and had *they* planned a tactical move to counter his considerable environmental advantage?

"I had divided my men into small cell-like units. I told them under no circumstances to concentrate. I spread my men into each hamlet where we had well-hidden firing positions to hold back the Americans. Each cell had some three or four soldiers. On 8 January, Crimp was a day old. I was at Goc Chang hamlet in An Nhon Tay village (in the Ho Bo woods). The troops had been pouring in by helicopter. They didn't attack right away. They set up positions and built a command post; then their troops advanced along the village paths, two to three soldiers walking ahead, more following behind. We saw they really *were* very big men. We waited until they were very close. We were in our spider-hold firing positions—the Americans never saw us at all. I ordered my men to fire, one GI fell down, the others just stood around looking at him. They were so bewildered, they did not hide or take defensive positions. They did not even know where the bullets had come from. We kept on shooting. In those days we did not have the AK-47 (later the standard Communist rifle) but very old Russian cavalry rifles, K-44s. The Americans just kept on looking. They were very naive, very brave. Although their fellows kept falling down, they kept on advancing. They should have retreated. Then they called for artillery. When the first shells landed we simply went into the communication tunnels and went on to another place. The Americans continued advancing, but we'd gone. That was the pattern; there was nothing special.

"All that day we fought like snipers and killed many of them. If we had had good weapons and fired continuously, bang, bang, bang, I don't know how the Americans would have reacted. Instead we fired pop, pop, pop, bullet by bullet. They were so naive that when they did lie down, it was just as they had been taught at military school, not the way soldiers really do it on battlefields. They went down on their hands, spreading their legs. They looked silly. We did not seek to attack whole platoons or companies. As we moved back they moved forward and we just shot more. I made a handful of my men work hard, but that first day American soldiers were killed like that everywhere. Later they were more cautious; they no longer walked openly along hamlet paths. But then they started to fall into our traps or were killed by wired hand grenades."

As Crimp was ending and its immediate follow-up, Operation Buckskin, was beginning, Associated Press war correspondent Peter Arnett reported precisely what Captain Linh was to describe seventeen years afterward:

> TRUNG LAP, SOUTH VIETNAM, 12 January 1966—It was a long bloody mile we walked today. At times it was an inferno. Riot gas drifted through the trees, burning where it touched a man's skin. The wounded writhed on the ground looking grotesque in their gas masks. It was a walk where death lurked in the trees where the enemy snipers hid, and under the ground where their mines lay.

Earlier that day a squad from B Company, 2nd Battalion, 28th Infantry, found one of Linh's claymore mines hidden in the jungle beside a dusty track. All day the squad had been plagued with mines, snipers, and tunnels. As the men milled around the claymore, forty-three-year-old Lieutenant Colonel George S. Eyster, commanding officer of the 2nd Battalion, 28th Infantry (the Black Lions), approached the group and warned, "Cut the wires, don't pull them." Then he took out a map and began talking to the company commander, Captain George F. Dailey. It was nine-thirty in the morning. Suddenly a sniper opened up from a tunnel spider hole—a small, shallow one-man fighting pit with a connecting escape tunnel—and Lieutenant Colonel Eyster fell with a bullet in the chest. As the dying officer was lifted gently on to a field stretcher, he turned to a journalist who was there and said, "Before I go, I'd like to talk to the guy who controls those incredible men in the tunnels."

That man was Lieutenant Nguyen Thanh Linh. "Those tunnels were everything to us in Crimp," he explained nearly two decades after Lieutenant Colonel Eyster's grudging words of admiration. "There were no set battles, but everyone who could fire a rifle did so. We used them for constant surprise sniper attacks and we used them, most importantly, for observation. Thanks to the tunnels, we could remain with the Americans, see how their troops behaved and reacted, watch their mistakes. Our observations helped us decide what kinds of booby traps to set and where to set them.

"You know, we even saw helicopters bringing special water for the Americans to wash themselves, and we realized the soldiers used nothing Vietnamese. I had been ordered by my superiors to provide intelligence about American battlefield tactics, and the tunnels made all this possible."

Linh's judgment remains harsh, but it is a fact that the general direction of training for the United States Army in the sixties was basically incompatible with what the troops were to face in Vietnam. GIs had been trained either for a set-piece confrontation with the Warsaw Pact powers on the plains of Central Europe, or for the kind of "human wave" battles they had fought a decade earlier in Korea. Military high technology, so liberating yet so full of constraints, was geared to saving American lives, while at the same time killing thousands of the enemy by remote control. The American army in effect entered the Vietnam War without a long-enough military memory. From the experience of state militias during the American Revolution, to the Spanish-American War; from the legendary Merrill's Marauders, the highly skilled and toughened American jungle fighters who served in the Burma-India theater in World War II, to the members of the OSS (the Office of Strategic Services), who on specific assignments fought alongside native guerrilla forces, the Americans had a long and honorable guerrilla-fighting tradition. Where and why this was forgotten in Vietnam remains a mystery. However, when Lieutenant Linh was peeping through fieldglasses at the Americans from the relative safety of his tunnels, he at least was following the oldest military dictum: Know your enemy. For the GIs, both the enemy and his terrain were, inexplicably, a dangerous military and geographical novelty.

By Tuesday morning, 11 January, the rubber plantation on the perimeter of Landing Zone Jack was beginning to look like a World War II movie set. A tight defensive perimeter had been established, Crimp had been renamed Buckskin, but the U.S. casualties continued to mount alarmingly from the apparently random Viet Cong attacks. The Communists still appeared and disappeared like magic. At the northern edge of the landing zone Haldane's men were well dug in. By now dirt-streaked and acutely tunnel-conscious, the GIs were quick to check any suspicious-looking holes. They found one, about a foot in diameter, that entered the ground at 45 degrees. The hole remained a curiosity—in fact, it was a tunnel's ventilation hole. At dusk, as the Americans settled down for an uneasy rest, they suddenly heard several grenade explosions and carbine shots—*from within their own perimeter*. Colonel Haldane sprinted over to B Company's sector, where the explosions had been heard, and was met by the ubiquitous Sergeant Stewart Green and a number of other B Company soldiers, all standing around a tunnel trapdoor. One of the GIs told Haldane, "We were just sitting there, almost on top of it, when the friggin' thing pops open, out comes Charlie, throws two grenades, reaches down, grabs a carbine, sprays us, and before we can pick up our weapons, he's back down in the ground and that goddamn trapdoor shuts over him."

Stewart Green, whom OJT had now developed into a reluctant expert on tunnels, was invited by Haldane to explore this one. He did not return for two and a half hours, and reckoned he had traveled a full mile and a half underground before returning. He had found what he called vestibules in the walls, but little else. Instinct alone prompted Green to ask for several rolls of communications wire, a field telephone, gas grenades, gas masks, flashlights, pistols, and compasses. Green and his squad went back down, now able to talk to the battalion, and to defend themselves. After having traveled a mile and a quarter (scientifically gauged by the length of wire played out), Green saw a light ahead. In curt messages to Haldane above ground, Green described the first recorded tunnel firefight between Americans and Viet Cong. The GIs put on their gas masks and threw their gas grenades. Even above ground Green's buddies could hear the sound of the battle. The squad fought its way back to the tunnel entrance—save for one soldier, who completely missed it in the dark—and pulled out. Green himself returned to find the errant soldier and bring him back. The Viet Cong, as usual, simply melted away.

The following morning, renewed exploration began to show just what the Americans faced in Cu Chi. Not only were they confronting an army of moles, but they had to deal with them in mole holes, perhaps the most extraordinary battleground the American soldier would ever encounter. Haldane ordered the tunnels to be closely explored. This thoroughness paid off. The men found a basket of grenades covering a trapdoor to a second level. They went in and found a lower chamber containing 146 service records belonging to the D-308 Viet Cong Company. They even found a third level, in which a tunnel branched away in two directions. One branch contained a small escape hole only large enough for a diminutive Vietnamese to crawl through. The other branch led back to the main shaft Stewart Green had discovered.

Later, A Company found another tunnel complex. One of its own soldiers was killed by a Viet Cong soldier who suddenly appeared out of a huge anthill. When the GIs rushed the hill, they discovered a tunnel entrance at the rear.

On Tuesday the 11th, in a tunnel somewhere in the Ho Bo woods, a Viet Cong called Tran Bang was making his diary entry. It described a situation far removed from Lieutenant Linh's optimism about the effective failure of Crimp. Tran Bang wrote:

> Have spent four days in tunnel. About eight to nine thousand American soldiers were in for a sweep operation. The attack was fierce in the last few days. A number of underground tunnels collapsed. Some of our men were caught in them and have not been able to get out yet. It is not known what has become of sisters BA, BAY, HONG

HAN and TAN HO in these tunnels. In their attempt to provide security for the agency TAM and UT were killed. Their bodies left unattended, deteriorated, have not been buried yet. In the afternoon one of our village unit members trying to stay close to the enemy for reconnaissance was killed and his body has not been recovered.

Fifteen minutes ago, enemy jets dropped bombs; houses collapsed and trees fell. I was talking when a rocket exploded two meters away and bombs poured down like a torrent.

We should fight them, we should annihilate them, you [U.S. soldiers] will have no way out. It is always dark before sunrise. After cold days, warm days will come. The most tiresome moment is when one moves up a hill. One must rise up, disregarding death and hardships, determined to defeat the American aggressors.

Oh, what hard days, one has to stay in [the] tunnel, eat cold rice with salt, drink unboiled water. However, one is free and feels at ease.

The entry is dated 1445 hours, 11 January 1966. The following day, the diary became one of nearly 8,000 items captured by the Americans.

On the same day that Tran Bang wrote down his bittersweet thoughts, the tunnels claimed one of their first victims, Corporal Bob Bowtell of the 3rd Field Troop of the Royal Australian Engineers. The troop was part of the 1st Battalion Group of the Royal Australian Regiment, brought in to act as a blocking force on the northern perimeter of the Crimp operation, an area covered with light scrub, rubber plantations, and secondary growth. The Aussies, with their traditional bush hats and British military background, made a distinct and colorful contrast to the GIs. They were all volunteers, and most were keen to find the action. Third Field Troop was led by a large, beefy, popular officer, Captain Alex MacGregor. He was known in the Australian military jargon as a hands-on type, an officer who truly led his men, and would ask from them nothing that he had not done or would not do himself. He was a front row rugby forward, built like an ox, and had already spent two years with an engineer construction squadron in Papua New Guinea, a place not generally regarded as being particularly homely or comfortable for a white man. In Vietnam he was one soldier who dealt with the prevalent foot-rot problem in a robust way: He discarded his socks and suffered the agonies of blisters for several days, but then, as calluses formed, his feet slowly developed a covering that was actually tougher than the jungle boots he wore. With him the captain had a small and enthusiastic team, including Sapper Denis Ayoub, his radio man, and Sappers Les Colmer and Barry Harford. Colmer was MacGregor's batman, but unlike the "butler" batmen of the British system, he followed his boss, often into fire. Sapper Harford was Colmer's friend; both had joined the army from Broken Hill, the large mining town in New South Wales. Although neither had been a miner, the mining background in their lives was to prove invaluable. Corporal Bowtell had been a friend of theirs.

On the first day of Crimp the troop found action without difficulty. Homemade grenades were spotted rigged as antipersonnel mines, with tripwires strung from the trees from ankle height to head height. On the second day they even ran across two mortar bombs activated by a grenade connected to an ankle-high tripwire. Later that day they found an area laced with punji stakes (razor-sharp bamboo spikes) set in concrete in the ground. A sapper of B Company demolition team stepped on one and it went straight through his foot.

By day three, the Australian infantrymen were beginning to take serious casualties. Captain MacGregor recalled that not only were the scouts of one leading infantry company killed, but when the stretcher-bearers were called for medical evacuation of the wounded, they were killed, too. In one action alone, four Aussies died. MacGregor and his engineer troop were called in when it became obvious that although the hot area had been surrounded, no Viet Cong had been sighted or killed. There was only one conclusion. They had, in the captain's words, "gone down." As the Australian ring of steel closed on the area, they found the tunnels.

Over the next four days, working with the Americans, the Australians slowly uncovered at least three-quarters of a mile of communication tunnels, bunkers, and underground chambers. MacGregor's men had been in the country for four months. This was already their fifth operation, and they were neither baffled by nor unduly apprehensive about the tunnels. They went down and explored. But there were mistakes.

They used a specially adapted commercial air blower called the "mighty mite" to blow smoke down the tunnels, and then watched carefully to see where the smoke came out of the ground so that they could begin a rough plot of where the tunnels spread. But the smoke stayed underground, and when the first Australian tunnel ferrets (as they were called) went below, they quickly became unconscious through lack of oxygen. This is how Corporal Bowtell died, in a tunnel war that was about to break out in earnest.

While exploring underground, Bowtell, a typically tall, lean Australian, unwisely tried to wriggle through a tiny trapdoor connecting one tunnel level with another. It measured sixteen inches by eleven inches, dimensions that would hardly have allowed a lithe Viet Cong guerrilla through, let alone a larger-framed Westerner. Bowtell got stuck and within seconds realized that lingering smoke from the "mighty mite" had expelled most of the oxygen in the tunnel. He shouted for help. Sapper Jim Daly volunteered to rescue his comrade, but by the time he got to the trapdoor, Bowtell was already unconscious. Futile attempts began above ground to sink an airshaft to the sapper. Daly was himself almost asphyxiated by the lingering fumes, but he had to try to cut Bowtell free with his knife by enlarging the tiny trapdoor frame in which the corporal's limp body was jammed. Four times he tried, but he failed to drag the corporal out, and finally, on the verge of collapse himself, he was ordered to stop. After Bowtell's death, MacGregor made sure no similar accidental deaths were ever to afflict the Australians. Jim Daly received a "mention in despatches" for "his sense of purpose, coolness in action and disregard for his own safety, which was an inspiration to all who fought with him."

Meanwhile, searching and destroying these incredible underground tunnels had to continue. Les Colmer and Barry Harford, the men from Broken Hill, volunteered to work with demolition explosives in the tunnels. Using his communications skills, Denis Ayoub rigged up a proficient underground telephone system. He found ammunition caches stored in small chambers, small booby-trapped Parker 57 pens, and even underground flag-making workshops, complete with sewing machines. Large rice caches were also found, every one of them booby-trapped—not just *around* the cache, but even *inside* the rice bags themselves. MacGregor made copious notes of what his men found. Only his bulk prevented him from leading the troop through the never-ending network of tunnels. It was MacGregor who realized the value to the Viet Cong of American combat detritus, after Denis Ayoub found a small tunnel workshop in which hand grenades had been made. The inner casing was made from a small discarded tomato juice tin, and the outer casing from an old beer can. The fragmentation pieces were blue metal road gravel, and the firing mechanism was from old French or American grenades. "Because of what we found in the tunnels," recalled MacGregor, "we ordered this policy of burn-bash-bury. We had twenty-four-hour ration packs with little tins in them. You never EVER left your tin around so it could be found, you never left anything the enemy could use. Your spoon, they would even use that for making weapons. We left nothing, absolutely nothing." This was a discipline the GIs could well have emulated more enthusiastically. As the war became harder on the Viet Cong, they used the waste so generously left around by the Americans more and more, and in some areas, they became dependent on it.

Tensions between the specialist engineers and the infantry began to show early in Operation Crimp. In an official Australian after-action report, the following laconic comments were recorded:

> In some cases, having secured tunnel entrances, infantry moved on to search other locations, leaving sappers underground with no immediate close-in protection. This does not foster confidence. One instance occurred where sappers were searching a tunnel under a house and the infantry commenced to burn the house. Sappers lose confidence under these circumstances.

There was some discord between the lanky Australians and their American comrades, too. Sapper (now Major) Denis Ayoub said quite bluntly: "The Americans taught us nothing about tunnel fighting in an hour that we hadn't already tried ourselves. Our determination to clear tunnels seemed to them to be little short of madness. They were quite surprised when our captain suggested that we were going to send guys down with a torch and pistol and a length of string."

While the Australians began to develop the earliest techniques for exploring and destroying some short tunnel systems, they had no real plan for dealing with the heart-stopping business of actually running into a Viet Cong guerrilla inside a tunnel. Denis Ayoub recalled the first time it happened to him, when he was behind another sapper who was leading in the exploration of a narrow communication tunnel: "One minute we were crawling through the tunnel, the next minute my mate, without a word, started to back up rather rapidly. No one could turn around in the tunnels we found on Crimp; you had to back out of the bloody things. So he started to back up, and I had to back up. No one said anything. When we got to the bottom of the shaft, he somehow managed to get past me and was first up and out. So I came up second, hoping to Christ that my legs weren't going to be left behind. When we got out, and my mate cooled down a bit, he told me he'd seen a man down there."

Fighting Charlie in his own tunnels was still a thing of the future. As American helicopters began to arrive to collect some of the thousands of Communist documents that had been found in the tunnels, Captain Alex MacGregor was ordering photographs taken of tunnel trapdoors and entrances, and of the booby traps found inside, and was busy making full notes of tunnel dimensions. Of all the tunnels intelligence assessments made during Crimp, the Royal Australian Engineers' was probably the most accurate and the most prescient. Unfortunately, despite their success, the Aussies were never again to be so involved in the tunnels of Cu Chi.

Alex MacGregor was to win the Military Cross for his courage and leadership of his engineer troop during Crimp. When the operation ended on 14 January, Australian deaths in Vietnam had doubled from eight to sixteen. The tunnels they had discovered turned out to be the huge complex that was part of the Viet Cong's Military Region IV headquarters.

The Americans were learning about tunnels, too. Three days before the operation ended, they brought in a huge mechanized flame-thrower to support an infantry task force attack to the north of Ho Bo woods. The flame-thrower was driven by Sergeant First Class Bernard Justen, then operations sergeant with the Chemical Section of the 1st Infantry Division. His flame-thrower, mounted on an APC, fired liquid napalm out of the nozzle, using compressed air. The droplets were ignited by gasoline. This system was known as saturation firing: "You didn't waste any as it shot to the target that way," said Justen. The diminutive Texan was eventually to specialize in tunnel warfare, but he admits that during Crimp he didn't quite know what was happening. "We knew nothing about the tunnels, and we had the wrong equipment. Everything that was learned was learned the hard way."

Justen used his flame-thrower to burn away jungle and growth near trenches. If this expensive technique exposed a tunnel entrance—some had trapdoors and some did not—then he would explore.

"We started going down checking tunnels out, and right in the middle of it, while we're going into one tunnel, they [the VC] would pop up somewhere else and the shooting'd be going on up above you. You could hear them up above ground shooting and you never knew if you popped up out of one of these holes whether somebody from our side might take a shot at you. So you used to tell the guy—in them days we didn't lay wire or nothing because we were working blind—we used to tell them to hold off if they saw us coming out from a different hole to the one we went in. Hell, you didn't know where you were going to come out. I went down there, I got real close to Charlie—warm food, papers lying around, even found a calendar with the day's date on, that's pretty damn close. But truth is, I'd rather run them out than meet them down there."

Justen was later to instruct others in tunnel warfare. He made drawings of what he found, including the tunnel water traps. The water traps, it turned out, were not to deal with drainage. They were rather like U-bends in the tunnel system, and they prevented tear gas or CS riot-control gas from blowing all the way into a tunnel complex. The early tunnel explorers had to navigate the water traps the hard way. Most just waded in, held their breath, and swam up the other side, always assuming they could do it on one lungful of air. "That really was the worst part of me," explained Justen. "You never knew what was waiting the other side, you never knew if in that black hole you'd get to the other side, and when you did, you came out soaking wet and stinking rotten. It was the worst part of it."

The commander of the 173rd Airborne, Brigadier General Ellis W. Williamson, was to write hugely enthusiastic after-action reports on Operation Crimp. Hindsight gives us all twenty-twenty vision, but history shows some of his optimism to have been either premature or hollow. "Most of January 13th was spent destroying and contaminating the tunnel and bunker system," he wrote eight days after Crimp had finished. "CS-1, a powder contaminant with long-lasting effects, was used for the first time and should prove quite effective. It was placed throughout the tunnel systems by placing a long line of detonation cord where desired. Crystallized CS-1 was then placed along the detonation cord just prior to the explosion. It is hoped that this approach will prove to be a lasting deterrent." It was an ill-founded hope. The water traps and the tightly sealed trapdoors connecting the various levels were to ensure that contamination usually failed.

In *his* after-action report, Colonel William D. Brodbeck of the Big Red One was considerably less sanguine, but more prescient. "CS riot-control agent was used without much success," he wrote. "Tunnels were baffled by the VC to prevent effective use of CS. Positive results were obtained when men went into the tunnels. A different combat technique is required when a man goes into a tunnel after a VC. However the same amount of courage is required in this type of fighting."

As Crimp and Buckskin drew to a close the "Sky Soldiers" remounted their noisy winged horses and flew back to base; the trucks and the APCs ground out of the hostile woods, leaving burned and empty villages. Most of the local population had been evacuated by the Americans because "they had lived under VC rule for many years, consequently they were thoroughly indoctrinated by the VC and willingly supported them."

Colonel Nguyen Van Minh of the Vietnamese People's Army is compiling the full military history of all the campaigns in the old Saigon—Gia Dinh districts throughout the war. He is a crewcut professional soldier, and his views about the Americans are almost wholly political. Nevertheless, there is some truth in his assessment of Crimp as an American failure. Nothing was lost that could not be replaced, he claimed, and such was the mobility and flexibility of the Viet Cong military structure that it could survive those short, drastic American hammer blows and re-emerge fighting.

Operation Crimp failed to clear the target area of the enemy for very long, failed to destroy his infrastructure, and highlighted the inherent weakness of the search-and-destroy tactic that was to become standard operating procedure for the U.S. Army. The operation's major achievement was the discovery of some parts of the enormous tunnel complex that ran underneath Cu Chi district, a discovery that concentrated minds on how to deal with the problem in the future.

Ultimately, what was self-evident was that the United States armed forces were not facing a bunch of Communist terrorists who had somehow infiltrated from the North and held a placid South Vietnamese peasantry at knife-point. The Americans had discovered a new enemy. He was better armed than they had imagined; he was far more elusive than they had imagined; he seemed to set his own conditions for combat; and he must have found willing support from the inhabitants of the Cu Chi villages to operate with the subtlety that allowed such room for maneuver. The Americans had begun to discover the real Viet Cong.

4

The Guerrillas of the Viet Cong

THE MORTALLY WOUNDED Lieutenant Colonel George Eyster called the Viet Cong "those incredible men in the tunnels." They were spartan and resilient guerrillas, whose existence was very different from that of their enemies. They dressed like the peasants, often in black silken pajamas and wore no badges of rank—a checkered scarf identified them as guerrillas. Their footwear was Ho Chi Minh sandals, cut from truck tires, with a strip of inner tube between the toes. They slept in roll-up hammocks, often made of U.S. parachute nylon and wrapped their daily ration, a little ball of rice, in similar material. They carried a water bottle, or canteen, usually made in China, and an improvised oil lamp, made from a perfume or medicine bottle with a wick, for the frequent journeys they would make underground. Some wore leather wrist-straps to enable their comrades to drag them easily into a tunnel if they were wounded or killed. They moved around on foot or on bicycles.

The cadres, or political officers, of the Viet Cong were in the main southerners, who had trained in North Vietnam for about eight years after the French surrendered in 1954, and had returned down the Ho Chi Minh trail to take up the fight. By the late sixties thousands of North Vietnamese soldiers would also make that wearying and hazardous journey to join Viet Cong battalions. (Some of these soldiers wore more conventional uniforms, with ammunition pouches and other accoutrements, even sun helmets.) All Communist troops in the South were known as the People's Liberation Army, under the command of COSVN, the party's southern headquarters. They were divided into local guerrillas, regional forces, and regular, or main-force, units. All structures were in threes, from three regiments per division to the three-man cell—of which three formed a squad, three squads a platoon, and so on. The three-man cell was a Chinese Communist idea; the group was intended to be mutually supportive (when one member was wounded, for example) but also to deny all privacy and to prevent desertion or deviation from the Viet Cong's puritanical standards of conduct. The political commissars enjoyed equal authority with commanding officers, and worked on the maintenance of morale, commitment, and group loyalty.

The guerrillas, male and female, were usually barely educated peasants and were recruited in their early teens. The Front devoted many hours a week to "educating," or indoctrinating, its soldiers, but encouraged discussion and criticism at such sessions. Both the southern guerrillas and the North Vietnamese grew up in what one American officer called a "tightly controlled cocoon of information" that convinced them of the justice of their cause. "Everything possible was done," said Le Vinh, a former Viet Cong political commissar, "to ensure that not a single soldier should have a single doubt as to why and for whom he was fighting." This training was based on the precepts of Mao Zedong, who had written: "The basis for guerrilla discipline must be the individual conscience. With guerrillas, a discipline of coercion is ineffective." Without adequate motivation the guerrillas would have found the danger and discomfort of their existence unbearable. In fact, thousands did defect to the government side during the latter part of the war, and this was one of the VC high command's worst headaches.

The Viet Cong depended for their survival on the collaboration and protection of the villagers. The NLF organized in the towns but drew most of its strength and succor from the rural villages, where 85 percent of South Vietnam's population lived. Murder or intimidation was ordered only for specific acts of collaboration with the government and was carried out by special squads; sometimes the deterrent purpose was emphasized by displaying severed heads with warnings. Guerrillas were involved in food cultivation, both to supply themselves and to assist the peasants they lived among—and beneath. Until a late stage in the war, the Viet Cong's weapons and equipment tended to be stolen, homemade, or improvised. After 1966 the Chinese-made AK-47 assault rifle became the usual Communist sidearm, shipped in down the Trail or by sea and through Cambodia. VC officers wore the Polish K-54 pistol.

Guerrillas hold the military initiative; the Viet Cong could choose the time and place of battle. In fighting the United States forces, their tactics were dictated by their extreme technological inferiority. Without air power or artillery, upon which the Americans relied, the Viet Cong resorted to ambush, hit-and-run attacks, and close-in fighting—"grabbing the enemy by the belt"; fighting close to the Americans protected them from air strikes or shelling. For a guerrilla army, stalemate—pinning down a larger force in its huge bases—is equivalent to winning.

The NLF campaigned vigorously among the people, making special efforts to undermine the loyalty of the ARVN troops and government officials, often by using their relatives to persuade them. It was an effective technique: Despite the wholesale conscription of young men, on average 21 percent of the conscripted ARVN soldiers deserted back to their homes each year. The Viet Cong often had at least eight hours' notice of any operation launched against them, and sometimes were warned many days in advance. The Viet Cong's own military operations were always rehearsed. Models of targets were built for briefings, and local guerrillas—or even children—would gather fresh intelligence on the spot. Arms and equipment were sometimes placed in tunnel caches, to be picked up by regional or main-force guerrillas on the day of the operation. Targets would often be approached through the tunnel network. Sappers would blast their way through the target's wire or other defenses, and whistles or bugles would signal the attack, which invariably took place at night. For obvious reasons, aircraft or helicopters on the ground were habitual targets.

Viet Cong morale and dedication continue to amaze their erstwhile adversaries. How did they fight so well against such odds and in such appalling conditions? How did the Communists come to bear such devastating casualties or carry out missions of such suicidal bravery? How, in short, did such a backward nation outface the world's greatest superpower and break its will to pursue the war? High-level political shrewdness is one answer. But in the field it was a triumph of organization and motivation by the Communist cadres—and the fact that the youths of Vietnam were already receptive to what they were taught. Most of the GIs had only a sketchy idea of what they were fighting for in Vietnam. But for the guerrillas, there were often personal blood-debts to settle—home villages bombed, relatives killed, or arrested and tortured, by a government funded and armed by the United States.

The Viet Cong fought on their own land, to which they felt closely tied. And Mother Earth herself became their protection in the tunnels dug beneath their ancestral fields and villages. "Your entrails, Mother, are unfathomable," wrote the poet Duong Huong Ly. The tunnels hid the guerrillas from searching enemy soldiers and from bombs and shells. In the tunnels were the sinews of their war—the arms factories, the rice stores, the hospitals, the headquarters. In the dark, damp chambers carved out of Cu Chi's clay was the essential statement of Vietnamese resistance to those whom they perceived to be the invaders of their land.

5

The Tunnels

CAPTAIN NGUYEN THANH LINH of the People's Army of the Socialist Republic of Vietnam spent five years in the tunnels of Cu Chi. Today, at forty-nine, he has a lean, sparse figure and a taut face. His sad eyes always forget to smile with the mouth. Something has gone from the man. He tires easily, as if he were a stranger to Ho Chi Minh City's crushing midday heat. At the 7th Military Region headquarters he sometimes catnaps during the long committee meetings, but no one chastises him. He has earned the respect and uncritical admiration of his peers and the new young officers around him. But at Phu My Hung, twenty miles out, in Cu Chi and on the banks of the slow brown Saigon River, Captain Linh comes to life as he explains the history and the philosophy, the tactics and the mechanics of the huge tunnel complex that was his home for half a decade. Of the 300 men under his command during Operation Crimp in January 1966, only four were to survive the war: two officers and two noncommissioned officers. His VC 7th Battalion was "wiped out" and reconstructed so many times that he lost count. "In Cu Chi we lost 12,000 people—guerrillas and civilians—in the course of the war," he points out.

Today Linh sits comfortably on the dusty red earth that marks one of the major tunnel sites. He explains the tunnels within a historical and sociological context. "They are something very Vietnamese," he says, "and one must understand what the relationship is between the Vietnamese peasant and the earth, *his* earth. Without that, then everything here"—his hand sweeps across the bunker complex—"is without real meaning. But I fear you will not understand." The mouth smiles slightly and the eyes stay dull. "You are from the West." It is not meant as an insulting remark; it is said with gentle despair, rather like the mixture of sadness and anger the Irish express in trying to explain their history of the British.

Vietnam is primarily an agrarian society. It is not a land of important cities or towns, nor does it have an urban-based technology. Vietnam is a land of peasants, whose deeply traditional lives are characterized by constant repetition, by the sowing and reaping of rice and the maintenance of customary law. The Vietnamese worship their ancestors as the source of their lives, their fortunes, and their civilization. In the rites of ancestor-worship the death of a man marks no final end. Buried in the life-giving rice fields that have without break sustained his family, the father lives on in the bodies of his children and grandchildren.

In this continuum of the family, personal possessions and private property hardly exist. The father is less the owner than the trustee of the land, which will beyond doubt be passed on to the children. To the Vietnamese, the land itself is the sacred, constant element. Western concepts of land-profiteering, of mobile societies, of land development or neglect, are beyond comprehension to the Vietnamese peasant. For the traditional villager, who spends his time in one place, bound by long tradition to the rice land of his ancestors, the world is a small place. The earth takes precedence, for as the source of life, it is the basis for the social contract between the members of the family and the hamlet or village. Without land, the villager would have no social identity; he would be a tramp, a landless vagrant. The people believe that if a man moves off his land and beyond the village limits, his soul stays behind, buried deep in the earth with the bones of his ancestors.

It was never military necessity alone, nor indeed the suitability of the local terrain, that led to the creation of the tunnels of Cu Chi; these were crucial factors, but it was also shrewd tactics for the new Communist cadres, returning south in the early sixties, to plan a life underground—an existence of both practical and symbolic significance. Strategy demanded it, the soil allowed it, and above all, history positively encouraged it. If, as General Vo Nguyen Giap believed, the enemy was to occupy the face of his earth, then his people would occupy its bowels.

For the Communist engineers, the cadres, and the peasants, the soil of Cu Chi had a huge natural environmental advantage for tunneling. Owing largely to its proximity to the nearby Saigon River, it is predominantly laterite clay, a ferric soil with a clay binder, which allows some air penetration. According to Engineers Corps Lieutenant Colonel Jerry Sinn, who examined the tunnels in detail in Cu Chi in the autumn of 1969, the clay was not particularly affected by large changes in the amounts of water present in it, and was consequently a remarkably stable structure for tunneling. It was further strengthened, rather like reinforced concrete, by the roots of various trees, a natural construction system the Americans called overbirth. "It was a super tunneling dirt," said Jerry Sinn gloomily. Captain Linh put it even more simply: "The earth in Cu Chi is sticky and doesn't crumble. The area is fifteen to twenty meters above sea level and for some six meters down we knew there is no water. The water table was usually found at about ten to twenty meters. We could not have expected better conditions."

Dry laterite clay has a dull reddish appearance. During the dry season in Cu Chi, the top surface along the village roads becomes a gritty dust, as uncomfortable and penetrating as sand. Yet the texture of the laterite clay round the tunnels was as hard as brick and seemingly impermeable.

There was nothing new about the use of tunnels by defenders against attackers. Indeed, Chinese guerrillas had successfully used tunnels in Hopei province during the Japanese war in the thirties. Whole counties were linked by underground defensive and communications networks. For the West, trenches and tunnels recalled the nightmare of World War 1, of mud and gas and death by the thousands as men were caught in holes in the ground by gas and artillery fire. Extensive tunnels, built by the Korean and Chinese forces across the waist of Korea near the 38th parallel, were widely used during the Korean War in the early fifties. However, never before had so daring a plan been conceived, as a result of which central government authority simply did not extend to a huge area of seventy square miles just outside the nation's capital. The tunnels made Cu Chi a no-go area by night and effectively out of bounds by day, without the use of extensive military support. It was as if Washington's authority did not reach to Philadelphia, or London's writ to Croydon.

The basic tunnel infrastructure, dug in the mid forties, had been little more than a series of backyard shelters and short interlinking hamlet communication tunnels. The tunnels of the sixties, however, were to be far more than convenient hidey-holes, safe houses for the Communists, or secure weapons caches. They were to be the linchpin of the entire regional campaign, and they would have to survive the high-tech assault of the most powerful and sophisticated military machine in the world.

On 28 September 1967, a detachment of the Korean 28th Infantry Regiment of the 9th (South Korean) Division captured a remarkable enemy document during a sweep north of Saigon. A full four months later it was translated into English and handed over to the American Defense Intelligence Agency and all the appropriate senior command structures in Vietnam. But by the time it had reached down to unit command levels in early 1968, it was almost too late in the war to be of much help. The Tet offensive was imminent and the fundamental nature of the land war would soon change. The document appears to be, on internal evidence, the only tunnels manual ever issued by the Communists. It is a ten-page technical and political booklet, revealing many secret details about the tunnels' structure and strategic purpose. The anonymous author displays the party's hopes and fears for the future of tunnel warfare in a style that reflects the authority, naïveté, and patronizing attitude that generally characterized the relationship between senior regional cadres and their village equivalents.

The *primary* role of the tunnels is stressed and restressed. "They are for the strengthening of combat vitality for our villages. They also provide more safety for our political and armed units, and for the masses as well. But their sheltering purpose is only significant when they serve our soldiers in combat activities. As mere shelters, their great advantages are wasted." And, even more significantly: "There must be combat posts and equipment inside the underground tunnels for providing continuous support to our troops—*even if the enemy occupies the village*." The document mixes political exhortation with what was to become a shrewdly accurate prediction:

> If the tunnels are dug so as to exploit their effectiveness fully, the villages and hamlets will become extremely strong fortresses. The enemy may be several times superior to us in strength and modern weapons, but he will not chase us from the battlefield, because we will launch surprise attacks from within the underground tunnels. . . . we can see that underground tunnels are very favorable for armed forces as limited as ours, in strength and weaponry.

The tunnels would be crucial for launching close-in attacks on the Americans and would also provide opportunities to seize their weapons; they would provide excellent mobility and (as the unlucky 25th Infantry Division was to discover) "we may attack the enemy right in the center of his formations or keep on fighting from different places."

Nobody, not even the centralized Hanoi planners, could predict the course of the war in Military Region IV, the area surrounding and including Saigon, from 1965 onward. To that extent the construction of the tunnels involved considerable extemporizing and engineering empiricism. The captured Communist tunnels manual envisaged a fairly rigid infrastructure, determining precise dimensions for tunnels and chambers and trapdoors. That the system grew and developed as it did, well beyond the original vision of this manual, is, perhaps, a testament to some residual sense of free enterprise among the builders. But at the outset, as the captured document reveals, the system was to be simple and effective: "We must plan for the eventual impossibility of fighting from inside the underground tunnels. A secret passage must then be available from which our troops may escape and fight in the open, or reenter the underground tunnels if necessary." The passages of the tunnels were not to be either straight or "snakelike," but were to zigzag at angles of between 60 and 120 degrees, "because if the enemy detects the entrance to the underground tunnel, he will set off mines and banglores (chain explosions) or pour in chemicals, both of which are certain to have disastrous effects on our troops." In fact, the use of explosives and chemicals did not have "disastrous effects"; zigzagging, however, did make a straight line of fire inside impossible, and helped deflect explosive blasts.

The dimensions of the communicating passages were clearly laid down. They were to be no wider than 1.2 meters, no narrower than 0.8 meters, no higher than 1.8 meters, no lower than 0.8 meters. The minimum thickness of the roof was to be 1.5 meters—"to avoid vibration caused by the explosions of bombs and shells and the sounds of mechanized units moving above."

A clever and finely engineered trapdoor system was devised by the Communists to create entrances and exits to secret passages and from one tunnel level to another. Where the water table allowed and local conditions necessitated it, tunnel complexes of as many as four separate levels were built. This remarkable feat was a tribute not only to the stamina of the diggers but also to their extraordinary practical application of certain physical principles, which allowed people to stay alive for years deep inside the ground, because the very rudimentary life-support measures actually worked. Air, sanitation, water supplies, and cooking facilities were sufficient to maintain a primitive but reasonably safe existence. It was crucial to the whole plan that even if the first tunnel level was discovered, the secret trapdoor that led down to the next would remain hidden from the enemy. That meant making trapdoors that were virtually invisible.

One of Captain Linh's favorite displays is to take guests into the underground by the Phu My Hung tunnel complex, stand them in a circle about twenty feet in diameter, and challenge them to find the tunnel trapdoor within that area. No one has ever done it. Linh then stamps on the ground and suddenly a grinning comrade lifts the trapdoor and pops out. The point is made. Only the most laborious, time-consuming, and dangerous probing with knife or bayonet would reveal a good trapdoor. The blueprint for trapdoor construction laid down by the manual was as follows: "With boards 1 cm thick and 2–3 cms wide, make two frames, one with horizontal boards and the other with vertical boards. Insert a nylon sheet between the two frames, which later will be glued together. Cover it with sponge rubber and fill all openings with wax. A single board should never be used for a frame [trapdoor] because it is not strong enough."

The sides of the trapdoor were usually beveled downward at an angle so that it could take considerable over-pressure. There was no sag. If the trapdoor was inside the tunnel, the VC placed earth on top of it and hid in the earth small finger wires, which allowed a soldier to lift the door. If the trapdoor was outside, then small plants would be encouraged to grow on it, or dead foliage would be cunningly "planted" to make it as one with its environment.

Ventilation holes were simplicity itself. They ran obliquely from the surface to the first level—obliquely to avoid monsoon rain flooding in. Some always pointed east toward the preferred light of a new day. Others, by instruction, "must be turned toward the wind." In the deathly blackness of the tunnels, these ventilation holes were to be the only physical reminder of the existence of the real world, with air and light, a few feet above. Internal ventilation holes were bored down to the lower tunnel levels.

Entrances to the tunnels were carefully and precisely engineered to cater for various contingencies. The Communists' tunnels manual explained:

> Because the activities of the militia and guerrillas require appearing and disappearing quickly, the entrances to the underground tunnel must be located like the corners of a triangle, so that each can support the other in combat. Our troops must also be able to escape from the underground tunnel through a secret opening so they may continue to fight.

The entrances also had to be able to resist fire, flood, and chemical warfare: "for this reason, we must locate the entrances to the tunnels in dry, elevated, and well-ventilated areas. Such an entrance will not be blocked by the chemicals that will otherwise kill the occupants. Also rainwater will not stagnate in the entrance so located."

The three trapdoors in the triangular entry system were to be an average of forty to fifty meters apart, and the entrances were to be strong. "We need to expend a great deal of manpower, time, and materials to make them so. The following dimensions are to be adopted: square entrance 1.5 meters for each side, rectangular entrance 1 meter x 1.8 meters, round entrance 1.5 meters in diameter." The authors of the captured document went on to complain:

> Recently local areas have observed no systematic digging procedure, some entrances were too large and remained weak, thus time, manpower and materials have been wasted... In some local areas the [tunnel] entrances were located only a small distance from each other... sometimes only 5 to 7 meters apart. The reason was that the digging was entrusted to separate families or groups of persons, who could not foresee the disastrous effects of their thoughtlessness... they seem to ignore the fact that close entrances attract the enemy's attention and do nothing but assist his discovery.

The attention to detail is dogmatic, but the fact remains that the tunnels of Cu Chi were the primary factor in fighting the campaign against the Americans, and if sloppiness or engineering imprecision infected the building of the system, the Communists would lose. Some first-hand evidence of the stability and efficiency of the Cu Chi tunnel system fell into American hands when a VC guerrilla, Ngo Van Giang, was captured by the South Vietnamese on 31 January 1968. In a sixteen-page debriefing statement, Giang is quoted at length by his interrogators on the subject of the Cu Chi tunnel network. He told his captors that where a tunnel became an open bunker, special roofs had been constructed by using 50-cm-thick bamboo poles followed by another 50-cm-thick layer of "husks." Then there was a layer of dirt 50 cm thick. On top of the dirt, they had planted flowers or used fallen trees as camouflage. Incredibly, according to Giang, if a 200-kg bomb fell within just ten meters of the tunnel, no damage would result. The husks and leaves used were excellent protection against bomb blast. Bamboo poles were also employed for their resilience. "In April 1966," Giang told his captors, "an airplane dropped a 200-kg bomb at Chua hamlet, and the bomb hit right on this type of tunnel. The dirt and husks caved in, but the cadre [inside] was not wounded."

Giang also revealed that the Communists had created a kind of tunnel hierarchy. There were what he called "high-level cadre tunnels," specially dug by VC engineers and specially reinforced. These were hideaway tunnels for about three cadres at a time and were specially bomb-proofed, using the husks and bamboo. Then there were tunnels for common cadres. These had to be made "by the individuals themselves . . . further there were no bamboo walls inside."

But even if accommodations were graded to some extent, the fact remains that by accident, design, or a combination of both, the Communists did create a series of underground fortifications strong enough to withstand most types of destructive warfare. For the Americans the sheer military frustration of dealing with the tunnels was to become intense. It was as if Goliath had *both* the club and slingshot, while all David did was dig a hole and hide, pop up every now and then to fight, and run.

The tunnels were usually dug the hard way—by hand. The tunnels manual tried somewhat patronizingly to formalize a system. It announced:

> The passages are dug in the following ways:
> With digging devices
> With the hands
> We introduce here the way to dig passages by hands.
> *Manual digging:* The passages are usually dug by:
> 2 persons who rotate in digging and shoveling the earth
> 2 to 3 persons who remove the earth (depending on how far the earth must be removed).

There was a primitive earth-lifting device that stood over tunnel holes during digging and allowed semimechanical earth *removal*, but not excavation.

Major Nguyen Quot is today with the 7th Military Region headquarters in Ho Chi Minh City. As a young captain (promotions in the People's Army are remarkably slow), he was assigned to the tunnels of Cu Chi. Like Captain Linh, he was to spend five years on that assignment. His eyes were to suffer badly from lack of light, and today he rarely removes his heavy sunglasses. Although the work norm for earth excavation was about one cubic meter per person per day, this obviously varied with the digger's health, age, the climate, and the soil. In Major Quot's experience only about half a cubic meter of dirt was excavated per working day, "although near a ventilation hole, they could dig faster and get more out." He says that everyone took part in the digging of the tunnels: old men, women, young men, and girls, even children. The process for earth removal was reasonably simple. A drawing hanging at Phu My Hung shows the method quite clearly. First a shaft was dug from the surface down three to five meters. A laborer would remain at the mouth of the dry well, as the first hole was called, with a basket attached to a long stick. The tunneler would place earth in the basket, which was then hauled up. At the same time a similar process would begin some ten meters away from the first dry well. Once both tunnelers had reached the required depth, they would begin tunneling toward each other underground. They relied on sound alone to help them meet in the middle. According to Major Quot, "Our tunnelers had good ears; they always met, and if they were a few centimeters out, it did not matter. Each dry well was filled after it had been dug, and remember, we could never tunnel up because you could not dispose of the earth. It was always down. In order to deal with the rains we allowed a slight downward gradient in the communication tunnels, so the water drained into the wells."

"To dig the tunnels we divided the work scientifically," explained Captain Linh. "Old men made baskets for carrying the earth, old women did the cooking, young men and women used their strength to dig the earth. Even children did their share by gathering leaves to cover the trapdoors. Our favorite digging tools were old worn-out spades and old hoes. A new hoe is about fifteen by twenty five centimeters, but after it has been used by the peasants to dig earth in the fields for a long time, it's nicely reduced to the size of a bowl."

The Saigonese poet and writer Vien Phuong spent much of the war in the tunnels. He is a medium-sized man with graying hair, scrawny arms, and tired eyes behind thick-lensed glasses. In 1962 he was working with the Viet Cong in the countryside.

He was fitter then, he comments, smiling. Today, at fifty-five, he is painfully thin. "Digging tunnels was our daily task; besides the tunnel where I lived, I had to have two or three spare tunnels, because if the enemy came to one, or bombings destroyed the other, I still needed one to go to. So we had to dig daily. The soil of Cu Chi is a mixture of sand and earth. During the rainy season it is soft like sugar, during the dry season as hard as rock. If I managed to dig down thirty centimeters a day in six hours it was a big achievement. It was easier to dig during the rainy season. I had a hoe as small as a saucer, and I had to kneel or sit down on the ground. I had to find hard soil at the root of a bamboo tree or where there was a termite nest. Such soil could stand the weight of a tank. We dug in teams of three: one dug the earth, the second pulled the soil out, and the third pulled it up."

And how were the thousands and thousands of tons of earth removed from the tunnels to be disposed of, hidden so that the Americans would not find the telltale evidence? The Communists knew full well that the Americans had spotter planes, and sophisticated new aerial-surveillance techniques that could easily "see" great mounds of freshly dug earth. High-resolution photography combined with infrared sensing techniques were sufficiently refined in the early sixties to pose a serious threat. The tunnels manual did not make a great fuss about earth disposal. It simply said, Get rid of that stuff, using your common sense:

> *Notice:* The earth removed from the underground tunnel should be made into basements for houses, furrows for potato growing, or banks for communications and combat trenches. It may also be poured into streams but must never be left heaped in mounds. In short, the utmost care must be taken to conceal the underground tunnel from the enemy's discovery.

And it was.

Tunnelers refined earth disposal to a new science. When the American B-52 bombing raids first began, the VC simply shoveled earth into the new craters. When U.S. ground patrols or the ARVN troops made disposal awkward, they used trained water buffalo to carry dirt away from tunnel sites. MacDonald

Valentine, who spent nineteen months attached to South Vietnamese Ranger battalions and was stationed at Cu Chi, was told by his Vietnamese scout, Phuc Long, that if enemy pressure left them no other option, they would smuggle earth out under the noses of U.S. patrols inside the common Vietnamese crock that usually contained fish sauce. The crock was the size of a coffee jug, and beneath a layer of fish sauce, the women would hide a bladder full of earth. It was as near as one could get to emptying a lake with a tablespoon.

Every twenty or thirty meters the tunnelers dug a water drainage hole to prevent flooding. It was 20 cm wide, 15 cm deep. But even more importantly, every hundred meters or so, in strategic locations within the tunnels, the special water traps were dug. These stagnant stinking pits, first uncovered during Operation Crimp, served to block the corrosive and often deadly fumes from the smoke bombs and CS riot-gas grenades that the Americans hurled into tunnels in an attempt to contaminate them. In effect, some of the most modern and noxious devices produced by Western chemical-warfare laboratories were often frustrated by the equivalent of a lavatory U-bend in the tunnels. The ordinary trapdoors linking the separate levels were also very effective blockers of gas fumes.

One of the most important secrets kept from the Americans during the entire war, according to Major Quot, was that the construction of the tunnels was such that each section could be sealed off. "The Americans thought that our armed forces were confined to one tunnel and that they were able to kill everyone down there by blowing down gas or pumping down a large quantity of water. But this was not so. It was important that the enemy never understood this."

In reality, this claim is a mixture of boast and fact. In the early days of tunnel warfare the Americans were certainly not aware of the secret exits. But it soon became obvious that trapped VC were not always being caught at tunnel entrances that were sealed by the attacking GIs. The only possible explanation was clearly the existence of hidden escape routes, which the Americans found only with considerable luck or ingenuity.

Although the tunnels were natural shelters against the U.S. bombing attacks, further special protection became necessary when the bombing increased in ferocity. So the tunnelers dug conical A-shaped shelters that were geometrically designed to resist both artillery shells and bomb blast. More important, their conical shape acted as an amplifier and magnified the distant sound of approaching B-52 strikes. This was the only real warning tunnel dwellers might get of an imminent attack.

Ultimately, the real security for the tunnel system depended on the precise and cunning use of camouflage. An undated captured VC document advised Cu Chi cadres as follows on the subject:

> If the duration of use [of the tunnel] is long, we should grow viable plants. Change dried leaves before [they get] dark, and blot out all suspicious traces before daybreak. Give a contrast to the camouflage by using high and low plants. Do not show a dull and prominent heap of earth. Plants and branches must be picked far from the fortifications and the troop's locations. When an emergency repair is necessary never pick up branches and leaves between the enemy and us, and especially do not gather a great number in one place.

An informant, code-named TU 10, was placed by American military intelligence somewhere in the Tay Ninh area from January to July 1967. On 28 July 1967 he spoke to his controllers at some length about the continuing success of VC tunnels camouflage, revealing some significant things about U.S. infantry technique when it came to tunnel warfare:

> Experience had shown the VC cadre that when friendly forces discovered any sort of hidden place they were inclined to destroy it and move on without further intensive search . . . tunnel and cache entrances located in residential areas were often placed under a cooking place, and if feasible, in a pig pen, the latter being more desirable because Americans hesitated to look in such places. A large corner post of a building or roofed animal shelter would sometimes be used to conceal the entrance to a tunnel or cache site.

Source TU 10 reported that it was a general rule (although not always adhered to) that foliage used in camouflage must be changed every three days. Often efforts were made (he did not say with what degree of success) to use "small bushes with many leaves" as camouflage, and where possible, living plant shoots, which would grow and remain green.

But Ngo Van Giang, the VC prisoner who had given U.S. intelligence useful information about tunnel construction, suggested there *were* ways for the Americans to discover tunnels, despite the excellent camouflage. Properly trained eyes could see evidence of trails, tree branches might be broken in the area, grass on both sides of the trails might be crushed, there might be several unexplained high knolls in the area, and in the tunnels area the dirt would be slightly more spongy.

The highly trained American Special Forces soldiers, the Green Berets, were specifically trained to break through even the most adroit camouflage systems. They lived rough, often in VC-dominated areas, and became renowned for their field and combat skills. Several were attached to infantry units that went out on search-and-destroy operations, and the Green Berets' ability to spot tunnel entrances was exceptional. But there were never enough Special Forces liaison NCOs to go round, and, if given the choice, they always preferred to return as quickly as possible to their primary missions.

"The tunnels began from a logical strategy," explained Major Quot. "First they were for individuals, then for families. Each family had responsibility for its piece of tunnel. Then various huts within the hamlet were joined by the tunnels, and soon we began to build tunnels that connected one hamlet with another. In the end there were main communications tunnels, secret tunnels, false tunnels. The more the Americans tried to drive us away from our land, the more we burrowed into it.

"We even had [street] signs underground so that strangers knew where they were, although guiding strangers [VC and NVA soldiers and cadres] was the responsibility of the local hamlet chief. It was for him to provide guides who would take the people from one district to another before handing them over to another guide."

As the intensity of the war in Vietnam escalated, Cu Chi district and the Iron Triangle area increasingly became the focus of attention for the frustrated Americans. Unable to dominate or secure these areas, they were to resort to the one factor in the military equation that was always in their favor—the ability to bring overwhelming firepower to bear upon the land. With artillery and air strikes, using high explosives, chemical defoliants, and CS gas, the Americans pounded the surface, while below, whole battalions of regional and regular Communist troops waited patiently. The earth cracked, groaned, and in places gave way. The landscape changed from jungle to dusty desert; entire villages disappeared and their inhabitants were moved out. But the physical integrity of the tunnels was to survive long enough for a shadow civilian and military Communist administration to live in the tunnels, conducting its business and defying nearly every attempt to force it up and out. It was an extraordinary triumph of the primitive in a decade that saw man walking on the moon.

6

Survival Underground

ONLY ONE YEAR after he married Nguyen Thi Tan in Hanoi, Captain Linh was ordered south to take command of the newly formed 7th VC Battalion in Cu Chi. Linh left behind a son, Nguyen Hoa Vinh; his wife was pregnant with a daughter he would not see until she was ten years old. When Captain Linh came marching home on 6 June 1975, his children refused to let him touch them for three days. "My wife and I treated our reunion like a new marriage. For ten years I had had no relationship with another woman. When we met again my wife only said to me, 'How thin you are.' Everyone in the street had come out to welcome me and my wife and I could say nothing in front of the crowd."

He is clearly proud of his ten years' service—five years underground—but too sensitive to have fully buried all the horror he lived through. For example, if the wounded couldn't be transported to a safe above-ground hospital, they had to be kept in the tunnels to recover. "They used to beg us to kill them," said Linh. "They used to scream for one look at light and one breath of air, not fresh air, just air. The wounded, their discipline diminished, their minds and bodies hurt, preferred death to lying underground. It was unpleasant to hear them.

We offered them nothing: neither death, nor light nor more air."

The Vietnamese rarely display emotion. Only very occasionally did the fixed, impassive faces of the villagers break into tears or shouts as they saw their homes or their families destroyed. For a Westerner to ask, "What was it *really* like, living in the tunnels?" is in itself to challenge Vietnamese, and therefore different, concepts of pleasure, pain, endurance, suffering, sharing, and self-discipline. There is common ground, of course—the wounded soldier begging for death as the only relief from hell under earth—but the cultural differences and subtleties make comparisons difficult. Vietnamese culture has its roots in the village, where material possessions are seen as a mark of selfishness, denying one's friends or neighbors the right to equality. This is not a political attitude but, like the close relationship with the earth itself, is based on long historical accommodation with the village experience, the lack of social and physical mobility, and an acceptance of one's role in life.

It is easier for a Westerner to try to understand the tunnels experience in a historical context as the final spasm in a ten-thousand-day war for complete independence from foreign domination. Only the certainty that Communist victory was inevitable protected mind and body from the true horrors of tunnel life. When victory would come was academic—perhaps in five more years, perhaps in ten or twenty. America was a formidable fighting power; one would have to be patient. But there were no doubts, no self-questioning.

To Asians steeped in Confucian concepts, time is an endless river flowing from an infinitely regenerative source. It is a commodity to be valued, but because it is of such unlimited abundance, one can hardly use too much of it. Time to Westerners is always precious; to the Oriental it is something that can be spent with generosity. Even Western calendars are different—they have starting and stopping points graphically shown in linear symbols. Each page has a beginning and an end. A year is a very long time. But the Oriental calendar is in the form of a wheel, a symbol with neither beginning nor end—a continuum. Quick victory is a Western concept.

The remarkable confidence of the Communists was based not solely on what they saw as the justice of their cause but also, more simply, on the fact that time was on their side. All they had to do was not lose.

For the thousands who were to live and die in them, the tunnels' paramount importance was to maintain the fight against the enemy. Captured VC documents carry a refrain, an exhortation to cadres to remind the people that combat had absolute priority; shelter came only second. So there were not only the sleeping chambers, air-raid shelters, latrines, hospitals, cleaning areas, and kitchens, but also chambers for political theater, military store rooms, conference centers, printing works, and even chambers to hide the precious water buffalo—and, above all, the chambers that became workshops to produce homemade armaments, with which the VC kept the fight alive until Hanoi sent down fresh supplies. Within this dark, subterranean metropolis there were primitive forges making antipersonnel mines. There were huge caches of rice. There were temporary graveyards. There were chambers where complete 105-mm field-artillery howitzers were kept stripped and oiled, ready for reassembly and action. Meanwhile, above, the tanks rumbled and flailed, the bombs hurtled down, the shells fell in devastating barrages. Later, the foot soldiers gingerly picked their way through the foliage, unaware that the enemy had literally gone to ground, taking his goods and chattels with him. When the Americans were around, not a whisper, nothing stirred, the earth belonged, or seemed to belong, to the dead. But once the Americans had gone, once night fell, the subterranean buzz and hum would begin.

First they'd light up the Dien Bien Phu kitchens. These were specially adapted "smokeless" kitchens, first used in the trenches during the war against the French, and subsequently refined and adapted for the sixties. When a fire was lit inside a stove, the smoke was ducted through several channels and finally allowed to escape from various and separated ground-level chimneys. The effect was to dilute the smoke so that it was scarcely visible from the air, even to the relentlessly sharp-eyed Americans in their reconnaissance planes. "The system worked extremely well," said Major Quot, "but it was most unpleasant for the cooks, and there were often leaks in the ducts, leading to some contamination within the tunnels."

According to a former VC guerrilla, Le Van Nong, now farming again on the banks of the Saigon River at An Nhon

Tay, it was much worse than Major Quot claimed. "The tunnels we were in stank and we stank. We met many difficulties. The tunnels were usually very hot, and we were always sweating. We took with us rice compressed into balls, hid during the day, and at night tried to cook the rice for eating the next day. If there was no time to prepare the rice, we went without food for the whole day until the next night, and we tried to come up to cook. It really wasn't possible for us to cook underground, the smoke was always asphyxiating, you just could not breathe, there was no air down there anyway. Sometimes we were driven to attack the Americans and make them go away, just so we could come up and cook at night, cook in the open. You cannot imagine what pleasure it gave us."

Colonel Dr. Vo Hoang Le, a senior Viet Cong medical officer, admitted frankly that it was difficult and unpleasant to cook underground. "Usually we ate only dry food. It was possible to cook properly above ground only; the smoke was unbearable if cooking was done underground." Eventually, the demands of the wounded increasingly dictated whether or not the Dien Bien Phu kitchens were ever used. Ironically, as the American military presence grew, it played a small part in solving the problem of food inside the tunnels. "They inadvertently supplied us with food that was most suitable for the tunnels," said Colonel Le, "because they always left food lying around after infantry attacks. It became quite plentiful in some areas. The Americans left tinned meat, dry rice, noodles with prawns, cigarettes and chocolate."

Captain Linh recalls that the Saigon River was always a useful source for fish and prawns, but it was difficult to fish without being spotted. "As we grew short of food, we grew manioc, banana, sweet potato, and cassava to help us. The Americans were clever and knew whenever they spotted these plants that we must be nearby, but we had no choice. It was dangerous to grow these plants near the tunnels and it was just as dangerous to starve. In the end, the only meat we had was from rats. They are delicious and provide plenty of protein. I found grilled rat had a better flavor than chicken or duck."

According to Captain Linh's account, few Westerners could have survived life in the tunnels for long without very special training and acclimatization. Although only a handful of GIs were taken prisoner in his sector, he had responsibility for them.

"We were kind to American prisoners of war; that was the National Liberation Front's policy. We had to look after them and send them back to Hanoi." (Once in Hanoi, U.S. POWs were not treated with generosity. Conditions were poor, and some were subjected to intense psychological pressures to speak against the U.S. government's actions in Vietnam.) "Once we had captured them," said Linh, "we kept them briefly in the tunnels, waiting for the chance to send them north. I had one who absolutely refused to go on to a rice diet. He insisted on being given a bread diet. We had no bread and we had no meat. He told me he could only eat bread and chicken. I asked him how much chicken he needed a day and he said about half a chicken. Well, half a chicken would have kept ten of my men for a day. Nevertheless, we made arrangements to steal bread and chicken for him. Once, I know, it came from the American base itself. I had two prisoners of war; they were given a higher standard of living than our soldiers because their health required it. I liked both the men, and we often spoke a little English. I think they liked me once they knew they would not be hurt or shot. Unfortunately they died of illness while being taken north. They could not endure the hardships of the jungle. They were with me for twenty days, then taken to the Cambodian border. They died there."

Next to food for survival, the manufacture of ammunition and weapons had priority in the tunnels. In the early days of the American presence, there were serious shortages. "We hardly received any supply of weapons from the North," said Captain Linh. "We received only mine detonators and delay fuses. We needed explosives and fortunately soon found them lying all around us on the ground."

One single battalion of the newly arrived 25th Infantry Division in Cu Chi fired, in the course of one month, no less than 180,000 shells into the Cu Chi district, averaging 4,500 daily. In one month, throughout South Vietnam, the Americans fired about a trillion bullets, 10 million mortar rounds, and 4.8 million rockets. And this was just the beginning of the war.

As Captain Linh noted, a great deal of this ordnance fell on Cu Chi. And considerable numbers, as is the nature of these things, failed to explode. For once it was the Viet Cong that began a course of on-the-job training. "We tried to understand the American science," explained Captain Linh. "We would have teams of watchers during a bombing strike, looking for the bombs that did not explode. They would try to mark the location. Then after the raid we would hurry to the spot and try to retrieve the TNT. Sometimes accidents occurred. Once eight of my men were killed when the bomb they were sawing exploded. All that remained of them was a basketful of flesh. But remember, of a thousand shells the enemy fired at us, only about a hundred caused casualties; a percentage of the nine hundred that did not hurt did not explode either. The Americans used their weapons to fight us and we used their weapons to fight back."

Captain Linh's cottage industry began to grow. "There were unexploded shells everywhere in the Cu Chi area. We organized special workshop chambers in the tunnels and we learned to take the ordnance in there. We dismantled their detonators, fitted our own, and changed the shells into powerful weapons, of which the Americans were very afraid. We exploded them with batteries or made booby traps with them. We also found claymore or directional mines, which did not explode because the bombers did not drop them from the proper height or at the right angle. Sometimes we even had more of these mines than we could use. With each claymore mine, suitably adapted in our tunnel workshops, we could inflict casualties of up to seven American soldiers. We did not need any great technical skill. They were very dangerous to the Americans, but harmless against us when we were in the tunnels."

Coca-Cola cans, in an act of ironic cultural inversion, were carefully turned into hand grenades for use against the Americans by the artisans who worked by candlelight and paraffin lamp in the special tunnel workshops. First they poured used bomb fragments into the tin, then TNT was poured into the middle, and finally a homemade detonator was placed on the top. Major Quot recalled: "At every hamlet underground in the Cu Chi tunnels we had a productive team making mines and hand grenades and repairing firearms. The claymore-type mine was of great importance to us. We made the DH-5 and DH-10 in the tunnel workshops. One had five, the other ten, kilos of high explosive and ball bearings. A properly made DH-10 could wipe out a whole enemy platoon. Even with rudimentary tools one person could produce from three to five mines a day. We even organized a little assembly line—one person specialized in taking the explosive out of the 'dud' American shells, another prepared it, and a third fitted the detonator into the mine itself." This underground arms industry was to be far more than just a nuisance to the Americans. It was to become the primary means for denying the GIs access to the tunnels complex.

The electrical power to run the workshops came principally from small hand or foot generators. "The signals unit had a small gasoline-driven generator," said Captain Linh, "but these were rare. Usually there were pedal generators, some hand generators from China, and batteries. We were never short of electricity in Cu Chi; we even threw away dim torch batteries and used only bright ones. We were 'presented' with batteries by the Americans; they were easy to pick up."

Major Quot recalled that there were several generators in the tunnel sections in which he operated. "We even had neon lights powered by generators," he said, "although that was a special luxury. We needed generators for running our signals communications, and also we used them for the film shows we had. You could not expect a man to crank a generator for three hours; we had to use the precious gasoline-driven one. We saw war films in the tunnels; one was *The Battle for Dien Bien Phu*. We liked the fighting films that Hanoi sent to us."

Most of the ordinary lighting came from oil lamps made from old American shell-casings, and a simple wick coiled into nut oil. A slightly larger and more popular lamp was simply a brown bottle about the size of a smallish medicine bottle with a drilled nut where the cap would be, and at the base a crude piece of metal as a weight. Again a wick, and nut oil, provided the light.

Only a few GIs ever penetrated the second or third tunnel levels. Jan Shrader, of the Combined Matériel Exploitation Center, attached to Military Assistance Command Vietnam, explored one second-level section, and recalled finding chambers over five meters high. "It was incredible, all that space, what they'd kept there or done in there I cannot imagine . . . the thing we found more than anything else was arms and matériel, but in very good storage. For instance, artillery ammunition for 57-mm recoilless rifles; each round was in an individually handmade little tin can with a sweated-lead joint and cap, also laboriously handmade. Each rifle we found was wrapped in rags and Cosmoline and very nicely done up with a little tag, a little metal tag tied with a little piece of wire; you wouldn't want to write anything on paper, because that wouldn't last very long in the tunnels, and they knew that because they had been doing it so damn long. So they had little pieces of soft metal that they wrote on with a stylus in their little symbols, of what was wrapped up in that package." Shrader also found tunnel workshops where fairly sophisticated armaments were being copied. "There were these workshops set up where they actually made small arms, Chinese copies of Thompson submachine guns and different French designs. They'd take a French machine gun which they'd captured from the French and set up a little tunnel workshop and start turning out copies by hand. They made hand grenades, ammunition, and lots of mines."

Sergeant Arnie Gutierrez did discover what some of the largest underground store rooms were for. "In the chambers, which were fifteen feet high, they were assembling artillery pieces and big mortars. They would be stripped down outside the tunnels, carried through, assembled during the night inside the tunnel, for maintenance or whatever, stripped, and then taken back through the tunnels and out again, reassembled and used. No wonder we never found their guns outside. In one set of underground chambers we found two 105 field guns. These two 105s were over forty years old and they were still in perfect condition. Can you imagine it, putting damn great field howitzers to bed every night in a tunnel? One reason our casualties ran so high, you could never figure where Charlie would get his weapons from, his rocket launchers and big pieces, fire them, then hide them, and then fire again. It was hard work for him to do it, but it was damn harder for us to figure it out. The first time we found this stuff deep inside a tunnel, we couldn't believe it."

In 1966, the Viet Cong managed to steal an M-48 tank from an ARVN unit north of Lai Khe, an event which caused understandable consternation on the government side. Three years later the Americans found it—in a tunnel. It had been buried about six feet down and tunnels had been dug around it. The tank itself was used by the VC as a command center; the batteries, the lights, and the radio were still working.

On 24 November 1966, ARVN military intelligence passed on to the Americans the interrogation report of a captured VC platoon leader. The prisoner had reported being ordered to turn on a generator to recharge batteries for a large signals unit in the Boi Loi forest (a few miles north of the Ho Bo woods). It was located deep underground and its members were involved in radio interception, telephone tapping, and codebreaking, and were fluent in many languages. This was a SIGINT (signals intelligence) unit. In 1970, the U.S. 25th Infantry found a North Vietnamese SIGINT facility hidden underground near the Thi Tinh River; all the radio communications of the 1st and 25th Divisions had been logged, and the intercepts translated into Vietnamese.

About halfway between Cu Chi town and Saigon, just north of Route 1, U.S. Special Forces Captain William Pelfrey was leading his unit on a routine search-and-destroy mission in the Hoc Mon area. It was 6 August 1967 and Pelfrey was taking part in Operation Kole Kole, an eight-month operation mounted by the 2nd Brigade of the 25th Infantry Division—a long, grinding exercise in attrition. The thirty-two-year-old Arkansas-born farm boy enjoyed life with the Special Forces and learned his jungle craft while serving in the northern provinces of South Vietnam. He'd already been in-country since December 1966, when, perversely, in his eyes, the brass had ordered him to leave Special Forces duty and rejoin an infantry unit for a while—"Get back to the army" was the way they had put it. He resisted as long as he could, and was then moved south, where he joined the 1st Battalion of the 5th Mechanized Infantry with the 25th Infantry Division.

Pelfrey, who was to win the coveted Silver Star, Bronze Star with "V" (for valor), Army Commendation Medal, and a couple of Purple Hearts during his double tour of twenty months in Vietnam, led his unit gingerly through the dry undergrowth. Just before ten the previous night three GIs had been wounded by VC mortar fire. The captain's instinct warned that there was something important in the area—it made him work his unit through the heat of midday, which earned him no applause. Just before 2:30 p.m. he noticed something odd about the way the bamboo was growing. It was just a little too neat. It was tall bamboo and it somehow looked a little too cultivated, almost as if it had been tied and trained for camouflage. It had.

The bamboo hid the entrance to a tunnel complex. Pelfrey ordered one of his men to blow the tunnel and the bunkers.

This often led to the discovery of new access holes, which themselves led to new discoveries underground. "Well, we found a complete munitions workshop underground," said Pelfrey. "They'd dug a whole bunker complex, covered each bunker with bamboo roofs, had a whole string of communication tunnels." Inside he found drill presses, little forges, a bellows system using charcoal—a complete workshop, where scrap metal was melted down in a pot and new casings made in sand molds. The grenades had handles made out of wood, with little firing chains on them. The drill presses were ancient upright models and hand-cranked. But they all worked. The official after-action report on the discovery somewhat grandly called the find a munitions factory. While it was certainly less than that, it did offer a perfect example of the light industry hidden inside the tunnels, which maintained supplies for the Viet Cong *and* maintained them under the noses of the Americans.

Lieutenant (now Lieutenant Colonel) David Sullivan of the U.S. 1st Infantry Division, a tall and wiry Iowan, made an unusual discovery in a tunnel in April 1966. He and an SP4 from his platoon came across a hardboard false wall underground. They worked at it with their bayonets for hours. When they broke it down, they found a two-foot-long wooden box with Chinese writing on it. Sullivan recalled: "The lid was nailed down; it was a weatherworn box. We prized it open. It was full of gold bars. Each was about five inches long and one and a half inches thick. We sat there just looking at them for a long time. I have to tell you, we began discussing ways of keeping the gold. First we thought we'd leave it there and collect it after the war. Then we thought we'd somehow distribute it through the platoon without anyone else knowing. Then we thought we'd mail it home and keep it. I'm happy to say that in the end right prevailed. All the schemes were impractical, and, let's face it, wrong. I went out and called a helicopter. It came and picked up the box, and you know something funny? We never heard any mention of that gold again."

The tunnels housed the living and the dead. As it became increasingly difficult for the Communist soldiers to bury the dead above ground, the bodies often had to be taken into the tunnels for temporary burial. They were generally buried in a foetuslike position in the walls of tunnels and covered with a few inches of clay or wattle. It was offensive to leave a dead comrade unburied above ground; furthermore, it helped frustrate U.S body counts if the dead were hidden inside the tunnels, and there they were at least laid to rest near the ancestral home. The VC also hid the bodies of killed Americans in the tunnels to demoralize their comrades, who regarded it as an absolute priority to retrieve their dead for decent burial at home.

In December 1969, Alpha Troop, 3rd Squadron, 4th Cavalry, had spent three days blowing up bunkers in the Boi Loi woods northwest of Cu Chi. "I saw what looked like an air vent into a tunnel," said Staff Sergeant Kermit Garrett. "We searched the area around, looking for a trapdoor, but couldn't find one, so we decided to dig around the air vent." Garrett and his partner, SP4 Mike Hanh, began to dig through the soil. Mike Hanh then came across wood, sawed through it, and then, unusually, he came up against concrete. After he'd hacked his way through that, Hanh found the hole and was first in. "I couldn't believe my eyes," he said later. "There was enough equipment in there to print a whole newspaper." They found a 1500-pound printing press in perfect working order; rows and rows of type, thirty-seven trays altogether, stacked against the walls of the huge six-foot high, thirty-by-forty-foot chamber; a table with bottles of ink and dyes in five-gallon cans; and stacks of pamphlets and papers—two tons in all.

Writer and poet Vien Phuong, who is now chairman of the Cultural Association of Ho Chi Minh City, explained that a considerable amount of printing work was needed during the war, and most of it was done using these underground presses. For several years the Communist Association of Artists and Writers of Saigon was based in the tunnels; they were responsible for their own living quarters and offices underground. "We moved around constantly, either because we were attacked or because we needed to expand. We had tunnel offices at Ho Bo, Phu Trung, Xom Thuoc. Some of our tunnel chambers still exist. There were very few printing presses and we used them mainly to produce information for the villagers. It was important to remind them that we had not left them, that we were still there, in the earth, beneath them." Phuong is a gentle and soft-spoken man. "When I got to Cu Chi district in 1962 there was already a major communication tunnel. Our office was there, and we had to dig a branch tunnel to the main one.

At the same time, the [Communist party] press office for Saigon also had its office underground near us. They too dug into the main tunnel system.

"It was a dreadful existence. One lived by the hour; one was alive one hour and might be killed the next. A person could be sitting and talking to you and be dead within five minutes. With the sheer quantity of ammunition the Americans used there were times when survival was just a lottery. The tunnels were the safest thing we had, but they were not impregnable. Personally, I had a small shelter in which I slept. It was 80 cm by 70 cm and one meter high. You can imagine what it was like for a man in that hole, night after night. I had not dug the shelter too deep, for we learned from bitter experience that the deeper the shelter, the greater the chance of being buried alive after a bombing attack, so I built a moderately strong shelter that could deal with the bomb fragments. When the enemy carried out their antiguerrilla operations above, I went into my sleeping shelter, lit a candle, and read books or wrote poems until the air was so foul I had to extinguish the candle and lie in the complete blackness of eternal night, listening to the tanks and guns above me. I did not know, and nor did my comrades, whether we had judged the depth of our tunnels correctly. One lay there, wondering if a tank would crash through the ceiling of your sleeping chamber and crush you to death, or worse, not quite to death.

"During the Manhattan operation [conducted in March 1967 by the Americans in the Long Nguyen base area just to the north of the Iron Triangle] a young man went mad in our tunnel. There had been a discussion among some of us whether we should go out of the tunnel in the evening for a few minutes to have our meal in the open. This was the greatest thing anyone could look forward to. But the Americans were around our tunnel entrances every day during Manhattan. One dead branch or one grain of rice dropped near the entrance would be sufficient for them to locate us. I felt we would be killed if we went up. That was my decision. The young man started to shout and became hysterical, saying he had to go up at that very minute, even while the Americans were still searching. He was going to go anyway, so I had him tied up."

But the real nightmare for the tunnel dwellers was the gas. Air was as precious as life, and was continually being contaminated by a variety of necessary activities—cooking, use of latrines, and so on. But when the Americans used gas, and the tunnel trapdoor and water-trap systems were inoperative or blown away or inefficient, then the tunnels became a place of slow, choking death. Whether the gas was acetylene or the anti-personnel CS riot gas, which burned the skin and tortured the eyes and nose, the effects were horrendous.

Vien Phuong remembered having to lie prone during gas attacks, staying alive only by breathing very slowly, sucking in the air remaining in a shallow layer on the tunnel floor underneath the creeping gas. Death, if it came, would be agonizingly slow asphyxiation, a dreadful retching in the stinking blackness of one's own ready-made grave.

Three members of the party press office were gassed in the tunnels. Vu Tung, a well-known Saigonese journalist; Huong Ngo, another Saigonese writer, and a Miss Tam, who had just joined the tunnel dwellers. All three were trapped in a large tunnel complex at Xom Phuoc when, according to Phuong, the Americans pumped "toxic gas" into it. When he and others were finally able to enter the tunnel after the Americans had left and sufficient time had elapsed to allow expulsion of the gas, they found Vu Tung, still wearing his felt hat, dead in a narrow communication tunnel. He had been trying to crawl out of the system. Huong Ngo lay dead, face up with a newspaper over his face, and Miss Tam lay nearby, with her face turned toward the earth.

Nguyen Van Binh joined the Viet Minh in 1951 and went to North Vietnam in 1954. There he received five months of basic training and finally returned to South Vietnam in October 1962, and was assigned to the Cu Chi district. He completed a ten-day course run by the regional North Vietnamese army cadre on the characteristics of various chemical agents used in warfare, and eventually he was assigned as the Cu Chi chemical defense officer, working from his base camp at An Nhon Tay village. He not only taught the theory of chemical defense training for all the VC units in his district but also involved himself in the practical. He had to identify visually any chemical agents dropped in his area by American aircraft and report these to the district chief. There were three main chemicals that he knew: a spray emitted from aircraft, which "killed trees and plants but was harmless to human beings and animals"—

presumably the now-notorious defoliating chemical Agent Orange; "smoke pellets" dropped from aircraft, which would cause tears, dry throat, and difficulty in breathing—probably Cry Baby tear-gas grenades; and finally, a powder dropped from aircraft in drums or sacks, which caused vomiting, dry throat, and general nausea. Cu Chi district and the Iron Triangle were to take the brunt of American chemical warfare attacks throughout the war.

The only individual defense against these gases was a locally produced gas mask made of nylon fabric (often taken from parachutes), with a filter consisting of cotton charcoal grains and linen. The masks were made with elastic bands for quick and easy pulling over the head and were usually found to be effective. Binh also referred to the use by the Americans of one mystery chemical, which he called "ypheric." This agent burned the skin, and the only defense was to hide in the tunnels for several hours until the chemical had settled on the ground. As the war grew in intensity, even the comparative luxury of homemade gas masks began to disappear. Combatants and civilians were increasingly forced to use strips of cloth soaked in urine, clamped over the nose and mouth. Occasionally, the VC would capture gas masks from the Americans.

Captain William Pelfrey, who was to spend some time fighting in the tunnels, saw them from a typically Western perspective. "It was foul down there. The Vietnamese used to urinate and defecate in the tunnels, the body odors and sweat were unbelievable. After you were down there thirty or forty minutes it was all right, but then when you'd come up and hit air, you'd just faint sometimes, literally faint."

Latrine systems were necessarily primitive. Where it was possible, large stone jars were buried in chambers and used as excrement receptacles. When full, they were simply plugged with earth and left. Often this luxury was not available, in which case one dug a hole and filled it up. It is difficult to imagine the sanitary conditions in the fetid and airless tunnels, where large numbers of people were often forced to stay for several days without a break.

"If our rice got wet, there was no place to dry it. We then had to cook and eat the rotten rice. Do you know what that means?" asked Vien Phuong. An American GI who had been exploring the tunnels came across a stench so awful, so overpowering that he instantly retched. He was convinced he had stumbled into another tunnel graveyard—in fact, he had come across a cache of rotten rice.

"Food went bad very quickly in the tunnels," explained Vien Phuong. "The most precious currency below ground was the plastic or steel containers the Americans left as litter on the battlefield above us. They were strong and we used them to keep our food dry. We covered each box with nylon sheets made from old parachutes. My own personal possessions for nearly five years were just those I could fit inside a shoulder bag. I had a big American army belt to which was attached an American water bottle. I had a nylon roof sheet made from parachutes, 2.5 meters long, which, where possible, was pegged to the roof to prevent earth falling all over me, especially during American operations. I had a nylon waterproof cape during the rainy season, a hammock, a lamp made out of an old menthol bottle, a dagger, a rifle, and a rice bag. The heaviest thing I had was the rice bag, which weighed ten kilograms. The main problems, the ones that never left us, were malnutrition and malaria."

Even the smallest irritants, literally, soon grew into one of the most tiresome and eventually insufferable problems. The tunnels were breeding grounds for tiny organisms, invisible to the naked eye; said to be half animal and half plant, and variously called Vets or Chiggers. They bred and survived—together with squadrons of mosquitoes—on the walls and ceilings of the tunnels. Upon physical contact, even with the clothed body, these organisms enter the body and live just under the skin, remaining there for about three months and causing—as the authors themselves were to discover—unbearable itching. Captain Linh, whose life was plagued by them, claimed the parasites lived originally at the very tips of tree roots. They were particularly unpleasant because they would enter any part of the body, causing acute local irritation, which, even when it subsided, would be easily triggered off through friction. They could be extracted only by a paramedic with a needle and some alcohol (when available) for disinfectant. Even Captain Linh was forced to admit: "After a time people were afraid of going down the tunnels because of these creatures. They caused us all much hardships."

Sometimes the tunnels *did* collapse under the weight of

tanks, and the victims were crushed or buried alive, and sometimes bombs and shells did make direct hits on the tunnel roof, with devastating consequences. Sometimes, people were just plain unlucky. The man who is now chief of police in Tay Ninh City was granted one day's leave by his VC commander to visit his wife, who was working as a nurse in the tunnels. They had only just been married and saw virtually nothing of each other. Because it was a marital visit, the couple were allowed a chamber for the night. While the couple were together, a stray bomb fell right through the roof. It didn't explode, but its fins severed the husband's leg.

In a comment that might have been made specifically about the tunnel dwellers of Cu Chi, Robert McNamara, when secretary of defense, reminding his audience of the ineffectiveness of America's bombing strategy in North Vietnam, said: "Their economy is agrarian and simple, their population unfamiliar with the modern comforts and conveniences that most of us in the Western world take for granted...their morale has not been broken, since they are accustomed to discipline and are no strangers to deprivation and death."

Even as he was making this prescient assessment, the district of Cu Chi was already on its way to becoming the Land of Iron.

7

Born in a Tunnel

DANG THI LANH was born in Saigon in 1945; twenty-two years later, on 23 February 1967, her first child was born in the tunnels of Cu Chi. The baby was a daughter, to be called Tranh Thi Hien; her birthplace was a hole in the ground at Phu My Hung near the Saigon River. The maternity ward was a tunnel chamber, its ceiling roughly hung with American parachute nylon to prevent earth falling on the mother. Tranh Thi Hien has grown up to be a healthy teenager. Her puppy fat and ruddy good looks give her the appearance of a well-fed farm girl; one would not guess she was once a skinny tunnel baby who screamed her way into life as battle raged above her head.

War had quickly brought death to the mother Dang Thi Lanh's family. *Her* mother and father were killed in separate, but coincidental, U.S. helicopter gunship attacks. Her only brother died during an ARVN operation in Bau Lach in 1964. But Dang Thi Lanh's face, with its hint of ethnic Chinese friendliness, betrays no shadow of the pain she felt at those losses. Small and sturdy, she was to have a second daughter after the war.

"I was with a cultural troupe in the tunnels: singing, dancing, and playing in a performance called *Cay Chong* (The Punji

Stake), which was all about the fighting. We performed inside a tunnel chamber, and the play was very successful. My husband, Tran Van Tien, was then a doctor's assistant working in Phu My Hung village. Sometimes we did not see each other for months. Once we were separated for a whole year. Before they destroyed the village, he could be working above ground and I below the earth, and we never met.

"I worked all the way through my pregnancy. During the Cedar Falls operation we had nothing to eat apart from dry rice and salt. I lived permanently underground during that operation; for fifteen days I did not see the light, or breathe the proper air. While the Americans were literally above us with their men and their tanks and their bulldozers, we still kept the troupe going. We did this every day and we even managed to rehearse. The chamber we used for the performances was on the first level, which was lucky because I was far too big with Tranh Thi Hien to be able to pass through the trapdoors to the second level. As we got nearer the time of the birth I found myself getting very tired and very hot. My leader agreed that I could do less. I knew the baby would come shortly and they promised me a doctor would be there.

"The day before my daughter was born I sang and I danced and I even managed to dig a little bit of tunnel with a short hoe from seven until ten in the evening. For the next hour and a half I cooked food for the thirty-six people in the troupe. I went to bed at about eleven-thirty, sleeping as usual in a hammock in a chamber I shared with nine other women from the troupe. The next day, I began to feel pains at about ten in the morning. My comrades called a doctor. I went to another tunnel, crawling through a connecting tunnel only one meter wide. It took a long time and I was very hot and felt bad from the lack of air. But then I went into a chamber they called the cool room because it had so many air holes. There was no bed but there was a hammock. The room was about eight meters by eight meters square and 1.8 meters high. The walls, ceiling, and floor were all covered with American parachute nylon. In order to eat I had to get off the hammock and lie on the floor. It was still rice and salt. Vien Phuong, the writer, was there."

Vien Phuong also remembered the occasion well. "She was a very good dancer and member of the cultural group. She had been dancing at Nha Be, but when we heard she was pregnant we called her back to Cu Chi because, though it is hard to believe, Cu Chi was safer than Nha Be. When she came back to Cu Chi we suggested she should go and live among the people, but she refused. She said she was a performer and anyway she was well known by the people and the puppets [those who worked for the South Vietnamese government]. She said if she lived in an enemy-controlled area she would be arrested. The woman was carrying her first baby. We were all living underground then; there were no more houses left above. When she felt her first pains we thought she would have the baby in the morning; usually the enemy raided in the morning. I knew it was time to get her a midwife nurse to deliver the baby, as the one nurse in our tunnel section could not do it herself. I left the tunnel to look for a midwife and bring her back. A plane was circling overhead and I was running and trying to hide from the plane. They only needed to see one person and the attacks would start again. Finally I got a message to a doctor at the military hospital. He arrived, but only just in time."

Dang Thi Lanh continued: "I think the doctor arrived at about one o'clock. I was already off the hammock, lying on the floor on a mat, and that's just where my daughter was born. There was hot water, medicine, and a bandage. The birth took about an hour. It was very painful, very painful. There was no change of clothing, we had only a handkerchief for the baby. I was worried about infection, with so much earth around, but it must have been clean enough in there for there was no infection. They put my daughter in another hammock and I was able to give her milk from my breast, but there was very little. The baby stayed with me for twenty hours and drank a little sugared water when I was unable to give her milk. After the big American operation was over they took me and the baby to Trung Lap, where the local mothers' association looked after us. It was an enemy-controlled area during the day, but at night it was controlled by the Communists. Six months later I returned to the tunnels, singing and dancing with the original troupe. My grandfather looked after Tranh Thi Hien.

"I stayed in the tunnels until 1968 and then joined the Tet offensive in Go Vap. After that I returned to the tunnels until 1970, when I returned to Saigon city to work for the revolution. I was caught that July and sent to prison for three months. I was tortured by the ARVN soldiers and an American who was in the cell. They beat me up and passed electricity through my body. Eventually, on 19 May 1975, I was reunited with my daughter. She was nearly eight years old. I had hardly seen her since I left her with my grandfather. All her childhood had gone by without me. Then I was reunited with my husband. He was very seriously wounded and has been unable to work since. We get a state pension; we live in one room. It was worth it. Would I do it again? That's a very hard question to answer. It was a valuable experience. Tranh Thi Hien is sixteen now, is at school, attends night classes, and wants to become a doctor. I had my second daughter, Tranh Dang Minh Hien, in a hospital. It was nice. It was all much easier."

8

The Tunnel Rats

TUNNELS FOR HAVING babies in, for hospitals, for hiding, for fighting—the American commanders arriving in Vietnam had never come across anything like them before. After initial bruising experiences, it became clear that they would need to develop a new military skill in tunnel warfare, and develop it fast.

In Operation Crimp in January 1966 the U.S. Army's commanders were astonished by the scale and extent of the Viet Cong tunnel systems, but they should have been prepared. As long ago as 1963, the ARVN, then fighting a losing war against burgeoning Viet Cong forces, had warned its American advisers of the tunnels' existence. There was, for instance, an ARVN briefing at the presidential palace in Saigon on 20 September 1963 by officers from the III Corps Tactical Zone. This was translated into English and transcribed at the specific request of the intelligence chief at the U.S. Military Assistance Command (MACV). The briefing described a two-month ARVN operation in the Iron Triangle, and other actions in the Ho Bo woods. The ARVN briefing officer was gloomy:

"Tunnels provide the enemy with an extensive means of resistance and are established in Viet Cong controlled areas.

To completely destroy a VC tunnel system, we must conduct a long-range operation and pay a dear price."

In the two-month operation, twenty ARVN soldiers had been killed, and sixty wounded, by mines and snipers; eight vehicles had been damaged by mines. The ARVN claimed ten Viet Cong killed. It had indeed been costly.

The briefing officer glumly continued: "We must admit that it is very difficult for us to discover Viet Cong concealed trenches and tunnels, because of their skillful and delicate organization. Short-range mop-ups in VC base areas conducted by units which have no knowledge of the terrain and accurate information rarely bring about desired results." The ARVN officer went on to describe the tunnels' structure and defenses with some accuracy, even pointing out that "it is useless to toss tear-gas grenades into trenches because they are provided with partitions which hold back smoke." ARVN "war dogs," he said, dared not enter the tunnels. He gave various bits of advice on tunnel detection, such as looking for freshly dug earth or cultivation in unlikely places. He went on: "It is necessary to probe separate graves located far from villages with a pointed stick. If the stick fails to strike the lid of a coffin, we are sure that the grave is a camouflaged VC trench."

One thing that emerged from the briefing with startling clarity was that no ARVN soldier ever ventured down into a tunnel to explore it or to engage the Viet Cong. The officers evidently never considered sending a man on such a mission. This was confirmed by former Viet Cong Captain Nguyen Thanh Linh, who said that the ARVN not only never entered tunnels, but even occasionally shouted greetings to Viet Cong inside, such as "Sleep well, you guys, so that you can go to work tonight!" The ARVN troops would even conceal tunnel entrances from their superiors, or fail to report their discovery, for fear of being asked to do the logical thing and investigate. In the 1963 briefing there was mention of "combating this system of VC warfare," without any real suggestion of how to do it, short of bemoaning the difficulties. The only tactic proposed was to surround a Viet Cong tunnel entrance and wait for the guerrillas to come out. It is hardly surprising that by the time the American army arrived in 1965 the Viet Cong were, literally, so well entrenched, their bunkers so extensive and so permanent.

The briefing found its way into MACV's bulging files, and references to it crop up in documents written years later. Brigadier General Richard Knowles, who in 1966 took command of the 196th Light Infantry Brigade, recalled debriefing Special Forces officers with Vietnam experience before he left the continental United States. "We used to listen to them by the hour," he said. "In the process I heard about the tunnels in considerable detail; apparently the South Vietnamese just left them alone. I was aware of the tunnels, but not of their significance to the Viet Cong effort in South Vietnam. We didn't appreciate the full extent of that till much later."

Brigadier General Ellis W. Williamson led the 173rd Airborne Brigade into the Iron Triangle in October 1965, and wrote afterward: "The Iron Triangle was thoroughly searched and investigated, and all enemy troops and installations were destroyed." Admittedly, his troops had entered the area and destroyed a number of dwellings and killed some of the inhabitants. But one of his company commanders, Captain Henry B. Tucker, made a more realistic assessment: "We burned the buildings, but we could not do anything to the fortifications; they were dug too damn deep." The proof that General Williamson was wrong lies in the massive operation that had to be conducted a year later over exactly the same ground, Operation Cedar Falls. And even after the devastation and depopulation of that great search-and-destroy exercise in 1967, the major thrust against Saigon during the Tet offensive of 1968 came out of the Iron Triangle.

In the U.S.Army, after each operation the commander must append to his after-action report (AAR) a list entitled "Lessons Learned." Operation Crimp in Cu Chi district in early 1966 proved to be a genuine and sobering education. Despite the upbeat and optimistic (if not self-deluding) tone of these army documents, and repeated claims of successes that often proved illusory, the references to the tunnels show how serious and how unforeseen a headache they presented. From the AAR of Williamson's 173rd Airborne Brigade:

> The fortification system within the AO [area of operation] was the most extensive and intricate one the Brigade has encountered. It included mutually supporting trenches

> and bunkers, and a maze of multi-level tunnels, some of which were constructed of steel and concrete. These tunnels were protected by command-detonated claymore type mines and the approaches and entrances were heavily booby-trapped. Many of the trench systems were capable of accommodating a VC battalion. The tunnels had been constructed over an extended period of time and were not vulnerable to artillery and air strikes—except for direct hits. They were of such great length and contained so many entrances that complete destruction would require large numbers of troops at least one month using great amounts of riot control agents and demolitions.

With some urgency, just two months after Operation Crimp, MACV published a confidential report entitled "Operations Against Tunnel Complexes," which was distributed to all U.S. commands in Vietnam. It drew on the experience of American and Australian units in recent operations in the III Corps Tactical Zone. It emphasized the problems of detecting and exploring "fighting" tunnel complexes in "war zones" and "VC base areas." This confidential report shows that the intractable nature of the war was beginning to dawn on the military analysts after one year in Vietnam. This is what they wrote:

> *These complexes present a formidable and dangerous obstacle to current operations* [authors' italics] which must be dealt with in a systematic, careful and professional manner. . . . Prisoner interrogation has indicated that many tunnel complexes are interconnected, but the connecting tunnels, concealed by trapdoors or blocked by three or four feet of dirt, are known only to selected persons and are used only in emergencies. Indications also point to interconnections of some length, e.g., 5–7 kilometers, through which relatively large bodies of men may be transferred from one area to another, especially from one "fighting" complex to another. The "fighting" complexes terminate in well-constructed bunkers, in many cases covering likely landing zones in a war zone or base area. . . . The presence of a tunnel complex within or near an area of operations poses a

> continuing threat to *all* personnel in the area. No area containing tunnel complexes should *ever* be considered completely cleared.

In Operation Crimp, tunnel exploration and destruction was entirely ad hoc. There was apparently no body of knowledge or experience upon which to draw. Soldiers improvised crawling and measuring techniques; some suffocated underground when smoke grenades had been used; others died from Viet Cong booby traps and mines. The MACV report listed the inherent dangers of underground exploration. As well as bad air and booby traps, it included, somewhat superfluously, "VC still in the tunnel." But its main recommendation was the creation of a specialist soldier, with a new military skill unique to the Vietnam War:

> A trained tunnel team is essential to the expeditious and thorough exploitation and denial of Viet Cong tunnels. Tunnel teams should be in a ready status to provide immediate expert assistance when tunnels are discovered. Tunnel team members should be volunteers. Claustrophobia and panic could well cause the failure of the team's mission or the death of its members.

The creation of those teams would prove one of the more extraordinary phenomena in the history of American arms: the birth of an infantryman who rejoiced in the undignified but menacing title of Tunnel Rat.

If Sergeant Stewart Green was the first reluctant tunnel explorer in Vietnam, Captain Herbert Thornton was the first of the new tunnel rats. Although the 25th Infantry Division originally called them tunnel runners and the Australian army called them ferrets, "tunnel rats" eventually became the accepted official term among the armed forces of the West. Far from derogatory, the name was a source of pride and esprit. Thornton had been the Big Red One's chemical officer when it arrived in Vietnam in 1965 and was based at Di An, just south of the Iron Triangle, east of the Saigon River. Herbert Thornton was forty in 1966, a round-faced, balding Southerner. He is lucky to be alive today. He was once crawling in a tunnel behind a soldier from the 25th Infantry who set off a booby-trap mine. Thornton was blown physically out of the tunnel and into the open air above, uninjured but deafened in one ear. His companion was buried and never found.

Thornton's chemical platoon was given special responsibility for tunnel destruction, and participated in Operation Crimp in that role. The infantry decided that the chemical CS gas—along with explosives—was the best way to deny the use of the tunnels to the enemy. When powder grenades were exploded, CS crystals lodged in tunnel walls, and the resulting gas would painfully irritate the skin and lungs of anyone passing through. The crystals were effective for about a week, though natural moisture would wash them away. Another tunnel-denial tactic was pumping acetylene gas into the tunnels with a Sears Roebuck orchard blower, an air compressor used at home for spraying pesticide onto trees. It was imported in large numbers into Vietnam and nicknamed the "mighty mite." The acetylene was then ignited and burned up the oxygen in the tunnel. In addition, demolition charges were used to blow up tunnel sections.

The policy of tunnel destruction was recognized as shortsighted when intelligence officers began evaluating items found in tunnels—documents such as Viet Cong tax records and personnel lists, as well as maps of U.S. bases, including Bien Hoa air base and Cu Chi. (North Vietnam's Premier Pham Van Dong once said, "The Americans like captured documents; we made sure they got plenty.") Consequently, Captain Thornton and his men were ordered to explore the tunnels before destroying them.

This task demanded not only special skills, but also—it was recognized—a special type of temperament and courage. The tunnel rats were obliged to perform the most unnatural and stressful tasks: to crawl through pitch-dark, narrow, low, earthen tunnels for hundreds of yards, facing the threat of sudden death at any moment. Heavily armed Viet Cong units hid in their underground refuges for most of the daylight hours. In addition, every tunnel was sown with mines and booby traps. There were fire ants, rats (real ones), and other creatures. In damp black holes dug for the slim and slight Vietnamese, most Americans found claustrophobic panic barely controllable. General Bernard Rogers, then an assistant commander of the Big Red One, described the rat's task: "Hot, dirty, and gasping for breath, he squeezed his body through narrow and shallow openings on all fours, never knowing whether the tunnel might collapse behind him or what he might find ahead around the next turn, and sensing the jolt of adrenaline at every sound. Surely this modern combat spelunker [cave explorer] is a special breed."

General Fred Weyand, who commanded the 25th Infantry Division in 1966, said of these men: "There's nothing more curious than an American soldier, particularly if he thinks there's an enemy down there somewhere. I found in each company, when it went out into an area of tunnels, the tunnel rat became a sort of oddball hero. You had guys who took great pride in showing their buddies they were unique in terms of courage; it's amazing what human beings will do in that sort of situation." Herbert Thornton himself: "It just takes a special kind of being. He's got to have an inquisitive mind, a lot of guts, and a lot of real moxie into knowing what to touch and what not to touch to stay alive. Because you could blow yourself out of there in a heartbeat if you didn't really keep your eyes open all the time. There were no bad days. They were all good days if you got through them."

Why did Thornton think tunnel specialists were needed? "At first we tried to put tunnel teams all over the division, and we had people getting zapped because they didn't have enough knowledge to go into a tunnel right." None of his chemical platoon, he claimed, was "zapped" in the one year he spent in Vietnam on that assignment. But other infantrymen, volunteers or under orders, from ordinary line companies did die in tunnels, sometimes in horrible and bizarre ways; one Viet Cong technique was to slit a man's throat or garrotte him, as he came up through a connecting trapdoor. Thornton took only volunteers into his squad. If you had to order a man into a tunnel, he said, he would come straight out and say it was only ten or twelve feet long even if it was much longer. But even experienced volunteers could lose their self-possession underground, start panicking and screaming, and scramble back to the entrance, to be absolved of tunnel duties from then on.

"I didn't like my people to be down there too long," recalled Colonel Al Hylton, who succeeded Herb Thornton as the Big Red One's chemical officer. "If they ever started panicking, as some of them did, I just said, 'You get the hell out of there!' You could tell when they were panicking because they would call up and say, 'I can't go any farther; I got to get out of here.' I'd call up on the field telephone line. I had a sergeant on top at all times, and if communication ever broke we went down to see what had happened. They would come out; some of them had obviously been crying, and even though they were volunteers, I would not let them go back until they had some rest and came to me and said, 'Colonel, I want to have a go again.' It's a job you can't force people to do. They volunteered because it was exciting, I suppose. They saw me, the old man, do it and figured if that old, gray man can do it, so can I! I never anticipated when I went to Vietnam as a chemical officer that I would be crawling around on my hands and knees underground."

Dead or wounded tunnel rats were dragged out with communication wires or ropes, or by the fireman's crawl, in which the wounded man's tied hands were hooked around the neck of the crawling rescuer. No dead tunnel rat was left in a tunnel, but extricating bodies exposed other men to the same danger. Many, but not all, tunnel rats were small men, suited to the narrow entrances and constricting space; many were Hispanic—Puerto Rican or Mexican.

The efficient Viet Cong intelligence-gathering inside Di An base soon let them know of Captain Thornton's special tunnel duties; despite his junior rank, he was a marked man. Reward notices were posted by the Communists, calling for Thornton's death; there was a price on the tunnel specialist's head. He survived, however, to become the tunnel guru. In March 1966 he was assigned to instruct soldiers of the newly arrived Tropic Lightning Division at the tunnel school in their base at Cu Chi. In 1967, after Operation Cedar Falls, tunnel-rat duties in the Big Red One were transferred to the 1st Engineer Battalion. The chemical detachment by then had defoliation commitments, and the engineers had demolition expertise. In the years that followed, esprit among tunnel rats increased to the point that they had a special cloth badge made and an (unofficial) sleeve insignia. The badge showed a gray rodent holding a pistol and a flashlight, and had a motto in dog Latin: *Non Gratum Anus Rodentum* (Not worth a rat's ass).

The 1st Engineer rats worked in teams of about a dozen men under a lieutenant or NCO. One of them was a "Kit Carson scout," a former Viet Cong who had defected to the South

Vietnamese government side, and who knew tunnels from first-hand experience. Junior officers of the Big Red One achieved distinction and decorations as tunnel rats. In the 25th (Tropic Lightning) Division, based just across the Saigon River in Cu Chi, the policy was not to allow officers to explore tunnels. In that division, each company had a volunteer tunnel rat, usually a private. He enjoyed some prestige among his peers, but no special status.

Tunnel rats volunteered for a variety of reasons—sometimes to make up for problematic lives back home, or to prove their manhood in truly testing conditions. Once their fear was conquered, and assuming they survived, some even came to like their work. They accepted the silent enclosure of a tunnel, where the Vietnam War was unavoidably reduced to the ultimate confrontation, single combat, one on one; for the rats, the light at the end of the tunnel was usually a VC with a candle. Colonel Thomas Ware of the 25th recalled one of his men: "There was one little pale-faced, pimply-skinned guy that'd go anyplace. I remember one time he was down there we heard a shot; we got him out and he was wounded. I'd go and visit him in hospital and he couldn't wait to get back. Next time I'd see him he'd be back in the tunnel again." Major William Pelfrey, also of the 25th Infantry, commanded a West Virginian tunnel rat called Private Short.

"He was north of Cu Chi," Pelfrey recalled, "and we'd run across a bunker complex. We blew it and opened up a hole and Short went down to check it out. He went in about thirty or forty feet and there's a trapdoor that led down to another level. He raised it and a booby trap went off and the tunnel caved in on him. He was buried, face down. We crawled down and tied ropes to his feet; we tried to drag him out, but couldn't. So we had to dig down from the top. He was about twelve feet down. It took us thirty minutes and was kinda frantic. When we could see his feet, they were wiggling. He was getting air because his hands were below his face. He was semiconscious when we got him out. He went to the hospital, but discharged himself. The hospital thought he'd gone AWOL, they sent military police looking for him; in fact he came straight back to his unit. His idea of R & R was to join me on patrol. You just couldn't keep that man out of the tunnels."

They were a special breed with a special and awesome task

that set them apart from the rest of the grunts. Among U.S. servicemen in Vietnam, only helicopter pilots and LRRPs (long-range reconnaissance teams) brushed with mortal danger so consistently or enjoyed such a reputation. The rats were professionals who did not hesitate to kill, loners who gained satisfaction from accepting a mission no other soldier would contemplate. Some were deeply aggressive men with dark and perplexing motives who found their true selves in the tunnels; others were well-balanced men who took on the job but were so scarred by the experience as to want to suppress it from their memories.

Harold Roper was a tunnel rat with the 25th Infantry in the early Vietnam days of 1966. "I felt more fear than I've ever come close to before or since," he recalled. "The Viet Cong would take their dead after a battle and put them down in the tunnels; they didn't want us to count their dead because they knew we were big on body count. Finding them wasn't pleasant, but we'd killed them so it didn't matter. It was worse if they'd been down there for a week—it stunk! Everything rotted very quickly because of the humidity. I came across rotting bodies several times. It didn't revolt me. I was just an animal—we were all animals, we were dogs, we were snakes, we were dirt. We weren't human beings—human beings don't do the things we did. I was a killer rat with poisoned teeth. I was trained to kill and I killed. Looking back, it's unreal. Unnatural. It's almost like someone else did it. It wasn't really me, because I wouldn't even think of doing anything close to that again."

Roper was seriously wounded by a mine, hospitalized, and repatriated. He was to suffer years of nightmares. Like many of the tunnel rats, he could not bring himself to talk about his experiences for nearly ten years. The collective experience of tunnel warfare was nearly lost. Only now have some of the rats been willing to recall, often painfully, what they had to do.

9

Not Worth a Rat's Ass

THE TUNNEL RAT was to stand proud and isolated within the ranks of the best-equipped army in the world. Not for him the standard infantryman's equipment of steel helmet, full combat dress, flak jacket, lightweight jungle boots, full webbing, water bottle, M-1 or M-16 automatic rifle and spare ammunition bandolier. To the contrary, the tunnel rat soon discovered that the less he took into the sweaty darkness, the better his chances of survival. The more they tried to arm him, the more he was to realize that neither firepower, personal armor, or newfangled high technology would ever give him an advantage over his invisible enemy.

After Operation Crimp, as tunnel rat volunteers began to step forward, experience soon showed that the knife, the pistol, and the flashlight were to be the basic tools for combat and survival inside the tunnels of Cu Chi. Indeed, the very reverse of high-tech weapons development took place within the tiny ranks of the tunnel rats. They had to relearn the whole business of carefully planned face-to-face combat, one on one, as they called it, without fire support, and without weapons superiority. The rats were to become obsessive about the most minute details of their equipment, lauding one pistol over another, one knife edge over another. They rediscovered the satisfaction of old-fashioned unarmed combat, where individual strength, guts, and cunning counted for much more than massive air and artillery support.

Every rat carried a flashlight, and carried it in a special way to avoid being a nicely lit target. If the flashlight was dropped and the bulb smashed, then panic could easily follow, so they learned how to change a bulb in pitch darkness by touch alone, and they learned how to do it quickly, and how to do it squatting, kneeling, or lying prone.

The only weapon the tunnel rats ever agreed about was the army's standard-issue Colt .45. No one wanted it, and very few used it. It was too big, too cumbersome, and too loud. Choosing your own pistol was a tunnel rat privilege and each sought the weapon he felt comfortable with. They disagreed about silencers. Some would not fire a pistol without one because of the deafening roar of the shot; others wouldn't use a silencer because the added barrel length made a quick draw awkward and hindered maneuverability within the tunnel confines—and indeed, there were times when they deliberately wished to advertise their presence in order that the VC be frightened out of the tunnel. Not many tunnel rats actively sought and welcomed tunnel combat, surely one of the most terrifying encounters imaginable.

PFC Harold Roper simply bought a Smith & Wesson .38 from a helicopter pilot for twenty-five dollars and used that, together with a shotgun, where appropriate. The larger pellet scatter of the shotgun made it potentially a more accurate tunnel weapon, although not necessarily as lethal as a pistol. Master Sergeant Flo Rivera appropriated his own German Luger and managed to arrange official issue of a four-gauge riot shotgun—"real handy that four-gauge, the noise blew your eardrums out but if there was anything at all in front of you, you hit it." Staff Sergeant Gilbert Lindsay, a Japanese-American, carried his own .38 but once in the tunnel he always carried it in the left hand. "I had this thing if the guy was going to cut my hand off—if I had this struggle with Charlie and if he had a knife and he cut my hand off—I'd still have my good hand to write with, wipe my ass, you know, do something. The idea of losing my right arm was like losing my friend, I was petrified." Major Randy Ellis, who led one of the tunnel rat squads in the Big

Red One, also favored an unsilenced Smith & Wesson .38 but was worried about its lack of firepower in the face of the VCs' AK-47. So he acquired an M-2 carbine with a "paratrooper" stock, which folded up to about twenty-two inches in length. This weapon was nicknamed the cannon, and if Ellis led a tunnel rat squad down a hole, the number-three rat always carried it. If the point man (lead man) suspected there was a VC ahead, he would call for the cannon. Sergeant Bernard Justen rejected a specially silenced .38 with a unique light-source sniper-scope, in favor of his own simple .25 Beretta. If the rats ever took a rifle below ground, it was a captured AK-47; the intention was to confuse the VC with its distinctive sound.

Despite the rats' satisfaction with the old-fashioned martial skills newly learned, their unit commanders constantly yearned for new technological solutions to problems that needed the application of common sense rather than silicon chips. In the event, home-based scientists were only too happy to produce new weapons systems, many of which turned out to be useless.

In 1962, the Limited Warfare Laboratory (known as LWL) was established in Maryland to develop counter insurgency hardware in a crash program to meet the army's operational requirements in a limited war. By 1967, nine out of ten of its projects were oriented toward the Vietnam battlefield. Some of its inventions proved useful: an effective leech repellent; foliage-penetrating radars; a 1,100-calorie meal in a ten-ounce packet. But many of its efforts directed toward tunnel fighting, while well-intentioned, were risible flops.

On 7 August 1966, after considerable research into the perceived demands of a new kind of war inside tunnels, LWL created and shipped to both the 1st and 25th division a Tunnel Exploration Kit for practical testing. It comprised three items: first, in place of the ubiquitous old-fashioned flashlight, or torch, there was now a revolutionary headlamp, specially mounted on a new kind of fatigue cap. In order to leave the hands free, a mouth-operated switch was supplied. You bit the light on and off. Second, the kit held a communications system with a sensitive "bone conductor microphone," worn on the bone at the *back* of the head, or strapped round the throat. Reception would be through an earpiece; necessary trailing wires would be secured through the pistol belt to a wire reel.

Third, there was a .38 revolver with a four-inch barrel complete with silencer and a tiny high-intensity aiming light. The kit came complete with ear plugs to be inserted when the weapon was fired.

Touched by such thoughtful concern for their welfare, the tunnel rats gingerly and suspiciously began to test the kit in combat conditions. Things went wrong from the outset. The headlamp bite switch didn't work properly; the lamp itself, which was firmly fixed to the fatigue cap, soon slid down over the rat's eyes because it constantly rubbed against the tunnel roof. Slipping was worse when the unfortunate rat began to sweat—which was inevitable the moment he entered the tunnel. The earpiece in the communications system was soon found to have the disadvantage of not staying snugly inside the ear but falling out, while the trailing wires snagged along the tunnel floor or round curves.

The specially adapted .38 was a total disaster. With silencer and aiming light mounted, it was far too large and awkward; the aiming light was either ineffective or useless because it was diffused and overpowered by the larger and stronger miner's lamp (unless it had tipped forward). The .38 silencer turned out to be ineffective, and even the gun's holster was too large and bulky for tunnel use. The Tunnel Exploration Kit was gratefully returned to the LWL, never to be seen again. One part of it, however—the communications kit—did make a brief and equally ill-fated reappearance three years later. A radiotelephone especially made for use in the tunnels was invented. Its rather grand name was TELACS (Tunnel Explorer, Locator & Communications System). A 1st Division tunnel rat squad was ordered to test and evaluate the complex system, which was intended not only to allow speech between those in the tunnels and those waiting outside, but also to facilitate electronic tracking of the rats as they crawled through.

Very quickly the rats discovered that the transmission system distorted the voice too much for anyone to comprehend it and the tracking mode system was too time-consuming for safety; then they discovered something the manufacturers might have thought of before they even embarked on the project—the kit was too bulky to take through the tunnel trapdoors.

Lieutenant Colonel James Bushong, who as a captain was chemical officer of the 2nd Brigade of the 1st Division in March

1966, was scathing about the kit. "The communications set was unsatisfactory; you had all that wire dragging along behind you. Besides, one of the things the bad guys liked to use a whole lot to make their booby traps with was our commo wire, and if you're in the dark, one piece of commo wire felt like another. We found using a human chain for communications far more efficient, and psychologically a little bit brighter.

"Then they came up with the miner's lamp. Wonderful as long as you were down there by yourself. If you were down there with someone else who was intent upon doing you harm, then keeping a spotlight for him to aim at on your skull may not exactly give you an advantage."

A full two years later, in July 1969, the Limited War Laboratory invented a new piece of equipment for the tunnel rat (or Tunnel Exploration Personnel, as it called them): a silent handgun, capable of "engaging fleeting targets without aimed fire." They came up with a "balanced, compact, six-shot, cylinder-loaded exposed hammer, selective double-action, modified Smith & Wesson .44 magnum revolver, weighing 38 ounces." It fired a special 15-pellet bullet with a shot pattern similar to that of a shotgun, but with smoke and flash virtually eliminated. Called the Tunnel Weapon, it deserved a better fate than it received, but by 1969, tunnel rat combat had become so refined that even the introduction of a potentially helpful new pistol did not interest the ultraconservative rats.

From the very beginning, the two demonstrators flown to Vietnam by LWL to sell the weapon knew they would have a hard time convincing the rats that the weapon was truly lethal. They were right. Rats who used it in combat liked its size enormously. It allowed them to reach quickly round tunnel corners and fire without themselves exposing more than a hand and an arm. It sounded like a cap gun when it went off (which was good)—but it did not always kill (which was not so good). In fact there were several times when it did not even incapacitate an enemy soldier after he was hit. The riot shotguns that some rats used always maimed, at least. There was also a dangerously high misfire rate with the ammunition.

According to the demonstrators, the differing tunnel rat techniques used by the 1st and the 25th also confused the tests. In the Big Red One, rats would often fire three rounds into the entrance of a tunnel, and around each sharp turn. A similar sequence was used when they found trapdoors or false walls. The 25th, on the other hand, tended to hurl grenades, mines, and gas into tunnel entrances "to discourage the enemy from firing on exploration personnel." The truth is that these rat techniques were not standard at all. By 1969 tunnel warfare had matured, and tunnel destruction was generally avoided until weapons, documents, and occasionally VC themselves could be brought out. In fact, the .44 magnum did not get much of a run from the rats, who were already impatient with all the false technological breakthroughs that LWL had shipped over. The Tunnel Weapon went the way of the Tunnel Exploration Kit, although there is a curious addendum to this story.

According to Richard Keogh, who was the 1st Division's ammunition officer, LWL did solve the ordnance problem and actually came up with some new, highly potent ammunition for the snubnosed .44. "It was a multiple bullet with four segments to increase the kill range," he recalled. "It didn't make a nice hole; in fact it just tore holes inside you. It was very good at a short distance. The barrel of the .44 was shortened to three inches and a sling swivel added. They only manufactured about seventy-five of these guns; they were in use for six months, and then suddenly they were withdrawn." It is likely that the new lethal and silent "segments" bullet that replaced the less effective 15-pellet bullet contravened the Geneva Convention on "allowable" weaponry.

The killing power of the hand weapons had become of great significance to the tunnel rats as they realized that nothing ever seemed to induce the VC to surrender in the tunnels. Major Ellis recalls that his squad were issued bullhorns to be used to talk VC out of the tunnel. "We figured that was a lot less risky than going in there. But in no instance were we ever able to talk anybody out of the tunnel. So eventually it became my concern that when we met a man in the tunnels, we would have to be absolutely sure that we killed him. Wounding a VC just didn't help. A couple of fellows showed up one day with this new .44 magnum. It had a stainless steel little shell, that kind of had little holes round the back of it. It was gas-propelled. It shot pellets and had a range of about twenty feet. They showed them to us and we fired at silhouettes above the ground, but it wasn't a killing gun."

Over at the 25th, Master Sergeant Robert Baer, an experienced tunnel rat, also found that the tunnel VC simply refused to surrender, even when obviously trapped away from any secret tunnel exit route. He devised one way of flushing them out into the open, by simply throwing smoke grenades or trip flares into the tunnels, which burned up all the available oxygen and sometimes led to reluctant surrender. But more often than not the VC preferred suicide to capture.

In May 1969, Baer was led to a shallow tunnel by a captured NVA nurse. There were two other NVA nurses and one Communist soldier in the hole. Baer's Kit Carson scout tried talking them out. Conversation was easy between the ground and such a small tunnel shelter. Baer's squad of eleven waited out of gunshot line near the hole. For nearly half an hour the Kit Carson scout tried and failed to get the three to surrender. Finally, Baer ordered an attack with fragmentation grenades. After the final warning had been given the three in the tunnel, Baer heard one single pistol shot. They threw grenades into the hole. When it was over and the bodies were taken out, they discovered that the two women had shot their own comrade in the back and used his body in a vain attempt to protect themselves from the grenades.

But it was the knife or bayonet rather than the pistol that became the tunnel rat's best friend. A weapon as old as war itself returned to fashion in the darkness, where feel, touch, and strong nerves determined whether you lived or died. The knife was used as a probe or as a silent killing instrument. Booby traps had to be felt for in the pitch darkness by delicately prodding the floor, sides, or roof of the tunnel in what became an instinctive search for tiny telltale wires, or for tree roots that somehow just didn't feel right. In blackness—only as loud as the mosquitoes—that sensitized the ears close to aural perfection, the tunnel rat usually moved with grotesque slowness, each new inch holding the threat of sudden detonation, that last and terrible flash before death. There was more than just an element of perverse satisfaction, even excitement, at meeting a challenge with such grim rules and such awful codes. The isolation in those endless black holes was often welcome. Many rats refused to take communications equipment; many who took it didn't use it. What was there to say and what was there worth hearing from the ground, when every faint rustle below needed instant interpretation and reaction?

Lieutenant Jack Flowers was typically contemptuous of all the attempts made to maintain tunnel–ground links. "Nothing ever worked," he said. "We used verbal communication between us when necessary. When there was contact, the man involved would fire shots. More than three shots and we knew he was in trouble. If six were fired we knew it was real trouble because there'd be no time to reload." Sergeant Arnold Gutierrez used his communications set, but not for speech. He developed a "click-talk" by which he switched his set on, once, twice, or more, in accordance with a prearranged code by which very basic information was transmitted to the ground. Sometimes he blew or gently whistled into his set, but he abhorred speech and allowed no two-way communication.

But the lack of communications did create a new hazard. Capless, covered in earth and sweat, usually shirtless, small, and sometimes Hispanic or Oriental-looking, the tunnel rat who suddenly popped out of an as-yet-unmapped tunnel hole could find himself quickly targeted by his own side! Sergeant Gilbert Lindsay was a classic example. "I kept telling the squad who waited up on the ground, 'Look, when I come up my hair's gonna be all dirty, I'm gonna be looking like Charlie,' and they said, 'Don't worry, Larry, we'll be up there waiting for you.' Well, once while I'm down there digging up stuff, the whole bit, it's chow time for them. So what did they do? They leave the fuckin' hole, sit down, and eat their C-rations. So along come brand new people from another unit. I start coming up and I shout 'Okay, I'm coming up,' no big deal. Okay. All of a sudden I come up, and pop my head out, and I look around and I see nothing but M-16s pointing at my skull and a lot of unfriendly faces looking down the M-16s. And all of a sudden your heart's beating, and you have to smile and shout, 'Hey, I'm like you, I'm American.' And they still ain't smiling, and I tell them who won the World Series in 1962 and who was the President of the USA, and all that shit. And then they start laughing, and I ain't laughing anymore."

In the early days of tunnel exploration, attempts were made to map the system, but it would have been easier to chart sandhills in the Sahara. Staff Sergeant Bernard Justen took compasses down below, but even with those he still soon lost all sense of direction. Harold Roper worked a little more scientifically. He would leave two of his squad on top, one with the walkie-talkie and one with a compass and pen. Roper himself had a walkie-talkie transmitter in the tunnel, and he kept the transmitter button permanently taped down so he could always talk into it. He had a compass and a pistol and simply maintained a running commentary on the compass bearings as he crawled through the tunnel. "It was like being in water, twisting and turning with your eyes closed. You completely lost your sense of direction."

"We tried the compass/radio system; we didn't know what we were doing," confessed Major Herb Thornton. "We always went in pairs; one did point and checked for mines and booby traps, the other talked into the radio, used his compass and tried to tell them above what the tunnel map was like. And they were up there, carefully trying to plot it all on a map board, and trying to tie it up with other holes found previously. We couldn't tell if we'd gone ten meters or ten miles after a while."

Ultimately, the tunnel rat's best piece of equipment was a body tuned to near perfection, where every part was guaranteed. The successful rat had to volunteer to go down and stay down and take risks that were unmatched by anything he would ever meet above ground. Even if he was small by American standards, he had to negotiate bends in the communication tunnels that would only just let a slim Vietnamese through. He had to conquer an instinctive tendency to hyperventilate and he had to remember that victory could be achieved only if he came to terms with his own fear. His fingertips and ears became to him what a walking stick is to a blind man. After a while, he could "smell" the enemy ahead, not just through odor but by sensing him, like a bat, that other creature of darkness that employs primitive sonar to avoid or detect objects at night. Major Jack Pryor forbade his tunnel rats to smoke, chew gum, or eat candy because it not only made them detectable but also impaired their ability to sense the enemy.

But it was Arnold Gutierrez who best expressed what really happened to the professional rat in those tense and lonely tunnels. "I could smell the Viet Cong, really, I could smell Charlie. It wasn't just his body sweat or the urine. There were times when I could hear the breathing, real quiet; you could hear a person breathe, and I'd know he was in there, and I didn't go any farther. I just said to myself: In this dark corner of a tunnel is where the animal belongs, a rodent belongs. I'm becoming like a rodent, but still I don't belong. Yes, I could smell Charlie. And he knew me. The type of cologne I used, the aftershave—that's when we stopped using it altogether. But there was more than that. There was the scent that told you there was somebody in the tunnels. We became so tuned up after a while that when the other person would flick an eyelid up or down, you really knew he was there, in the corner, not even hiding anymore. Just sitting and waiting. They were the ones you never killed. You just backed out and told them up above the tunnel was cold."

10

Stop the Americans!

BY 1966, VIETNAM HAD been at war with various enemies for nearly a quarter of a century. The Japanese had been followed by the French, and now the United States with its unimaginable power and fury had arrived. Within a year after the marines hit the beach at Da Nang, 850,000 tons of supplies were being hauled in every single month for the Americans, their ARVN allies, and the token troops from Australia, New Zealand, the Philippines, Thailand, and Korea. GIs ate some ten million field rations every month, used 80,000 tons of ammunition, and burned 8 million gallons of gasoline and oil. In May 1966 there were a quarter of a million GIs in Vietnam. The average soldier used up 340 pounds of food, clothing, ammunition, fuel, and supplies every day. Planes were being lost at the rate of one a day, at a cost of between $1 million and $2 million. There were now two famous American infantry divisions near Saigon, the 25th and the 1st. Included in their military tasks was responsibility for neutralizing the tunnels of Cu Chi. Each division needed $100 million worth of equipment to keep going, including 6,780 rifles at $122 each, eighteen light tanks, 362 jeeps, and four huge road graders.

In and around their two hundred kilometers of tunnels, the

Vietnamese were less well endowed with money or military hardware. The Cu Chi tunnels' defense system was evolutionary, owing its effectiveness to a mixture of tenacity, flexibility, and cunning. Its technology often reached back to the European wars of the Middle Ages.

Conventional defense for the tunnels was out of the question. The VC had neither the men nor the weaponry, nor was it ever the policy of the Communists in South Vietnam to face the Americans in large, fixed-location, set-piece battles. Anyway, tunnel-searching kept lots of GIs busy, a large investment with meager returns. Primary defense requirements were, as the Communist tunnels manual had stressed, camouflage and the maintenance of silence about precise tunnels location. Deaf and dumb villagers, the VC's equivalent of Sicilian Omerta, or silence, were the first line of defense.

Nevertheless, the tunnels did need a defense system; they could not be left unprotected at the mercy of every GI foot patrol that stumbled upon a tunnel entrance or telltale ventilation shaft. The slow development of a tunnel defense strategy eventually owed much to Captain Linh's careful observations of the Americans during Operation Crimp.

"They marveled at everything they saw," he said, "everything seemed strange and new to them—the jungle, the fruits, the water buffalo, even the chickens. Again and again they would stop and stare, even pick things up. Not only were they easy targets for our snipers, but I realized the best way to kill them was with more booby traps. After Crimp we made more and more of them. I was sure they would work well for us."

Despite the original shortage of explosive materials (soon remedied as the 25th Infantry began shelling Cu Chi), the homemade booby-trap business began to boom. Those with access to explosive powder, detonators, and a crude tunnel workshop, produced, first and foremost, the DH-5 or DH-10 mine. These were modeled on the successful American claymore mine, and were to be used primarily against the American light armored tracks and half-tracks, and inevitably, against unwary infantrymen. They were detonated either by pressure or—and this was a surprise—by command (remote-detonated). Major General Ellis W. Williamson, who commanded the 173rd Airborne Brigade, recalled vividly how he first got to hear about them. "We'd been in-country only a few days when this young and overly excited lieutenant came up to me and says, 'These mobile minefields are running us crazy.' He'd lost a lot of his men and he didn't know how to fight back. And I said, 'Mobile mines, what are you talking about?' We'd studied all about mines, but nothing about mobile minefields existed in the literature. Now suddenly this lieutenant, right in the middle of battle, tells me the minefields are moving. A concept none of us had ever dreamed of. And he was right, absolutely right."

Conventionally static, or earth-sown, minefields had been expected in Vietnam. What the general discovered was not just an isolated command- or remote-controlled mine, but a procedure by which the Viet Cong could not only detonate their mines electrically from a command center but also, if the enemy chose not to go sufficiently near the mines, physically transport the mines somewhere else. The concept of the "moving minefield" was another example of the optimum use of limited resources. A limited supply of mines went a long way under these circumstances.

The DH-5s and DH-10s were made out of crude steel, shaped like a saucer and containing five or ten pounds of high explosive. The mines stood on bipods pointing directionally, or they would lie buried a few inches underground. They inflicted dreadful injuries. One American medical officer's report explained:

> [They were] packed with hundreds of steel pellets and a few pounds of explosives . . . the terrific force and the pellets propelled by it made the explosion of a command-detonated mine equivalent to the simultaneous firing of seventy twelve-gauge shotguns loaded with double-O buckshot. Naturally anyone hit by such a weapon was likely to suffer the traumatic amputation of something—an arm, a leg, his head. And many did.

Tunnel rat Lieutenant David Sullivan of the Big Red One recalled a particularly devious Viet Cong booby trap. A tunnel entrance would be exposed to lure the Americans. When a rat team was sent down to investigate, the guerrillas in the tunnel knew that other GIs would gather round the entrance for communication or on guard. A claymore mine hidden in a nearby bush would then be detonated by wire from inside the tunnel. Sullivan lost several men like that: The VC waited until they heard the rats in the tunnel and then blasted the men still on the surface. In the confusion, the rats aborted the search, and the guerrillas escaped into the tunnel system.

One of the most feared variants of the DH-10 was the notorious Bouncing Betty, conical, with three prongs jutting out of the soil. When a foot struck a prong, a small charge was detonated, which shot the mine into the air about three feet, where it then exploded, showering shrapnel at groin level. It was a terrible mine.

For sheer ingenuity in adapting to local warfare conditions, a guerrilla farmer from the Cu Chi village of Nhuan Duc was to win the top award. To Van Duc invented a helicopter booby trap. It was known as the cane-pressure mine and for a while it was a successful (and to the Americans, quite baffling) answer to the problem of how to destroy the helicopters that brought troops and supplies into the jungle. At first, as the American heliborne assaults brought more and more troops to fight in the tunnel locations, the VC had tried with no success to lure the choppers into a booby-trapped landing zone. Inside the zone four hand grenades, each cross-linked by a friction fuse wire, would detonate in a daisy-chain sequence once the helicopter landed. But To Van Duc's invention was to that system what the space shuttle was to the Dakota.

Mindful of the simple physical principle that the blades of a helicopter create a considerable downdraft, the farmer suggested placing DH-10 mines at the *tops* of trees in an area where the helicopters could be expected to fly fairly low, or one to which they could be lured to fly low for surveillance. A highly sophisticated friction fuse was connected to the branches of the tree or fairly tall bush, which bent under the helicopter's downdraft, detonating the mine, which then exploded under the machine.

Confirmation of the efficacy of this system—and a reasonably successful attempt to counteract it—came from tunnel rat Captain Bill Pelfrey, the Special Forces officer attached to the 25th Infantry Division at Cu Chi. In December 1966, he was with a unit opening up landing zones for heliborne assaults. It was his company's mission to secure hot landing zones long enough for the helicopters to land. "Previously, we'd been losing a lot of helicopters to mines and booby traps. They had a pretty ingenious little mine that they'd rigged so that when the helicopter tried to land, the wind from the rotors would shake the bush and that would set off the mine."

He usually found these mines in bushes. "The mines were well camouflaged with foliage. The way you could spot them was this: If they'd been there a day or two, the foliage began to wilt and die, and you could spot the difference. When we found them we usually defused them by blowing them up with a small, quarter-pound charge."

The mines and tunnel booby traps were cheap to make, psychologically effective, and did crude but considerable physical damage. One was a simple artillery shell dug into the ground and pressure-detonated by a man's body weight. "One of the regiment's battalion commanders stepped on a booby-trapped 155-mm shell," wrote the medical officer. "They didn't find enough of him to fill a willy-peter bag [a waterproof sack little larger than a shopping-bag]. In effect . . . he had been disintegrated."

By Viet Cong standards these were highly sophisticated traps. At the other end of the evolutionary scale of weapons were those that owed more to the Wars of the Roses than to the high-tech war in Vietnam. There was the crossbow and arrow, originally used by aboriginal tribesmen in the highlands to kill animals. It was adapted by the Viet Cong for tunnel defense. A concealed pit contained a bow with its ends embedded in the sides; an arrow was held under tension in the bow, and a simple release mechanism was activated by a tripwire running across the track. Historically contemporaneous was a medieval macelike device: a heavy mud ball with spiked bamboo stakes sticking out of it. This was attached to a tree by a seemingly innocuous jungle vine. When freed by the tripwire, the ball swung hard across the track.

Then there was the coconut mine, a hollowed-out nut packed with explosive powder and then covered by a rock as the missile—not lethal but scary. Or there was the bamboo mine. This was a large bamboo joint, cleaned out and filled with nuts, bolts, broken glass, or scrap metal, together with a small amount of plastic explosive or powder explosive. A friction fuse operated by a tripwire detonated this package.

The most common Communist booby trap was the wired

grenade, used in tunnel entrances or in the tunnels themselves. In the early days of the war the grenades were homemade, with wooden handles, or adapted Coke cans, with powder filled from dud U.S. shells. On jungle tracks and paths near the tunnels a favorite tactic was to place the grenade, with the safety pin removed, inside an appropriate tin can. A pull on the tripwire extracted the grenade from the can, which then automatically primed itself and exploded. Inside the tunnel a similar system would be used at the entrance or in the blackness of the tunnel itself. Often the tripwire was made out of jungle tree roots. The detonation of even a small grenade inside a tunnel caused unspeakable damage to anyone nearby and could cause an asphyxiating cave-in.

There was even the single-bullet trap, one cartridge held up by two bamboo pins, resting on a small wooden base, pressure-detonated by foot. And there were the infamous punji stick traps around all the tunnels. Sometimes the Viet Cong dug tiger-trap pits; if a GI fell into one, he became impaled on the spikes. The trap was kept to a reasonable size so that it could easily be camouflaged with twigs and foliage, but its depth was sufficient so that the victim's foot would descend with enough force for the stakes to pierce the toughened sole of the GI's jungle boot. A more sophisticated version had stakes buried in the wall of the pit, but facing downward, making extraction of the foot even more painful. Sometimes the sticks were smeared with excrement to aid infection, sometimes with a poison the VC simply called Elephant's Trunk, which they claimed caused death within twenty minutes of entering the bloodstream. There was even a bear trap, made out of poisoned punji sticks or metal spikes. The victim stepping on this would hit two boards, or steel plates with wooden and metal spikes attached. The boards would then pivot, burying the barbs into the leg just above the area protected by the boot. At face level, there was the bamboo whip, about five feet long with a fish-hook barbed spike at the end. This was held back taut by a wire linked to another cross-trail tripwire.

Sometimes the Viet Cong resorted to original if somewhat gruesome local psychological warfare. On one occasion following an American attack on a tunnel complex, Captain Linh watched impassively as a GI, alighting from a tank, stepped on a DH-5 mine, which blew the unfortunate soldier's leg off.

After the man had been "medevaced" and the patrol left, Linh retrieved the leg. On a discarded American C-ration box he wrote the word "dangerous" in English, then hung the leg and the sign on a tree that had been defoliated by shelling. For effect, he added a skull and crossbones. It was during the dry season, and the shriveled leg hung there for several weeks, acting, Linh claimed, as a useful deterrent.

There is some evidence, tantalizing but inconclusive, that the Viet Cong may have tethered bubonic-plague-infected rats in the tunnels as a primitive form of biological warfare against the GIs who went down to explore the complexes. Early in March 1967, a foot patrol from A troop, 3rd/4th Cavalry, of the 25th Infantry Division, entered a tunnel in Hau Nghia province, about one mile northwest of Cu Chi town. Inside they found three dead rats, all leashed round the neck. A syringe and phial containing a yellow fluid were also found, together with cages for catching the rats. The patrol commander immediately contacted intelligence specialists attached to the 521st Medical Detachment (Intel), who took over the analysis of this bizarre find. One of the rats was found to be a carrier of bubonic plague.

One benign explanation for the find may be that the guerrillas themselves, who often lived on rat meat, needed to know if they were eating plague-carrying rats. If, on the other hand, it had become widespread knowledge among the GIs that plague rats were being used by the Viet Cong in the tunnels, then tunnel-searching might well have become a considerably more laborious and slow process than it was already. Even though American and allied servicemen were all automatically injected against bubonic plague, a very careful watch was kept for its appearance, as the terrifying disease was prevalent throughout most of Vietnam.

Unfortunately, the recently declassified military correspondence relating to the strange story of the leashed rats is incomplete. There is evidence of considerable concern at the highest military levels in Saigon and Washington. Copies of the memoranda were sent directly to the officer commanding the U.S. Army Medical Research Command at Fort Detrick, Maryland.

Inside the tunnels there were occasionally false walls, thinly plastered with clay, on the other side of which waited Viet Cong with bamboo spears. As a tunnel rat made his way slowly forward, the VC would spy through a hole in the false wall and spear the victim. A similar fate awaited the unsuspecting GI who fell victim to a trap the Americans laconically christened "Sorry 'bout That." This was a pit into which the victim fell. Next to it, and separated only by a thin clay-plaster wall, was another pit inside which a VC waited. The moment the GI fell, the VC would spear his hapless victim to death.

Booby traps and ambushes took a disproportionately high toll among infantrymen and remained a source of great anxiety to military tacticians in Vietnam. Throughout the war, booby traps were responsible for 11 percent of all American deaths, and 17 percent of all wounds. The mortality rate was kept down only by the superb American helicopter medical evacuation system.

Real damage was often caused by the high rate of wound infection. Major General Spurgeon Neel, former deputy surgeon-general to the U.S. Department of the Army, explained, "Massive contamination challenged the surgeon to choose between radical excision of potentially salvageable tissue and a more conservative approach which might leave a source of infection." The vicious booby traps inside and just outside the tunnels generated sufficient fear among the ordinary grunts seriously to affect their military effectiveness. A high-tech infantry that usually fought only by day and was helicoptered out by night was not necessarily going to go out of its way to discover long tunnel complexes. Everyone knew about the booby traps . . . and what the grunt eye did not see on patrol, no officer's heart was going to grieve about.

In a revealing study conducted by Lieutenant General Julian J. Ewell, former commander of the II Field Force in Vietnam, it was shown that at least half the booby traps found by the 9th Division's GIs had been found by detonation—in other words, the men had set them off. Forty-six percent of the resultant casualties were multiple, caused by the bunching of the troops, who just did not know any better. In 1969, booby traps were the single most important casualty source in the 9th Division. When the 25th Infantry Division arrived at Cu Chi and discovered how serious a problem the tunnel booby-trap defenses were, they created a special school, called the Tunnels, Mines, and Booby-Traps School. It was run inside the perimeter using actual VC tunnels that had been dug under the division

HQ. At a more senior level, commanders of the 25th conducted elaborate booby-trap statistical analyses, a sort of sophisticated market research program; data was fed into their brand-new military computer, "thus giving them the capability to present and study the problem with minimum clerical effort," noted the generals.

If the tunnels' outer defenses failed to deter, the next line of defense was the so-called spider hole. Spider holes were superbly camouflaged pits, dug to shoulder depth near each of the three tunnel entrances, and linked by short communications tunnels to the main tunnel. One, sometimes two, Viet Cong snipers stood, perfectly protected, and shot at intruders; when it became too dangerous to stay, they scuttled through the communication tunnel back into the main tunnel complex. No sophisticated detection or weapons system could easily or mechanically find, fix, and destroy the ubiquitous spider-hole sniper. He could be (and frequently was) mortared, shelled by artillery, napalmed, or besieged by tank. But the longer he fought, the more he fulfilled his primary function, which was to engage large numbers of the enemy and keep them busy, distracting them from the real prize, the tunnel complex over which he kept his lonely vigil.

The tunnels were not impregnable, but their strength, based on sound engineering principles, and their clever and exploitative defense systems gave them a military longevity far greater than they actually deserved. For a full five years they allowed the Communists to exercise effective control over the district of Cu Chi. The Americans and their ARVN colleagues held only a short lease above ground. The freehold belonged deep in the permanence of the earth.

11

Animals

THE ANIMALS AND insects of the Vietnamese jungle quickly found the tunnels of Cu Chi to be a satisfactory environment. Many were already well adapted to the subterranean life; now the host, Man, left inviting traces upon which they could feed. Often they found themselves sharing the same space as the fighting men on both sides.

MASTER SERGEANT ROBERT BAER

"The last tunnel I went into—I have this deathly fear of rats, and I crawled down, started going down the hole, and I could hear a noise and that alerted me to get the old adrenaline going. And the hole went down about six feet and then it turned to the left and opened into a room about four yards square, and I got to where I just saw the opening and I let the flashlight roll down ahead of me. So the flashlight is laying on the ground at the bottom of the hole, shining into the room, and at the opposite corner, I peeked round. In the corner was a rat up on its hind haunches, just baring its teeth. I swear this was the biggest rat I've ever seen. Well, I just flipped out, I just completely flipped out. I was firing, yelling and screaming, and firing my .45, and people were pulling me out and I'm still firing and got up on the top, and like I say, I always have my explosive stuff right there at the top of the hole. I grabbed the 'frag' and threw it down, and grabbed the concussion grenade and threw it down, and rolled away. I must have been a sight because I was petrified—I can't remember ever being that scared. That's when I gave it up. That was the last hole I ever went into. That damn rat, he made a believer out of me."

LIEUTENANT JACK FLOWERS

"In the Cu Chi tunnels the VC used to take boxes of scorpions with a tripwire and that was a booby trap. You tripped the wire, the box would open, and the scorpions would come into the tunnel. One of my men got stung; he came out screaming and never went back in another tunnel. But scorpions don't kill you, plus we always had a medic on the surface."

CHI NGUYET (SISTER MOONLIGHT)—GUERRILLA

"In our area as in many others there is a specially fierce type of bee. They are more than twice as big as ordinary bees. They don't store honey, but their sting is terribly painful. We studied the habits of these bees very carefully, and trained them. They always have four sentries on duty and if these are disturbed or offended they call out the whole hive to attack whatever disturbs them. So we set up some of these hives in the trees alongside the road leading from an ARVN post to our village. We covered them over with sticky paper from which strings led to a bamboo trap we set on the road. The next time an enemy patrol came, they disturbed the trap and the paper was torn from the hive. The bees attacked immediately; the troops ran like mad buffalo and started falling into our spiked punji traps. They left carrying and dragging their wounded.

"From the post they must have radioed for help because the ARVN district chief sent a company by road from another post and more by helicopter. By that time we had set up quite a few hives. When the enemy came, they saw piles of dirt that looked like freshly dug traps so the officer ordered the troops to clear away the earth and uncover the traps. But the hives were hidden under the earth and there was a terrible commotion when the bees were disturbed in such a rough way. They attacked, hundreds of them, and in no time at all thirty enemy troops were out of action. They had to withdraw again. We were very encouraged by this and started to rear the bees specially for our defenses."

COLONEL DO TAN PHONG

"We used the hornets against the Americans for a while in 1966. Training them was a long process. When I asked one of my trainers about it, he told me it was possible to train the hornets because after a time they recognized the personal odor of the trainer and so they didn't attack him. The trainers used long poles to move the hornets' nests to the places where they foresaw the enemy troops would go through. The hornets were valuable. Western people not used to our climate got fever from their stings."

STAFF SERGEANT PEDRO REJO-RUIZ

"The thing that bothered me most was that damned centipede, but it was not a centipede. I don't know. I had to shoot it, whenever I saw it I used to shoot at it. It wasn't a snake, it had legs like a centipede. I used to shoot at them. It was over half a foot long. Kind of greeny color. I used to open up on those. I didn't want them close to me."

SERGEANT BILL WILSON

"I got bitten by a centipede once. That sucker was probably a good eight inches long and I thought I was going to die—thought I was poisoned; my whole arm was numb. I crawled out of there and I was hollering for a medic. I thought, I'm going to die for sure."

SERGEANT GILBERT LINDSAY

"They had this big hole and I had this weak flashlight, and I was checking to make sure there was no more booby traps or anything, and all of a sudden I felt like I was being watched. And I took my flashlight, it was very weak, and I turned to shine it on the wall and there were these two gigantic spiders. I think I was more scared of spiders down there than anything else. When you're face to face with them, this close to them, you know, close to the wall, they're pretty damn big. I remembered my bayonet, I took my bayonet and tried to stab them. I wasn't going to shoot them, you know. It was no good going bananas over two spiders, and then they went into the hole I was digging. And to hell with that. I just put the dirt back on the hole. I'd been digging because my detector showed there was metal down there, we'd already found some mortar shells. I didn't care what was in that hole after the spiders had gone in; whatever it was is still down there with the spiders."

MASTER SERGEANT ROBERT BAER

". . . and one hole that seemed to be darker than any hole I'd ever been in and for a moment I thought I was losing my equilibrium because it seemed like the hole was moving in on me, and as I shined the light around more, I found out it was just a mass of spiders—just these spiders. The whole chamber, the walls and the top, were one great black moving mass of spiders. I'm sure they were there naturally. You know, they're black spiders with a purplish or aqua blue spot on them, they're about as big as my thumbnail. They got on to me, too, and if they bit me I don't know, because I never got sick or anything."

STAFF SERGEANT RICK SWOFFORD

"Yeah, I remember when we went in a big tunnel, I went down in it and there weren't nothing down there. But the Vietnamese didn't bother me, I wasn't scared of them, cause I'd have shaped them [blown them up]. But the doggone snakes and spiders and stuff—went down this one and I bet you there was a million spiders in that thing, and they got all over my body, and I had to come out backwards, and I turned round and I was just covered with spiders, and they had to beat 'em off me. I'll never forget that, that's when I almost quit the tunnel rats. Spiders. And in a foreign country like that, I didn't know whether they were poisonous or not."

STAFF SERGEANT PEDRO REJO-RUIZ

"I seen some spiders down there you won't believe it. In fact I shot at them, the spiders as big as my hand. I just shot them. Bam."

CAPTAIN HERB THORNTON

"We used insecticide in there, too, because of the huge fire ants. What we'd do if we encountered fire ants, they were on you before you'd know it, and we would simply pull out these little bottles of insecticide and stab it with our bayonet, just puncture it. They'd just blow up all over you, so you've got to get your mask on first, because it's a substance that would make you nauseous. Mind you, so did the fire ant. When we could get it, we'd use masking tape and we'd tape around our cuffs and close any entrance that we could, to keep these ants from getting into our boots. Because when you're crawling along on your hands and knees, by the time you realize they are there, they're all over you, and they really bite flesh. The insecticide helped if you had it, but the eyes, nose, ears, and mouth were always vulnerable to fire ants."

SERGEANT BILL WILSON

"There were a lot of things that scared the hell out of you. The bats used to scare the hell out of me. You'd be crawling through a really small tunnel, you had just enough room to crawl and you'd kick all these bats up and they'd come flying at you and they'd go right down your back and you could feel them, and they'd get tangled in your hair . . . you could feel them all the way down your back, over your butt, down your legs, and gone. They used to give me the shivers."

STAFF SERGEANT RICK SWOFFORD

"Sometimes you'd be scared and open fire and the bats started coming out through the tunnel. One bat grabbed a man in the groin area here, and just bit him, and he took his .38 and blew him away."

NGUYEN TRUONG NGHI—GUERRILLA

"One kind of venomous snake sometimes encountered in the tunnels was from forty to fifty centimeters long, triangular-shaped body and red in color; another kind was about thirty centimeters long, red and black in color and had a round body. Persons bitten by these snakes died instantly."

CAPTAIN HERB THORNTON

"They had snakes down there, they really had snakes. I remember finding them tied up in a sewing room and in one hospital chamber. They had the bamboo viper, which was very poisonous, and everyone is very knowledgeable of them. Well, if you're climbing down a tunnel with a flashlight in your hand and you see a damn snake of any kind the first inclination is to kill the thing. And since you can't get a good swing at a snake in a tunnel, you're going to shoot him. Well, that tips them off down the tunnel that you're coming. The snakes were held in place with a piece of wire. Charlie, he had a way he could lift the wire and pull the snake out of the way."

LIEUTENANT JACK FLOWERS

"They would take a snake, we used to call them one-step, two-step, or three-step snakes, and they were bamboo vipers. They weren't very long, but they had a very potent bite; once bitten you could only take one or two more steps. The Vietnamese somehow tied the viper into a piece of bamboo with a piece of string and as the tunnel rat goes through he knocks it, and the snakes comes out and bites you in the neck or the face and then the blood gets to the heart very quickly. You just had to make sure when you went through a tunnel you not only looked at all sides with your flashlight, but you also looked at the ceiling."

STAFF SERGEANT PEDRO REJO-RUIZ

"He was an infantryman and the snake crawled into his pants so what they did, they touched the snake and when the snake moved its head they grabbed him through the pants. They grabbed the snake and they cut the pants off him and they killed the snake. In the process the GI fainted. In the ceiling they used to hang—well, we used to call him quarter-step snake because you take one quarter of a step after he bite you, you're dead. They used to take a piece of bamboo about that long, take the snake, tie him by his neck, insert him into the bamboo tube and they put the tube in the ceiling. And then you hit the tube and the snake is on you."

NGUYEN KHAC VIEN

"Well-equipped and specially trained, these 'tunnel rats' however did not take the invisible and the unforeseeable into enough account . . . one day a tunnel rat handling a mine detector cautiously entered a tunnel . . . although trained to avoid traps on the ground, he slowly proceeded forward. Suddenly his head touched something like a big salami; he reached out to push it away but this long cold thing wound round his neck. He had no time to scream or unsheathe his knife, the snake had already knotted tighter around his neck and badly bit his face. Outside, the other tunnel rats waited for their comrade. At last the team leader pushed one of them into the tunnel. This man emerged soon after, panting and pale, dragging after him the violet-colored corpse of the tunnel rat."

MASTER SERGEANT ROBERT BAER

"One hole, I pulled out a six-and-a-half-foot boa constrictor and we killed it, and then everyone in the tunnel rat section skinned it and we all had snake headbands and stuff."

12

Cu Chi Base Camp

By the end of 1966, as Captain Linh and his unit of battle-weary and underfed troglodytes lay in their vermin-infested tunnels beneath the district of Cu Chi, a few miles away American soldiers lived in an air-conditioned comfort beyond the reach of his imagination. One of the largest and most impressive fortified base camps the Americans built in Vietnam was at Cu Chi. It was one of the ring of bases that General Westmoreland had decided to place around Saigon.

The huge sprawling base camp that became a temporary city in the middle of the countryside was a military creation unique to the Vietnam War. On the one hand, from 1965 on, massive troop formations were deployed with armor, artillery, and helicopter support, with all the consequent maintenance, logistical, and supply requirements. On the other hand, there was no front line. The war occurred wherever opposing forces made contact. It was an "area war," and the only secure area for an American commander was his base camp, supplied by heavily defended convoys of trucks. "Because of the nature of the war," explained Westmoreland, "tactical units had to be scattered throughout the nation at widespread locations. The lack of a sophisticated transportation system necessitated major units establishing their own logistical bases rather than one central depot serving a number of units." In other words, large parts of South Vietnam could not be, and never were, secured. The Viet Cong's commanders took a pragmatic and sanguine view of the U.S. bases that they spasmodically bombarded with rockets and mortar shells. Camps always provided lucrative targets. Any missile fired into a base was certain to do some damage to men or equipment and keep the Americans nervous and on their guard. No U.S. base, even in Saigon itself, would escape bombardment.

Cu Chi base camp was built in 1966 on an area known to the Vietnamese as Dong Zu, meaning the paratroops' field. The ARVN paras had trained on the huge disused peanut farm in the Diem days. It lay between Cu Chi town, about twenty-five miles northwest of Saigon, and the disused Fil Hol rubber plantation, which in turn touched the southern bank of the Saigon River, across which was the Iron Triangle. Its location was not only between the main strategic road and river approaches to Saigon, but close to what were rightly considered to be some of the worst hotbeds of Viet Cong activity—in Communist eyes, liberated areas. The abandoned rubber plantation would be a constant origin of rocket and mortar attacks; a little farther north the so-called Ho Bo woods embraced the village of Phu My Hung, site of the Viet Cong's Saigon area headquarters, two hospitals, and training depots.

Cu Chi base was, in fact, in the heart of the most tunnel-riddled countryside in South Vietnam, scene of the most destructive operations of the war. The tunnel network was to plague the Americans from the moment of their arrival to the time they left.

Adjoining Cu Chi base was the village of Nhuan Duc. Arguably, Nhuan Duc was the most front-line village in South Vietnam. In 1976 it was honored as a Heroic Village by Vietnam's national assembly, and it was the home of several medal-winning Viet Cong heroes during the war, including To Van Duc, the farmer who invented the cane-pressure mine that disabled so many helicopters. Today, some agriculture has resumed in Nhuan Duc; during the war just about everything above ground was obliterated. Decades will have to pass before the forests and plantations are as thick as they were in 1965. Before the 173rd Airborne Brigade and the 3rd Brigade of the

1st Infantry Division mounted Operation Crimp in January 1966 to clear the area to build Cu Chi base, the entire locality was bombarded by artillery and with high-explosive bombs from specially adapted B-52 strategic bombers. All the houses were destroyed. The women, children, and old people of Nhuan Duc were moved out by ARVN soldiers to the strategic hamlet at Trung Lap. But the able-bodied men and girls remained hidden in the tunnels, ordered by the NLF to stay close to the enemy. Their attempts to continue to cultivate some green vegetables at night were frustrated by crop poisons sprayed from aircraft. A white area was created. Operation Crimp was meant to sweep the area clear of Viet Cong and make it safe for the 25th Infantry Division to establish its base at Dong Zu, next to Cu Chi town. But Crimp was a partial failure; many of the guerrillas were not displaced, nor was much of their underground fortifications found or destroyed. When the new division arrived in early 1966, it unknowingly pitched its tents right on top of an existing network of Viet Cong tunnels.

Huynh Van Co, an enterprising twenty-nine-year-old local guerrilla, could not believe his good fortune. He and the other two members of his cell decided to hide in a tunnel for a week with a little store of dried rice. Each night they stealthily emerged from their trapdoor and created havoc with directional claymore mines and grenades, killing and wounding GIs in their tents, who had no idea where the attack originated. Mortar shells lobbed in from outside the perimeter by other Viet Cong added to the confusion, and helped disguise Huynh Van Co's infiltration. Co and his men made a point of stealing food from the Americans each night before returning to the tunnel in the darkness and hiding and sleeping for the day. This went on for seven nights until the three-man Viet Cong cell withdrew back through the tunnel, which rejoined the larger system known as the belt near the village of Trung Lap. Neither they nor their tunnel was ever detected.

Huynh Van Co went on to become a captain in the Viet Cong main force and to command a platoon of Dac Cong—special forces, or commandos. He was killed in 1969 by napalm dropped from a U.S. aircraft while he was fighting ARVN troops. His citation as a Hero now hangs in the little bamboo-and-corrugated-iron house of his sister, Mrs. Huynh Thi Bia, in a leafy hamlet a mile from Cu Chi town. His faded photograph, showing a youthful and strangely innocent face, sits next to a cobwebbed official portrait of Ho Chi Minh. The citation, signed by Premier Pham Van Dong, reads "The nation remembers."

Another local hero was Pham Van Coi, who led a daring attack on Cu Chi base at night in April 1966, while the Americans were still vulnerably under canvas. Neighboring Vietnamese villagers who remember him unanimously credit him and his two colleagues with killing dozens of Americans. All three survived the raid. Pham Van Coi commanded the Nhuan Duc guerrillas until he was killed in an ambush in 1967.

The siting of Cu Chi base over existing tunnels was, to say the least, fortunate for the Viet Cong. The American 173rd Airborne Brigade had operated in the Cu Chi area since January 1966, and its job was to facilitate the arrival of larger units. Its commander, Brigadier General Ellis W. Williamson, observed the arrival of the 25th Infantry Division with amusement. "They brought quite a lot of little shelters," he said, "little huts and things, with them from Hawaii. They started putting these things up and we were very envious of them. We were also somewhat critical of them. We couldn't understand why in God's green earth they couldn't sit down and make themselves secure where they were. The 25th Division came in, set up in Cu Chi, and was constantly feuding and fussing with the enemy around its own headquarters. We literally laughed at them. We thought: What kind of an outfit is it that can't even secure its own headquarters? And it began to come to light that the tunnel system was in fact a reality.

"The 25th Division didn't realize that they had bivouac'd on a volcano. There they were, right on top of a very explosive situation. They just couldn't imagine how it could be that they put out patrols—had men walk and walk over an area absolutely devoid of any enemy, and then that night—brap! brap! brap! The quartermaster tent gets shot up. The ordnance tent gets shot up. A support unit gets itself all bunged up. And everybody says: 'Where did they come from? My perimeter is secure. Nobody penetrated my perimeter last night. I know they didn't.' But there they are. Come under the ground and climbed up."

The commanding general of the 25th Division, Major General Fred Weyand, himself admitted that his choice of site for the divisional base had caused problems at first. "We used to talk laughingly about when we moved into Cu Chi base, thinking that the area was already secured. But in a sense we had to fight our way in there. Once we got in, we thought we could bed down and sleep in open tents. That turned out to be wrong. The Viet Cong could, at that time, with impunity come up in the middle of the night and fire away and cause us that kind of grief. We realized that there were tunnels. And gradually we realized the extent of them. Now, as that realization dawned, we dealt with the problem as best we could."

He sent for the newly formed tunnel rat section of the 1st Infantry Division to help seek out Cu Chi base's underworld. Sergeant Bernard Justen used a napalm flame-thrower to burn up some of the tunnels they found. In his words, "Ain't nobody going to argue with a flame-thrower." He sent one of the rats to explore a tunnel and the man came to the surface—to the astonishment of all concerned—in the middle of the 25th Division's motor pool. Justen added that the GIs got little sleep in the early days of the base; the nightly attacks went on.

Before long, construction crews with bulldozers and concrete began turning Cu Chi base into a more permanent structure. But the tunnels were still there. Colonel Thomas A. Ware was a battalion commander with the 25th Infantry. He recalled: "When the division built that camp they were uncovering tunnels for months, if not a year. One of my best lieutenants was killed there. His platoon had seen this VC fire a rocket-propelled grenade and pop down into his tunnel. They were right behind him, and this lieutenant went down there and tried to get the trapdoor up. They shot him, killed him with an AK-47 through the trapdoor. They just fired up. You had to be pretty cautious about trying to get too brave and show too much initiative there." At length the 25th succeeded in stopping up all the tunnels, if only with bulldozers leveling the site for buildings. All, that is, except those Viet Cong tunnels that would be used for training future tunnel rats. The problem of access to the base from underneath was licked, but its troubles were far from over. There were to be more attacks from both inside and outside the perimeter in the years that followed.

For four of those years Cu Chi was the headquarters of the American unit that had begun arriving in the early spring of 1966—the Tropic Lightning Division. The 25th Infantry Division is in a sense America's Foreign Legion; it has never served on the American mainland. It was formed from existing smaller units in the islands of Hawaii in November 1941, one month before the Japanese attacked Pearl Harbor—and machine-gunned the 25th's barracks. In 1942 the division was thrown into the Pacific war and earned its (now official) nickname Tropic Lightning from the speed with which it relieved the U.S. Marines on Guadalcanal. Division troops saw continuing action in the South Pacific and the Philippines and, after the Japanese surrender, occupied Osaka. In 1950 the 25th was sent to the snows of Korea and saw prominent action throughout that war. It returned to its home base, Schofield Barracks just outside Honolulu on the island of Oahu, in 1955. The division's identifying shoulder-flash is a bolt of lightning superimposed upon a red taro leaf (taro is a leafy root crop native to the Pacific islands); its motto is "Ready to strike . . . anywhere, anytime."

In Hawaii from 1955 to 1963, the 25th was prepared for counter-guerrilla jungle war in Asia and was the only unit in the U.S. Army to undergo such training. With shrewd anticipation of Communist insurgency in Asia, the Pentagon had 25th Infantry troops experience jungle conditions and learn to handle tropical dangers like insects, snakes, and diseases. The Special Asian Warfare Training & Oriental Center (SAWTOC) was established in the foothills of Oahu's Koolau mountains in 1956. It was modeled on the British jungle warfare school in Malaya. In Hawaii, in addition to the guerrilla warfare training center with its twelve mock Asian villages, there was a Code of Conduct Station—a simulated North Korean prisoner-of-war compound, in which the GIs were subjected to controlled humiliation and brutality. So-called Red torture techniques were demonstrated to the troops by guards in North Korean uniforms—all of Asian ethnic origin. Some of the GIs were seriously disturbed by the frightening realism of the camp, which was kept secret for several years. When it was exposed, public protests followed, and it was closed down.

By 1962 the "special war" in Vietnam between the Communists and the ARVN (with U.S. advisers) was in full swing. Units of the 25th were then sent to Camp Cobra at Korat in Thailand, then an ally of the United States in SEATO. There a simulated area of Vietnam was constructed, complete with a

Potemkin village called Ban Kara Eboo, populated by truculent and aggressive GIs in peasant dress, along with a few helpful Thais. The emphasis of the training was on civic action: cajoling villagers into transferring their sympathies to the government, and therefore betraying any guerrillas whose whereabouts they might know. The setting was authentically Southeast Asian, but it was hopelessly unlike the reality of the situation in Vietnam. It overlooked the centuries-old xenophobia of the Vietnamese, and their tradition of wily dissimulation in the face of authority. Nor did it anticipate the Viet Cong's greatest tactical asset—the tunnel system. And ironically, for all the 25th's training in guerrilla warfare, many of the operations in which the division would take part in Vietnam would be "big war" operations, with thousands of troops, armored vehicles, and helicopters crashing across the countryside in search of an elusive enemy.

In early 1963, the Tropic Lightning sent a hundred aerial door-gunners to Vietnam at the request of MACV to "ride shotgun" on helicopters carrying ARVN troops. They were the first Americans committed in a capacity other than as "advisers." In 1965, the main deployment of U.S. troops to Vietnam began, and a brigade of the 25th was airlifted to Pleiku in the central highlands, where General Giap's most potent threat was then perceived to be. The bulk of the division, however, was destined for Cu Chi, which became its headquarters in the spring of 1966, under the command of Major General Fred Weyand, a lanky and slow-talking Californian. Weyand commanded the division until March 1967, and went on to become a corps commander, and later the last commander of all American troops in Vietnam. Because it stayed at the base throughout the war, the division earned the nickname the Cu Chi National Guard.

The site of Cu Chi base was carefully surveyed. Officers of the 25th Infantry studied maps of the area back in the comfort of Hawaii, and an advance party under the division's support commander made an on-site inspection. The base would be what the army called semipermanent. The location had been chosen with an eye not just to defensibility but to water supply, drainage, and other real-estate considerations. "I selected Cu Chi," said General Weyand, "as an area that was well away from the populated center of Saigon, to act as a sort of lightning rod for the enemy. We picked the specific area because of the topography. It was the one place that was above the water table, where we could put trucks and tanks without having them sink out of sight during the monsoon season. Our artillery could reach out, so an area of about 5,000 meters in diameter around would be cleared of any continuous real activity." Unfortunately, it was precisely because the land was twelve meters above the water table that it was possible for the Viet Cong to have burrowed so many tunnels underneath it.

Cantonments were designated in the base for the various battalions, and road and telephone networks laid out. But perimeter defense took priority. Bulldozers cleared surrounding farmland to ensure a field of fire. Observation towers were built looking out over it, and firing positions with overhead cover, an earth rampart, barbed-wire entanglements, floodlights, and minefields were put in place.

Given that they were at war, Tropic Lightning soldiers lived in conditions of luxury undreamed of by earlier generations of GIs serving in the tropics. Before the division left Hawaii, it had obtained precut tent and latrine kits, which were erected at Cu Chi. But these were used only while the wooden huts and air-conditioned steel offices were being built. The division also brought along ice-machine plants, sixty-five-cubic-foot walk-in refrigerators, ten-kilowatt generator sets, ice chests, and folding beds; in addition there were filing cabinets, desks, chairs, tables, safes, tools, and communications equipment. Until a proper water supply was installed, showers were taken under improvised water-tanks made from bomb casings. Construction crews built maintenance shelters, fuel storage tanks, ammunition bunkers, roads, and helicopter pads. The army would boast that Cu Chi had virtually all the facilities found at any permanent U.S. Army base, including clubs for officers, NCOs, and enlisted men; a USO club, a radio station, barber shops, sports fields, miniature golf courses, swimming pools, and chapels. Running the camp became a complex task in itself, consuming time, resources, and manpower beyond, as one commander put it, "the organic capabilities of battalions, brigades, and divisions." For one combat commander the base devoured so many resources that it became "the tail that wagged the dog."

When it was completed in mid-1966, Cu Chi base was an

imposing place. It covered 1,500 acres and its perimeter was six miles around. At any time, over 4,500 men and a few women lived, worked, and played inside it—not counting the army of Vietnamese workers who performed all the most basic tasks. Outside the main gate was a sign that read ALOHA. 25TH U.S. INF. DIV. HAWAII'S OWN. Inside was the divisional headquarters, an elegant and broad-fronted one-story building with three gables in its sloping tin roof. In front of it stood a lifesize bronze statue of a GI between two flagpoles, one flying the Stars and Stripes, the other the three red stripes on a yellow background of the Republic of Vietnam (a flag which gave rise to the unkind gibe "When they're not red, they're yellow"). In front of these was a parade ground with a huge helicopter landing pad shaped and painted exactly like the divisional shoulder-flash—yellow lightning upon a red taro leaf. But despite these and other attempts at beautification, the base was never peaceful. Artillery fire boomed constantly from the big guns inside the perimeter, "harassing and interdicting" any activity in the free strike zones within a huge radius of the base. The air throbbed with the clatter of arriving or departing helicopters.

Rocket and mortar attacks on Cu Chi base usually came from the direction of the Fil Hol plantation, and early on the army established an outlying observation post called Ann-Margaret (after the movie star), facing the forest of rubber trees. Ann-Margaret consisted of ten deeply dug bunkers surrounded by minefields. Each platoon of the 25th Infantry had to spend a month in this outpost. Tragedy struck soldiers of one platoon, who mistakenly walked into a minefield laid by earlier units. Each man going to help a wounded comrade was blown up by the Bouncing Betty mines, which exploded at waist level; some were killed, the rest grievously injured. Because of the mines, medics and ambulances refused to approach. The eventual helicopter rescue took twenty minutes to arrive. In 1967, observation post Ann-Margaret was abandoned as being unprofitable to maintain.

As the 25th Infantry established themselves in Vietnam, they realized the need to give their constantly rotating troops special training in local conditions, and even to share some of their hard-learned knowledge of Viet Cong tactics with ARVN local forces. At Cu Chi base they were proud to show visitors the Tropic Lightning Academy, a controlled and encapsulated little version of the war. It included the Tunnels, Mines, and Booby-Traps School. In an area of heavy vegetation on the western side of the base, 500 feet of Viet Cong tunnels were maintained by local Vietnamese—but this time for the Americans, and for a payment of eighty piastres (less than a dollar) a day. Prospective tunnel rats were given supervised and safe experience of underground claustrophobia, complete with false walls, seeming dead-ends, and harmless booby traps.

When Lieutenant Colonel James Bushong was the 25th's divisional chemical officer, he was responsible for training tunnel rats. "The main thing about the tunnel rat school," he said, "was that guys who were sent there who did not have that little bit of craziness, or whatever it took to survive and do well on that assignment, were weeded out early enough." Sergeant Arnold Gutierrez was also an instructor at the tunnel rat school. He said that few of the students had the stability for the job, and most crawled back out of the training tunnel as soon as they went in; they would not go back and, in Gutierrez's words, "flunked." Out of fifty students over five months, he remembered only five graduating as tunnel rats.

Alsatian or German shepherd dogs were schooled in the 25th's private tunnel system, as part of the dog-training school at Cu Chi. Hitherto, the U.S. Army had used dogs only as watchdogs or to sniff out drugs in its own barracks. In Vietnam they became scout dogs, or combat trackers, and they and their handlers were much in demand to give early warning of the ever-likely Viet Cong ambushes. At the school, the dogs were trained to respond to ultrasonic whistles inaudible to men, and to detect Viet Cong by scent. This was made easier when defoliants and other chemicals had been sprayed on VC-controlled areas like the Iron Triangle; the dogs could recognize anyone who had been in such an area. However, the Viet Cong found an ingenious way to foil the dogs. Having acquired quantities of American toilet soap on the black market, or stolen it from base camps, they made a practice of washing with it, thus giving off a scent immediately recognizable to the dogs as friendly. Pepper spread on the ground distracted bloodhounds from tunnel entrances.

Dogs proved to be of little use in tunnel exploration. The main reason was their inability to spot booby traps. In tunnels, dogs were often killed or maimed by wire-triggered grenades; this was so distressing to the handlers that they refused to send dogs down tunnels. (This failure had been one of the reasons for the abrupt creation of human tunnel rats in 1966 after Operation Crimp.)

Cu Chi base also contained the 12th Evacuation Hospital, a 400-bed establishment of a dozen wards housed in Quonset huts. They were arranged around a U-shaped compound connected by covered walkways. A soldier wounded out in the countryside was first treated at a battalion aid station. There he was bandaged up, given morphine, and put onto a "dust-off" medical helicopter to be taken to the evacuation hospital. He could be on the operating table within an hour of being wounded. There he would find the latest equipment, the best facilities, and the most experienced surgical teams available. The "12th Evac" served Cu Chi, Tay Ninh, and Dau Tieng bases. It had two intensive-care units, one for medical-surgical cases, the other for burns. One ward was always kept empty for a sudden influx of casualties from a big battle, an emergency known as a "masscal," or for prisoners. During the dry seasons of 1966 and 1967, there was a masscal about once a month. Dozens of wounded men, bloody and bandaged, were laid on their stretchers outside the operating rooms. There the army surgeons did triage—estimating whether a man needed urgent surgery or could wait an hour or two, or whether surgery would be wasted on a man unlikely to recover. A masscal was a frantic and noisy occasion of shouted instructions and bloodstained overalls. There was also a ward for Vietnamese civilians; they tended to be caught in the hail of bombs and artillery that would descend on any area thought to contain Viet Cong. The hospital had about thirty doctors and sixty female nurses, some of whom were married to officers of the 25th.

Some of the more startling pieces of military hardware housed behind the ramparts and barbed wire of Cu Chi base were the UNIVAC 1005 and NCR 500 computers, the first time they had gone to war. The army's war managers placed increasing faith in their ability to solve the intractable problems of the Vietnam War. They were mounted in expandable mobile vans parked outside the division's tactical operations center. Every little contact that the 25th had with the surrounding Viet Cong was fed into the machines to create a huge intelligence bank, which, it was hoped, might analytically predict where the enemy might next be found, and which type of operation would be most likely to succeed against him. The computers contained constantly updated lists of known or suspected Viet Cong sympathizers, and interfaced with other military computers in Vietnam, such as the Hamlet Evaluation System, maintained at U.S. Army headquarters in Saigon. HES categorized supposed degrees of sympathy with the Viet Cong in each village across the country. The evaluation was notoriously overoptimistic. It relied on suspect intelligence supplied by often corrupt ARVN local officials, who tended to portray the running of their areas of responsibility in the most flattering light.

Supplying the occupants of this colossal base with their expected comforts, and the wherewithal to fight, became a military operation in itself; they called it Operation Roadrunner, and it sapped a significant part of the 25th Infantry's energies. Cu Chi base was resupplied by road from nearby Saigon and Long Binh, the army's biggest depot in Vietnam. An average of four convoys of about sixty vehicles, known as the Cu Chi Express, would make this short but hazardous journey each day. For the first two years that the 25th was at Cu Chi, there was a constant attrition of men and vehicles from Viet Cong mines and ambushes. There could be no travel after dark. After running over mines, crippled or burning vehicles would halt a convoy and make it a sitting target for mortar, rocket, or small-arms fire. Former 1st Infantry Division commander General John H. Hay ruefully admitted that "effective convoy operations were possible only because of the mutually supporting artillery fire bases along the route." Search-and-destroy operations had to be conducted just to clear main roads. By 1968, the 25th had developed procedures to reduce convoy losses. Ammunition and fuel vehicles were placed at the rear so that the entire convoy would not be blocked by burning trucks, and tractors were brought along to move disabled vehicles off the road. The convoy commander would accompany his vehicles by helicopter, and gunship cover was arranged ahead of time over potential ambush sites. Roadside vegetation was progressively cleared by bulldozers fitted with Rome plows, which cut down trees.

Battle-weary troops from the countryside were given privileged treatment on large bases at rest centers known as Holiday Inns. Waikiki East (named after the Hawaiian beach) was one such at Cu Chi base, where company-sized units could stand down and relax. It was within walking distance of the main post exchange, a large swimming pool, and the enlisted men's club. Units that had been out in the field for over a month were given forty-eight hours to recuperate. Their fatigue uniforms and boots were renewed. Personnel officers sorted out pay and other problems. Every evening saw a steak barbeque and entertainment by pop groups from Saigon, or by visiting American entertainers. Cold beer was consumed in quantity and Vietnamese dancing girls gyrated to the blare of electric guitars. Every grunt could also look forward to five days R & R during his one-year tour in Vietnam. Men were flown out monthly to Bangkok, Tokyo, Manila, Australia, Hawaii, and other suitably supplied venues.

There were even pretty young American girls around the base. Known as Doughnut Dollies, they were American Red Cross recreation volunteers. They wore light blue seersucker outfits, floppy field hats, tennis shoes, and big smiles. They entertained the troops with games and refreshments. These friendly girls were a popular feature of many army bases in Vietnam.

Despite the comforts they enjoyed on the base, soldiers of the 25th Infantry were occasionally reminded of the prevailing hostility of the surrounding population they had supposedly come to defend. Admittedly the children smiled, and teenagers hung around the GIs hoping for castoffs of their wondrous technological and consumer civilization; but every GI knew that no Vietnamese could be completely trusted. Soldiers were not allowed off base unless given official permission for some specified duty. Cu Chi town itself was off limits, and there was no traveling under any circumstances after seven at night. Contact with the Vietnamese was normally restricted to flying to villages in force to search homes for Viet Cong; or dealing with some of the thousand or so civilians allowed to work inside the base. These had such jobs as laborers, barbers, laundry-workers, bookkeepers, waitresses, mortuary attendants, and "shit burners," whose task was to ignite the contents of fifty-five-gallon drums that contained the base's sewage, having first mixed in gasoline. Soldiers also constantly smuggled prostitutes, or boom-boom girls, onto the base. One system was to drive one in in an ambulance, the beds of which would then be utilized by a succession of young soldiers, at three to four dollars a time. Sometimes the whores were smuggled into the base inside an empty water-tank trailer. Colonel John Fairbank, formerly the information officer at Cu Chi, remembered one occasion when GIs put a dozen girls inside an empty gasoline tanker; by the time they had got them past the military police on the main gate, the girls had all died from asphyxiation. There were "laundries" and "car washes"—Eve, Fairlady, Sexy—lined up just outside the base to service those GIs who had permission to go out. Marijuana and heroin were cheaply available at such places—a trade which the U.S. authorities were convinced was one way in which the Viet Cong financed their war. By the main gate a little restaurant run by the wives of Korean construction workers served as a cover for a brothel for the officers, in case visiting chaplains or movie stars asked embarrassing questions. Cu Chi hosted not just clergy and entertainers. Robert McNamara came, as secretary of defense, in 1966, and there was a stream of reporters and television crews. The base was, after all, conveniently near to Saigon.

But despite these distractions the 25th was at war—and not just with an unseen enemy outside the wire. There was a fifth column inside as well, an enemy that found it easy to operate within the comparatively lax security system that took into account the entertainment needs of the soldiers and the necessity to use local labor to service the huge complex. The Vietnamese workers on the base lived in nearby strategic hamlets. In theory they were screened by the national police. In fact, some were guerrillas using tunnels round the base, and most workers were in touch with their local NLF organization. The Viet Cong cracked down heavily on fraternizing with the Americans, except on a commercial basis. For example, a Vietnamese girl who worked in the PX was known to be seeking permission to marry a GI. One morning her head was found on a post outside the main gate, with a note that said, "This is what happens to Vietnamese people who go around with the enemy." A special mobile punishment unit of Viet Cong was responsible for such executions.

The Vietnamese workers on Cu Chi base lined up to be counted and checked as they arrived and left each day. However, an explosive device or booby trap was found inside the base once or twice each week. Mess hall walls seemed to be a favorite place to leave them. One such bomb caused dozens of casualties in a mess hall on 5 January 1969. Today, few of the civilian workers are happy to admit that they ever worked for the Americans. Mrs Le Thi Tien, for example, is a self-employed seamstress with one child in the village of Phuoc Hiep, a short distance up Route 1, north of Cu Chi town. During the war she worked as a waitress in the officers' club on the base. She recalled: "I had to work there because my family was so poor. Most of the villages in this area were destroyed by bombs, so we all had to live temporarily in the villages along the road. I was forced to work for the Americans to support my mother, who was blind. I was told to observe everything in the base and report it to the local cadre." The man to whom she reported was Ho Van Nhien, who is still the party cadre in Phuoc Hiep today. "Each village sent in spies," he said. "I had many report to me. Some were laborers filling sandbags. They reported whenever the Americans launched an operation. The bar girl (Mrs Le Thi Tien) reported whatever conversations she overheard that she could understand. I reported back to the district committee so that they could prepare to deal with any attack." He described how intelligence messages detailing future search-and-destroy operations were written on small sheets of paper, wrapped in nylon, and hidden in the hair of women couriers, who attracted less suspicion from the police. Another of Ho's agents worked at the graves registration point, the mortuary on Cu Chi base, preparing American dead for shipment home. By this means, the Viet Cong had a far more accurate picture of American casualty figures than was ever made public. The camp barbers, too, were well placed to gather intelligence.

Sergeant Arnold Gutierrez recalled an episode concerning a barber. He and a patrol were in the Boi Loi woods and came under sniper fire from a tree. Gutierrez had the radio and was the prime target; he was wounded in the elbow. The patrol sprayed the tree with machine-gun fire and brought the sniper down. It turned out to be a thirteen-year-old girl, and—worse still—the daughter of one of the camp's Vietnamese barbers, a friend and confidant of the men. The girl had been in the tunnels since she was ten. That night the barber was hanged.

In January 1967, during Operation Cedar Falls, tunnel rats found a VC document that named dozens of sympathizers working inside Cu Chi base. It included all fourteen of the camp's barbers.

For attacks from outside, Cu Chi's intricate defensive perimeter turned out to be well justified. Because of the formidable American presence that descended on the area and the semipermanence of the buildings and structure, as well as the wholesale devastation and depopulation of the surrounding countryside, the Viet Cong always saw Cu Chi—like other U.S. bases—as an affront and a challenge. Truong Ky, a top Viet Cong staff officer, announced in 1967: "We will continue to encircle and hug their bases wherever they establish them." The interrogation report of Viet Cong prisoner Ngo Van Giang (made in January 1968) bears this out. He said: "Some permanent U.S. troop bases are near VC areas. Prostitutes around these camps make it easy for us to learn the defensive system and the strength of the post. At night, the Americans fire flares to assist in their observation of the area, but unconsciously they also help our sappers observe how to enter the post."

Not only did the Viet Cong lob mortar shells and rockets into Cu Chi base camp but, incredibly, they executed daring raids on it from the surrounding tunnels. These were carried out by parties of thirty or forty guerrillas at most, and often by smaller groups, even by the classic Viet Cong three-man cells. Some caused enormous damage, to helicopters and tanks for example, and loss of life among the American soldiers. The raids were profoundly unsettling and of psychological and propaganda value far beyond their military importance. The Viet Cong demonstrated to the Americans that none of their installations was impregnable; that their adversaries were self-sacrificially brave; and that the Viet Cong would keep coming back, even after the annihilation of their villages and apparently fearsome casualties. Twenty years earlier, Ho Chi Minh himself had warned the French: "You can kill ten of my men for every one I kill of yours, but even at those odds, you will lose and I will win."

Once the Americans had succeeded in blocking up all the tunnels that ran underneath Cu Chi base, the Viet Cong created a complex structure of tunnels, trenches, and firing positions all around it. This ring of tunnels they called the belt. (The same technique had been used against the French at the siege of Dien Bien Phu in 1954.) The belt connected most of the villages surrounding Cu Chi base, including Trung Lap, Nhuan Duc, and Phu Hoa Dong. Every fifty meters, branch tunnels headed off toward the base itself. One set of branch tunnels ended in well-defended firing positions placed in the banks of the stream that ran along the northern side of Cu Chi base. The firing position that ended each branch tunnel was well concealed and surrounded by punji traps and mines. These nests of resistance commanded wide fields of fire and often overlooked, and hence dominated, one or another of the roads that crisscrossed the district. Because the branch tunnels led back into the main Cu Chi tunnel system, Viet Cong using firing positions to harass the enemy had a safe escape route when detected or shelled. The tunnels themselves had the multilevel structure that prevented damage from explosives or CS gas.

The belt was constantly used for infiltration by main-force Viet Cong from the more secure areas of War Zone C in Tay Ninh province or from Cambodia, to attack Cu Chi base itself or to proceed to other attacks in or near Saigon. One of those who worked and fought in the belt was Mrs Vo Thi Mo, the one female guerrilla who survived the squad that stayed behind in Nhuan Duc. In 1966 she was still a teenager but dedicated to the cause she had espoused. "Our fighting area was the belt around Dong Zu (Cu Chi) base. My duty was to lead the way for the regular troops from Nhuan Duc to Dong Zu. In the daytime I went to Dong Zu openly by myself to observe the road, the fences, the terrain—the ways by which one could penetrate the base. Then at night I guided the reconaissance group to observe the base. The regular forces mounted attacks. My duty was to guide the troops on their way back and help carry the wounded. Sometimes I went there legally, with puppet identity cards, on a Honda moped. Inside the base I was guided by liaison agents. I collected information from women inside the base, like cleaners and prostitutes, about the Americans' activities. I ran fifteen secret cells. That way we knew in advance the names and times and places of some of the big operations, like Cedar Falls."

As late as February 1969, after three years of Cu Chi base's existence, the camp was the victim of a daring and destructive Viet Cong attack that penetrated right inside its security perimeter. It came from the least expected quarter: not from the notorious Ho Bo woods or Fil Hol sides, but from the side facing Cu Chi town, which was normally government-controlled. Local guerrillas like Mrs Mo had guided the Viet Cong main force around the belt to the side chosen for the attack. They slept the previous day in the tunnels. In the dead of night, Dac Cong, or special force, sappers crawled forward to clear a path through the protective minefield and barbed wire, unobserved by the patrolling sentries. Then the thirty-nine Viet Cong, three squads of thirteen, some of them women, entered the base. Their main aim, as with so many Viet Cong attacks, was to destroy their enemies' most feared and hated weapon—helicopters. They knew exactly where to find them. Using satchel charges, the guerrillas blew up fourteen of the big troop-carrying CH-47 Chinook helicopters on the ground, all those in Cu Chi at the time. The realization that the Viet Cong were "inside the wire" created some panic. The defenders fired ghostly parachute flares into the air to illuminate the base and help spot the attackers. Firing broke out on all sides; there was the whoosh and boom of rocket grenades. A medical orderly in the 12th Evacuation Hospital later recalled that night: "Guys confirmed that the VC were inside the base. They said the enemy had killed some of our people and had blown up some helicopters. That the VC were inside our wire scared the wounded guys pretty bad. It scared me, too, and for the rest of the night, whenever the door opened on either ward my heart flipped and I froze, half expecting it would be VC. The shooting and the rockets and the flares kept up for hours." Thirty-eight Americans were killed, but all but thirteen of the attackers escaped safely and unharmed when they melted away before dawn. They left in a direction different from the one they had taken to reach the base; they knew that artillery fire would rake the area from which it was thought they had traveled.

By a cruel stroke of irony, the commander of the 25th Infantry by that time was Major General Ellis W. Williamson. He was the officer who had commanded the 173rd Airborne in 1966, and had been so scornful of the 25th's early tribulations with tunnels underneath the base. The destruction of so many helicopters during his command was, he said, heartbreaking.

But back in 1966, when Cu Chi base was just completed, that raid was three years away. By establishing such a huge base (and others like it), General Westmoreland had grafted a little piece of America onto Cu Chi. But the Viet Cong were not displaced, and emulated the Americans by fighting and playing just as hard.

13

Pham Sang—The Story of an Entertainer

ON CHRISTMAS DAY, 1966, Pham Sang, an entertainer, was boosting Viet Cong morale in a tunnel beneath Cu Chi district within artillery range of Cu Chi base camp—while Bob Hope was doing the same for the 25th Infantry Division. Pham Sang arranged that word-of-mouth invitations be delivered to cadres and guerrillas, to attend a small entertainment underground.

Up above, thousands of GIs were sitting in the sunshine on the same Vietnamese earth, beer cans in hand, emitting piercing rebel yells at the obvious charms of the current Miss World. They hooted at the wisecracks and patriotic sentiments of the army's best-loved comedian, dressed in a grotesquely over-decorated fatigue jacket and armed with a golf club. "When I landed at Tan Son Nhut," quipped Hope, "I got a nineteen-gun salute. One of them was ours." Through the roars of encouragement he continued: "We have a very mixed audience today at Cu Chi." The grin, the famous pause, then: "We're so close to the fighting we had to give the Viet Cong half the tickets!" A classic one-liner, nor far removed from the truth. Ten minutes into Hope's show, two VC who had sneaked in through Cu Chi's base's perimeter were killed and one was captured; the artists heard the firing.

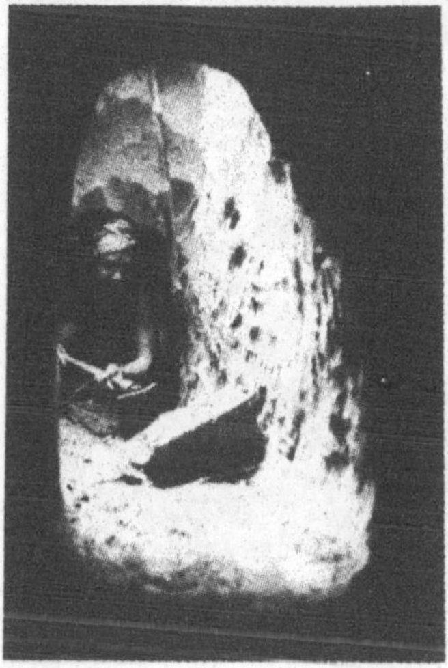

Tunnels in Vietnam were dug by hand, using hoes as scoops and baskets to take out the earth. Sometimes the Viet Cong could only manage a few feet a day, yet they dug over 200 miles like this. A captured VC document stated "tunnels will turn hamlets into fortresses." There were large "conference chambers" at ground level (*below*), protected by camouflaged roofs, but when the land was shelled and bombed they became too dangerous to use.

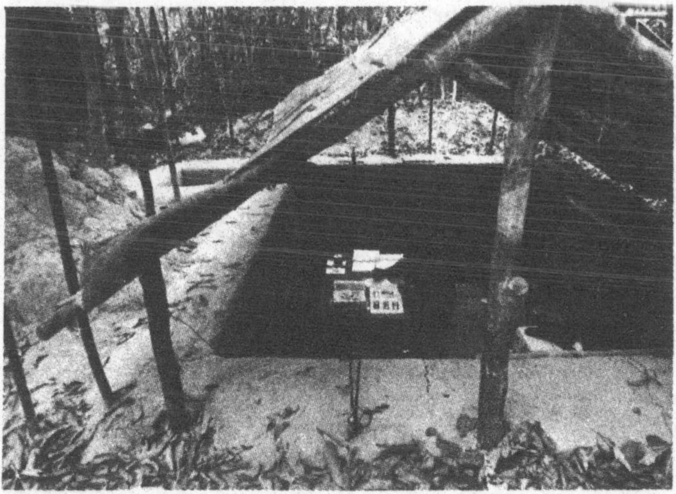

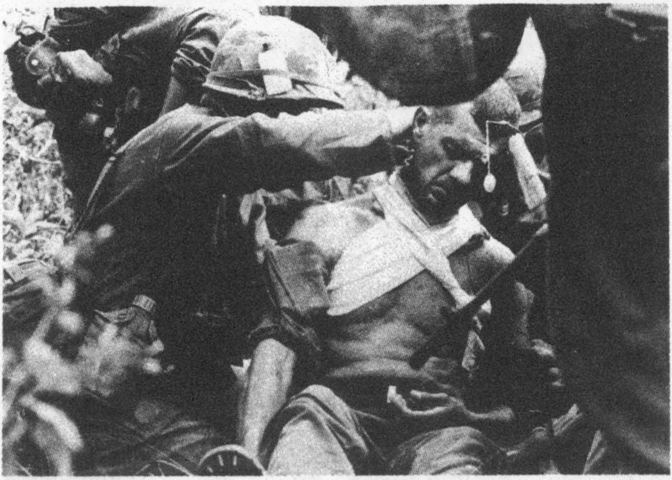

Lieutenant Colonel George Eyster, commander of the "Black Lions" Battalion of the U.S. 1st Infantry Division, lies mortally wounded after being hit by a sniper during Operation Crimp, the first full-scale operation in Cu Chi district in 1966. His dying words were: "Before I go, I'd like to talk to the guy who controls those incredible men in the tunnels."

The guy Eyster praised. Captain Nguyen Thanh Linh, commander of the Viet Cong's Cu Chi Battalion and in charge of tunnel defence during Crimp. Linh helped perfect tunnel engineering and lived and fought in the tunnels for five years.

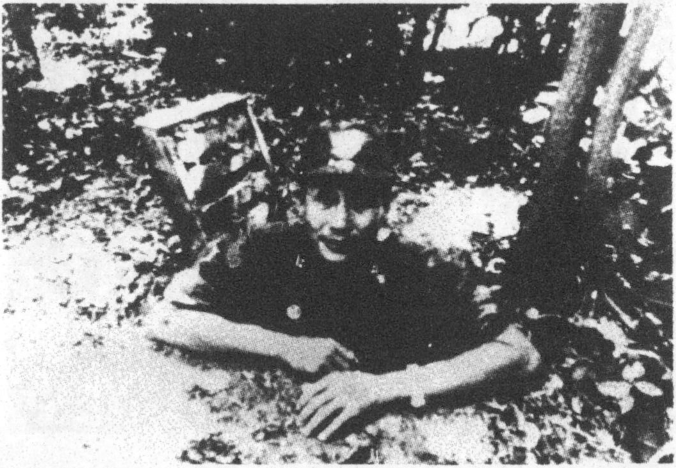

Major Nam Thuan, a veteran Viet Cong tunnel fighter (*left*). He personally destroyed an American task force sent to flush him out from his tunnels. Another senior Communist tunnel veteran—Major Nguyen Quot (*right*). Like his comrades he was promoted through the ranks and spent a decade fighting from the Cu Chi tunnels complex. He once lived five months underground without a break.

In the early days of tunnel warfare, VC cells like this one fought hard to acquire precious American weapons. The VC girl guerrilla wears the identifying black and white check scarf. The women were discouraged from hand-to-hand fighting with the GIs.

Instant death faced these Viet Cong tunnel fighters who emerged after American air raids to salvage dud bombs to extract the explosives. Despite the smiles, one mistake blew them to pieces; scores died like this. The water from the kettle is to cool the friction from the saw as it gently breaks open the bomb casing.

Death above but life below. Tranh Thi Hien (*on the right*) was born inside a tunnel in 1967 as war raged on the ground. Her mother Dang Thi Lanh (*left*) was an actress who played to the guerrillas in the tunnels. She sang and danced until a few hours before the birth.

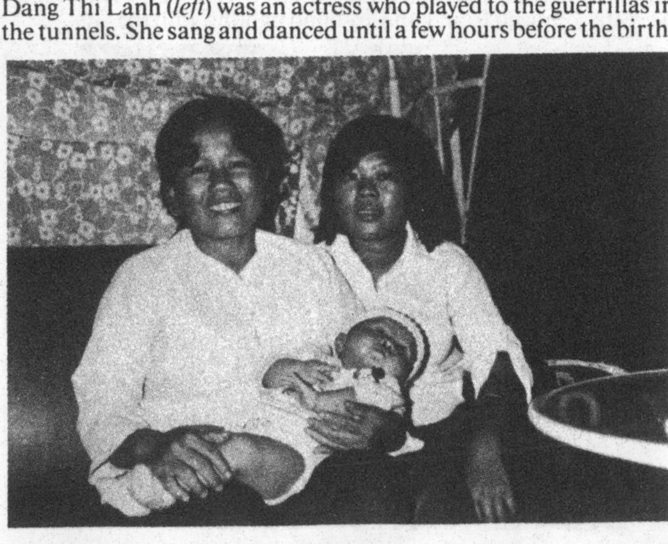

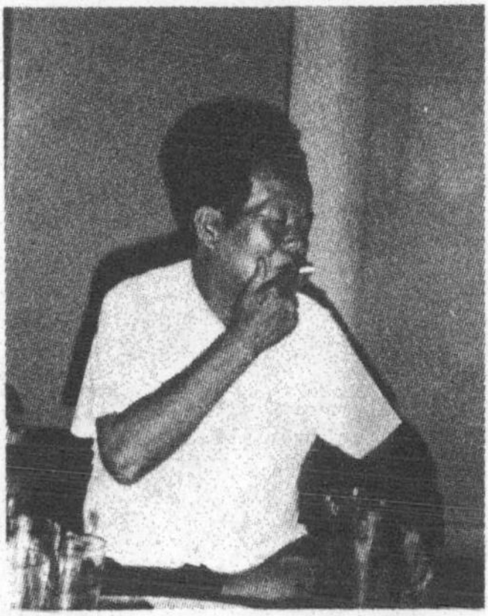

The remarkable Pham Sang (*top left*), a tunnel entertainer who did below ground for the Viet Cong what Bob Hope was doing just above for the GIs. A party hack, Pham Sang found his courage and some independence of spirit during the tunnel campaign.

Vien Phuong (*top right*) was another major contributor to the cultural life that grew inside the tunnels. His poetry and stories provided a rare account of the appalling difficulties faced by those who lived and fought there. Most of his comrade-writers died during the campaign.

A rare photograph showing a cultural troupe performing in a tunnel at An Phu, Cu Chi. These shows continued despite stringent blackout precautions and lack of oxygen. When the tunnels crumbled, old bomb craters became the stage.

On Cu Chi base in 1966, the divisional headquarters of the 25th "Tropic Lightning" Infantry Division from Hawaii. They built the fortress above the tunnels and were soon attacked from within. There were air-conditioned offices, ice machine plants, golf courses, and swimming pools. But nothing stopped the Viet Cong spy network from operating inside.

Major General Ellis W. Williamson (*left*), who commanded the 173rd Airborne Brigade to clear the ground for Cu Chi base. "What kind of outfit is it that can't even secure its own headquarters?"

Lieutenant General Fred C. Weyand (*right*), who commanded the 25th Infantry Division. "We realised that there were tunnels. And gradually we realised the extent of them."

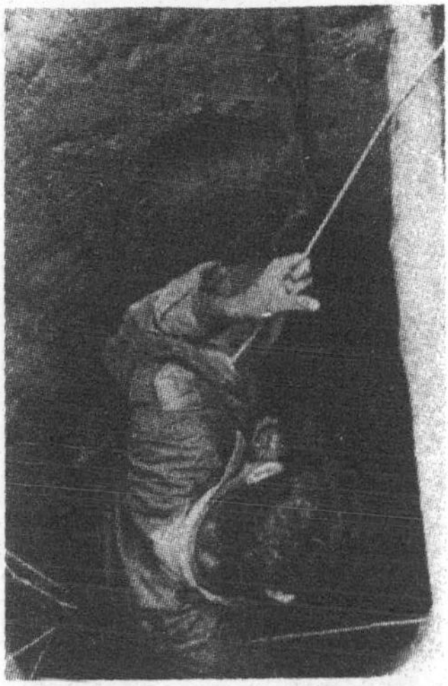

Captain Herbert Thornton (*top left, bald, center*) in 1966—the father of the tunnel rats. He was blown out of a hole and left permanently deafened by a grenade.

Entering a tunnel the hard way (*top right*). This was the most vulnerable moment. The tunnel rats faced grenades, bullets, punji stakes, or spears through the groin.

Sergeant Flo Rivera (*below*) with a captured Communist flag from a tunnel headquarters. He broke every rule to turn his tunnel rat squad into heroes.

Tunnel Rat Lieutenant Dave Sullivan in 1966 (*left*)—he found Communist gold bars inside the tunnels.

Tunnel Rat Sergeant Arnie Gutierrez (*right*) killed his first guerrilla inside a tunnel. "I'm not kidding, you could hear a man blink down there."

Holding the ubiquitous flashlight, a tunnel rat fires a special tracer bullet. Men fought and died in the inky blackness of those strange tunnels.

Helicopters close in on the village of Ben Suc (*left*) as Operation Cedar Falls begins on January 8, 1967. This controversial operation was the biggest of the war. Its mission—to clear the Viet Cong out of the Iron Triangle and the tunnels below it once and for all.

General William Westmoreland (*top right*), who called the VC "an army of moles," decorates a youthful Lieutenant Colonel Al Haig. Haig's battalion led the assault on Ben Suc. The civilian population was sent to the "safety" of strategic hamlets. But when they had gone, the tunnel fighters remained.

Pham Van Chinh commanded the Ben Suc Viet Cong guerrillas and stayed in the tunnels below his flattened village.

Rome Plow bulldozers—"hogjaws"—stripped eighty-yard-wide avenues across the Iron Triangle. VC tunnel fighters caught by the plows while hiding behind bushes were sliced to pieces.

Lieutenant General Jonathan O. Seaman (*bottom left*), who was in charge of Operation "Cedar Falls." He said he had turned the legendary "Iron Triangle" into a military desert: 750 Viet Cong killed; 280 prisoners. But when it was all over, the survivors came up from the tunnels once more.

Seen from the air (*below*), the insignia of the 1st Infantry Division and the US Army Engineers (a huge castle) were carved in the jungle by bulldozers during "Cedar Falls."

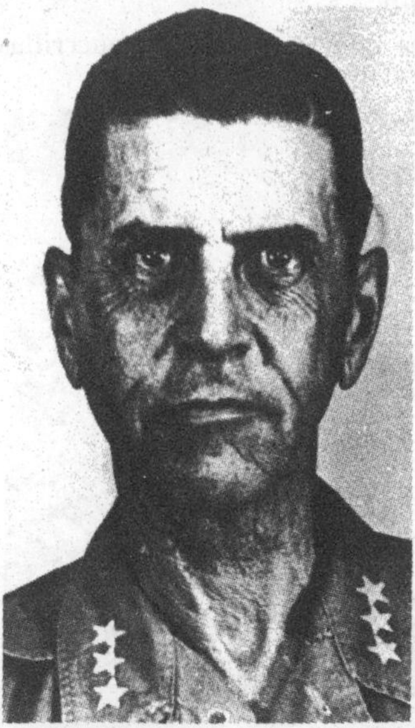

One of the biggest finds during "Cedar Falls" was a tunnel complex believed to be the underground headquarters of the Viet Cong's 4th Military Region. Tunnel rats of the 196th Light Infantry Brigade sent for their commander, Brigadier General Richard T. Knowles (*left*), who supervised the search. Platoon Sergeant James Lindsey (*center, with field phone*) was killed inside this tunnel two days later by booby-trap explosives.

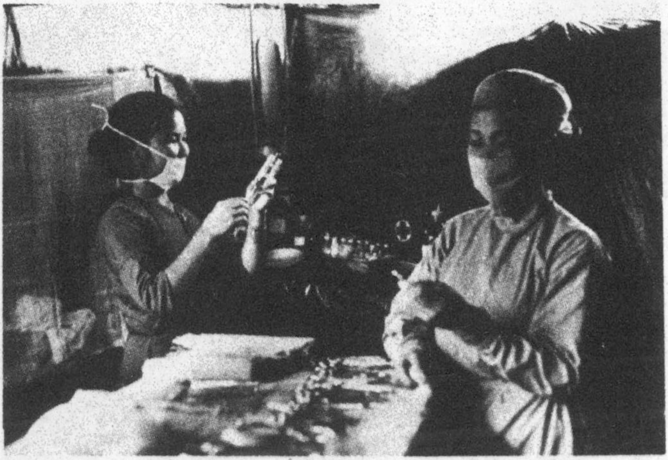

Two Viet Cong nurses prepare for an operation inside a tunnel hospital. The medical equipment was mostly American, bought on Saigon's black market. Parachute nylon hangs on the walls of the hospital to keep earth and infection away.

Dr. Vo Hoang Le, the famous tunnel surgeon, and his wife Nguyen Thi Tham in 1974. He performed hundreds of operations inside the Cu Chi tunnels. Amputations were done without anesthetics ("half died of shock but half lived"), and he did brain surgery with a household drill. He has become a national hero in Vietnam; she died from her wounds in 1982.

Tunnel rats, including Sergeant Bill Wilson (handling phials), inside the captured tunnel hospital at Lai Thieu in April 1967.

Vo Thi Mo, the tunnel guerrilla. A ruthless killer who softened long enough to let three GIs escape from her rifle sights.

"Rat Six" and "Batman" standing together. "Rat Six," Lieutenant Jack Flowers (*center*), is congratulated by Major General Orwin Talbott, commanding the Big Red One, on receipt of his bronze star. "Batman," Sergeant Robert Batten, is on the right. Later Batman was to warn his officer: "You're not a killer…and that's your problem…you'll screw up somewhere." His officer was indeed to be ordered back to the United States after one nightmare tunnel operation.

The sign that hung on the door of the 1st Engineer Battalion Tunnel Rats' "hootch" at Lai Khe base. They saw themselves as hard-drinking, mean-mouthed, fast-shooting sons of bitches. The reverse was true. They were cool, calculating, and ruthless.

Tunnel Rat Sergeant Pete Rejo in action. He was one of the meanest, working alone, hating and killing the Communist fighters in the holes. His squad called him the Human Probe. "I loved it down there…when they told me they had a VC down there, I came unglued."

The nucleus of the 1st Engineer Battalion Tunnel Rat team in 1969. Left to right: Kit Carson Scout Hien, Sergeant Pete Rejo, Lieutenant Randy Ellis, Kit Carson Scout Tiep, and Rick Swofford, the demolitions man who blew the lid off a tunnel like a scalp from a skull.

U.S. high technology warfare ultimately triumphed. Pictured above is the AH-1G Cobra attack helicopter. Some, like this one, were painted with a shark's mouth and swept low across the defoliated scrub killing anyone caught out of the tunnels. Captain Nguyen Thanh Linh called them "Red Headed Beasts." "We feared them very much; they killed many comrades." Once a decoy dummy VC soldier was used to lure a Cobra into a waiting ambush, and it was shot down. But it was the B-52s that finally destroyed most of the tunnels. This enormous crater (*below*) from just one B-52 bomb shows why. After 1969, B-52s, freed from bombing the North, "carpet-bombed" Cu Chi and the Iron Triangle in South Vietnam. The tunnels' infrastructure could not survive this kind of onslaught. But it had taken nearly five years for the tunnels to be smashed. And when they were—it came too late for the Americans. The tunnels had already made their vital military contribution, and the Americans had decided to quit Vietnam.

Hope's entourage included the Golddiggers, a troupe of thirteen leggy girl entertainers; they sang and danced to Les Brown and his Band of Renown. Superstars like Raquel Welch and Jill St. John had only to trip on stage in the then-fashionable miniskirts and the audience broke up. Singers like Connie Francis or Nancy Sinatra crooned the latest hits.

Pham Sang, in the theater of the earth, the tunnels, performed songs such as "He who comes to Cu Chi, the Bronze Fortress in the Land of Iron, will count the Crimes accumulated by the Enemy." His audience rose to its feet only if there was room to stand. Two of his wartime songs were intensely popular: One was a love song, "A Rose in the Land of Iron"; the other a satirical number about Saigon's revenue collectors entitled "400 Piastres of Tax." Both he and Bob Hope were there to sustain the fighting spirit of weary and homesick boys. The Hope show was sufficiently big and professional to be filmed by an American TV network. The Viet Cong tunnel entertainers, however, performed in cramped caverns, on bare earth floors. While Bob Hope had the beauty of a Vietnamese sunset as his stage lighting, Pham Sang's only stage illumination came from small lamps made from bamboo cane filled with nut oil, and slow-burning wicks.

The Vietnamese tunnel entertainers were a unique group of artists who volunteered to share the life of the Viet Cong tunnel inhabitants. They were in the main Communist party members, strongly opposed to what they saw as the deliberate erosion of traditional Vietnamese culture by the Diem government. These entertainers were recruited as early as 1960 by the National Liberation Front. Within the next five years the arrival of the American soldiers with their alien cultural backgrounds, and the continued neglect of Vietnamese historical inheritance by successive Saigon governments, resulted in further confusion, which the Communists took advantage of. The party believed the Vietnamese needed to be reminded of their colonial past, with its foreign domination and exploitation. By mixing their brand of socialism with traditional Vietnamese nationalism, they hoped to create a new culture. As far as the tunnels were concerned, not only were audiences captive, but morale frequently needed boosting. What Bob Hope was doing at the headquarters of the 25th needed doing inside the tunnels, too, for similar reasons and often with similar results.

It was the rubicund and enthusiastic Pham Sang who was originally instructed by the NLF to create a theater and song-and-dance ensemble at Phu My Hung in the district of Cu Chi, where he was then working as a civil servant. He was first transferred to the propaganda department of the Hoc Mon district committee, and soon became secretary of the district front committee. Pham Sang began the war, but was not to end it, as a bit of a party hack. He is one of the very few leading tunnel entertainers who survived.

His was a non-theatrical background. In 1955 he was in prison for political crimes against the new government of President Diem. Out of sheer boredom he taught himself to write plays about guerrilla warfare. Unlike plays in the prevailing political style, his works were not three-hour pieces of great polemic content, but unusually tight fifteen-minute productions. It was this kind of dramatic format that tunnel productions needed, given the numerous interruptions caused by shelling, bombing, or ground assaults.

The district committee nominated Sang as the most promising and prolific songwriter and playwright of the area. Soon the neighboring provinces of Tay Ninh and Binh Duong began mounting his productions. His stewardship of the Phu My Hung tunnel entertainment group gave the one-time civil servant a unique opportunity in his new career. As manager, writer, hirer and firer of the talent, he was in a comfortable position to have his works performed. By 1965 and the arrival in Vietnam of the Americans, his ensemble had grown to over a hundred young men and women. The Front ordered him to divide the group into three troupes of some thirty each. Subsequently, as the facilities down below became increasingly odious and cramped, the troupes split into much smaller numbers.

Such was Pham Sang's growing fame and importance as an actor-manager-writer that wherever he traveled, local people dug a special tunnel chamber for him to stay in and write more music and plays. In an underground society that could hardly afford privilege, politically or environmentally, this was a rare honor.

By 1966, Pham Sang could really work only in the tunnels, for above it was becoming too dangerous. Below, he would write endlessly by the light of a converted penicillin-bottle oil lamp. Like all creative artists, he maintained a running battle with those he regarded as philistines, such as the tunnel security guards. They seemed to care more about his little bottle lamp than they did about his songs and plays. They ordered him to make a lampshade for it, and even when that was done, they further commanded him to cover the flame completely with material, leaving only a tiny hole the size of a coin for light to shine through. It was almost impossible for an artist to write under these conditions, and he complained bitterly. But still the security men scolded him, warning him of developments in technology that sounded more like fiction than his own plays. They spoke of low-flying American spotter planes that could detect tiny light sources that were invisible even to the human eye, and of American night-scopes capable of magnifying available light 70,000 times. Pham Sang found it hard to believe. After all, he was under the earth. "How can I write if I am not allowed to have light?" he grumbled. "All my best works against the Americans are written at night in the tunnels, that is when I need light most." Like many of his artistic colleagues, the stage had become his world. Fighting, well, that was for soldiers.

His works were soon being performed in front of mixed audiences of soldiers and civilians, who themselves took great personal risks in making their way to the tunnels. Performances usually took place in tunnel conference chambers or even specially dug theater chambers, which could accommodate scores of people. If shelling or bombing began during the shows, the audiences could take to the smaller, safer communication tunnels. Some crawled to special bomb shelters inside the tunnels that had the greatly strengthened conical roofs. Sometimes, Pham Sang's ensemble was able to rehearse above ground in the lull between operations, or while the Americans changed over from day to night operations. But in the main, shelling was a considerable impediment to the continuity of Sang's productions. By 1967, the 25th Infantry alone was raining shells at the rate of nearly 200,000 a month into the Cu Chi district.

The most appreciative audiences were made up of men from the 267th (Quyet Thang) Regiment, the regional force that defended much of the Cu Chi area. Pham Sang was personally popular with many of the young soldiers, for whom Sang's songs were the only light relief from the alternating monotony and danger of their lives.

It was with the help of friends from the 267th that Pham Sang hit upon what everyone thought was a clever and audacious plan. Together with his close colleague Bay Lap, who was then in charge of the Cu Chi District Music Ensemble, Pham Sang decided it was time to give the enemy a chance to appreciate his songs and plays. It was also time the troupe did more to proselytize the puppets, and Sang was reasonably certain that his art would transcend the political gulf. Some of the tunnel shows had taken place only 200 meters away from the enemy military posts. Pham Sang became convinced that he would be able to organize an *above-ground* performance close to an ARVN military post that stood guard over a strategic hamlet. It was not inconceivable, thought Sang, that the sheer quality of the revolutionary performances might woo some of the misguided ARVN soldiers over to the Communist side. Such an event would not go unrecognized at district, or even regional, party headquarters.

First, he and Bay Lap needed to find a suitable location. It had to be within a couple of hundred meters of an ARVN post, yet also it needed to have suitable vegetation to act as cover, and to be near a tunnel entrance for speedy retreat. Once this location had been found, Pham Sang used his friends from the regiment to procure precious loudspeakers, microphones, and generators. Bay Lap's authority was crucial in forcing other tunnel sections to allow the precious equipment out of their hands for a few hours. Eventually all the necessary equipment was gathered together and the singers waited inside the tunnel.

Sang had chosen the period just after four-thirty in the afternoon, when the light was clear and the air beginning to cool a little. The equipment was carefully brought from the tunnels to the cover about 150 meters from the ARVN guard post. The singers moved stealthily into position; a handful of boys from the 267th crawled into the undergrowth to guard the ensemble. At a signal from Pham Sang the electricity was switched on and loudspeakers blurted out patriotic songs at full volume to the astonished ARVN soldiers. Interspersed among two songs were political commercials, enticing the South Vietnamese to defect to the Communists. It was, in retrospect, Pham Sang now admits, perhaps a somewhat naïve exercise. In the event, after a short silence, the entertainers received their answer. A barrage of small arms and rifle fire was hurled at them. In the ensuing undignified scramble to dive back into the tunnels and save the equipment, considerable pride and a couple of loudspeakers were lost. The experiment was not repeated, and Pham Sang's political future stayed on a plateau for some time to come.

Inside the tunnels, shows would run for five minutes; then all lights were put out to allow some air replenishment through vent holes, and then the show would start again. Sometimes the air was so bad the audience was ordered not to join in the patriotic singing, to conserve what little oxygen there was. When the American planes flew over, the security guards ordered the show to stop, but audiences would wait patiently for the all-clear. Some people walked up to seven miles through hostile ARVN-dominated territory just to attend a performance.

One of the most popular songs of the period—another Pham Sang creation—was called "Cu Chi, the Heroic Land." The lyric went:

> We are Cu Chi people who go forward to kill the enemy.
> We go through danger, bullets, and fire to fight for our native land.
> Our country is a fortress standing against the Americans,
> Cu Chi is a heroic land.
>
> Let's grow manioc plant all over the bomb craters and make them green.
> We kill the Americans with their own shells and bombs.
> We kill the enemy and increase our production,
> Those were our glorious victories.

Some songs were love songs. But Bay Lap, a sterner follower of the party line than Pham Sang, insisted that even love songs should carry a message. In the end, Pham Sang wrote a hybrid lyric—it was, he admitted, not his finest—the first line of which was: "I love you, I miss you and wait for you, liberation fighter, let's fight the enemy together." Bay Lap felt strongly that the main purpose of this song was to encourage the soldier to fight and the girl to work harder. Pham Sang, who was beginning to feel the first stirrings of artistic integrity in a socialist environment, wanted the song to be mainly romantic. He lost. Bay Lap is today the deputy director of cultural affairs in Ho Chi Minh City; Pham Sang is right out of show business.

Tensions were now beginning to develop between Pham Sang and the party. He believed his entertainers were not always getting a square deal; he did not like being told specifically what to write—there had to be some individuality in the theater; and it seems likely that he was beginning to have one or two tiny doubts about the general course of the revolution. According to him: "The Cu Chi District Committee patronized the Cu Chi cultural troupe, but troupe members did not enjoy a definite status as actors and artists do now (1983). There were times when we suffered much hardship. During the dry season, whenever it was possible, we gave performances. During the rainy season and in great fighting, we could not always perform. So we were forced to earn our living as laborers.

"My actors and actresses and singers became seasonal workers, plowing, sowing, harvesting rice in 'safe' areas. They were real actors and now they had to do these kinds of work. They even had to take turns as hired hands. There were no regulations as we have now. Now artists and actors can collect their monthly ration of rice. The Front only fed us if we were in a desperate situation. Some of my colleagues worked as slaves to support themselves and their comrades, like Ut Tho, who is now in charge of a cinema in District 5. He worked as a laborer season after season, just to stay alive."

By 1968, unequivocal instructions from COSVN pointed out sharply that the tunnels were primarily for battle purposes. By implication, their use for entertainment was a very low priority. In order to retain the use of tunnels for his productions at all, Pham Sang restricted tunnel performances to those for party hierarchy, civil servants, and soldiers. The others, the bulk audience—friends, peasants, and Sunday workers—had to take their places in the revolutionary new al fresco theaters created in B-52 bomb craters. Some thirty feet deep, these craters were narrow at the bottom and very wide at the top. Pham Sang realized the architectural potential—they were miniature amphitheaters. The main advantage was they were available without party harassment or grumbling. Small stage areas were flattened in the hard earth at the bottom of the bomb crater. The crater slopes were gentle enough to sit on, and special shallow tunnel shelters were built into the sides of the craters.

So opened a handful of the most extraordinary theaters in the history of the stage—a testament to the endurance and innovation of the actor, one that gives new meaning to the oldest theatrical cliché of all: The show must go on. Although there were no stage props, no curtains, and no lights, the theaters were a huge success, better ventilated than those dreadful tunnels and somehow a more defiant symbol. Pham Sang was happy for his art, Bay Lap for the political credit. Security was less strict and audiences were by now almost disdainful of the shelling. In fact, even when shells landed less than a hundred meters from the performance, the audience would stay, and while *they* stayed, the players played on. If the explosions crept too close, the audience ducked into the crater tunnels and waited; even then they would often continue singing the songs. They were remarkable nights, and to this day, when what is left of the original Cu Chi ensemble gather for their yearly meetings in Ho Chi Minh City, tears come to the eyes of the raconteurs as they recall those fine hours.

By late 1969, Pham Sang was finding it increasingly difficult to move his diminishing troupe around an area which had now become the scene for ferocious bombing or shelling strikes by the Americans. The Tet offensive had failed to end the war—indeed conditions had become much worse for the Communists after Tet. Now large mechanized sweeps across the land were being mounted by the battle-hardened 25th Infantry. Sang was changing, too. He had enjoyed the early years as a party hack. A Viet Cong victory had seemed inevitable. It would be followed by important political appointments, and Sang did not imagine he would be ignored by the grateful party. But by 1969 his character had developed and matured. An artist by temperament, Sang had never felt the tug of the military. For him the sound of the trumpets meant the raising of a curtain rather than a call to arms. But the fighting and the sharing of hardship, the cries of the wounded in the tunnels, and the haunted eyes of the young soldiers had left an impression. He hated the Americans as much as ever, but he had also spotted hypocrisies and inconsistencies within the party. Bay Lap, a former friend, epitomized those who, as far as Pham Sang was concerned, were able to further their careers through this endless and dreadful war. How far had he himself gone down this path? How was it that after four years of fighting he still had not fought a battle? Would patriotic songs alone eventually drive the Americans out? These thoughts were uppermost in his mind.

He was in charge of the Cu Chi Sub-Zone 1 Cultural Troupe, a sadly diminished and mixed bag of some thirty performers, when he was ordered (he used to volunteer) to give shows at Phuoc Hiep village and at An Tinh village near Trang Bang. To reach these villages he would have to lead his troupe across Route 1 to the north of Suoi Cut, which he negotiated without difficulty. All of them arrived at An Tinh just before midnight, and managed to scrounge beds for the night in the villagers' huts. At seven the next morning, however, the Americans landed by helicopter at the other end of the village, which caused the prompt cancellation of Sang's show. Coincidentally, his own niece, Vo Thi Mo, was the commanding officer of an all-female village defense platoon. Pham Sang went to see her to discuss the problem. She told him that naturally the women would stay and fight. By implication there was nothing to prevent Uncle Pham and his entertainers from fighting, too. Sang ducked out, saying somewhat tactlessly: "How can you fight? You are just a few women. If you fire your guns the Americans will come and wring your necks." The insult, that the women did not even qualify for death by shooting, was unfair, the more so as Pham Sang was himself beginning a long retreat.

Pham Sang took his troupe and recrossed Route 1, heading for Suoi Loi in Vuon Trau hamlet, which is a part of the village of Phuoc Hiep. He justified his retreat by claiming responsibility for the safety of his entertainers, but he knew there was a streak of something else that made him run. Unfortunately, in the course of his attempt to put as much distance as he could between himself and the Americans, he bumped into the commanding officer of the 7th Regiment of the North Vietnamese army, who naturally assumed Pham Sang and the troupe had arrived to entertain his men. "We are so happy you have arrived," he said to Sang. "Please stay for the night and perform for us tomorrow evening." Pham Sang said: "The Americans have landed across the road. This is not time to perform our plays." But the commander wouldn't hear of it: "Do you know what is our strength? You should not be scared. We are two regiments here. Do you think we can't protect your troupe?" So Sang and his group bedded down for the night and the NVA soldiers fed them.

The following morning, one lone spotter plane circled overhead. Twenty minutes later the Americans landed in two waves of eighteen helicopters each. Tanks and infantry supported by artillery had also moved up and were now surrounding the hamlets of Mit Nai, Vuon Trau, and Suoi Loi. Suddenly the optimistic assurances of the NVA colonel began to look a little hollow. Even two regiments of Vietnamese would not be sufficient to guarantee protection from what the Americans were throwing in.

Pham Sang's troupe of thirty dispersed and he retired for a while to a secret underground shelter that had been specially dug for him because of his fame and his status. The NVA commander sought him out there and, ignoring his own advice of the previous day, suggested Pham Sang might after all be safer if he tried to leave, as a long and fierce engagement was about to begin. Once more Pham Sang prepared to run.

"I went by myself and soon met a younger man, and asked him if he knew the country well. He said, 'I know this area well—this is my native hamlet.' I said, 'Let's get out of this place together then.' So I let him lead because he said he knew the area. He led us straight to a place where the American tanks were coming in. I asked him, 'Do you know any other way?' and he did not answer me. I suggested we hide in a clump of bamboo trees and wait until dark to find a way out. Even though there was plenty of country all around, one tank moved straight toward our hiding place as if it knew we were there. If I had not rolled over, it would have passed right over my stomach. My companion was shaking like a leaf. I pulled him to my side, but he would not stop trembling. I told him: 'Fuck your mother! Our soldiers are fighting and sacrificing their lives and we are doing nothing but hiding ourselves. If we have to die here, then so be it.' Yet just as I spoke what I thought were heroic words, I looked up and saw an American tank so close that I could see speckles of rust as small as straw on the track. The American at the machine gun was swiveling it round, and my companion jumped out and shouted, 'I surrender.' I told myself, 'That's the end of me.'"

It was at precisely this moment in his life, lying face down in the dirt, humiliated and within a muscle twitch of death, that Pham Sang found courage for the first time in the war. The party hack, the writer of songs and plays that motivated others, suddenly found motivation of his own. He could surrender, he could die, or he could do what he had urged others to do for so long. He could resist.

He just managed to see and hear his unlucky companion being roughly interrogated by the Americans. While the GIs were fully occupied with their prisoner, Pham Sang was able to crawl undetected into a bamboo clump nearby. In the undergrowth he left a small radio set, his clothes in a bag, and a large part of the past. He took with him his gun, two hand grenades, and a sheet of camouflaged (American) parachute cloth. Even as he was inching himself away, he heard his companion betray him by name. The Americans ran over to search the bamboo clump, found the discarded equipment, but not the man. They returned to their unfortunate prisoner with renewed vigor.

Pham Sang managed to put a little more distance between himself and the Americans but then realized to his great alarm that the Americans were deploying themselves to stay and hold the area and spend the night there. It would have been madness to move, and Sang stayed where he was for the moment. One GI came extremely close to where he was hiding and began digging a trench for the night. Sang pulled the pins out of both of his hand grenades and held them ready. If he was discovered he would take the American with him, or he would throw one grenade, run and then throw the other at any pursuers. Incredibly, the American didn't see him. A Vietnamese would have seen me ten times over by now, Sang thought to himself. The Americans must have very bad eyesight. After the American had dug his trench, he took out a mosquito-repellent spray and sprayed the area, at one stage so close to Pham Sang that it was only with a superhuman feat of self-control that he didn't cough and retch as the acrid spray went over his face.

When the American moved off to rejoin some comrades, Sang gently put the pins back in the grenades and tried crawling to a new position. It would have been easy to surrender; there would have been less pain. Instead, for the next six hours, from seven at night until one the next morning, Pham Sang, the great Communist actor-manager, dragged himself through the American lines. Bleeding from numerous cuts and scrapes, half-demented by thirst, carrying now only the tools for killing or suicide, he wriggled like a giant worm through the lines, until finally he finished up exactly where he had begun that endless day, at Suoi Loi. He returned just as both Communist regiments were preparing to break out of the American trap. Within an hour the counterattack began, concentrating on a 500-meter front through marshland, where the Americans could not use their tanks to full advantage.

By now utterly exhausted, Pham Sang could only limp painfully back to the small tunnel that had originally been dug for him the day before. First there would have to be sleep. He sank gratefully into the stinking pit that would cover and protect him through what was left of the night. Even as he closed his eyes, he heard footsteps approaching above. Only he and the small guerrilla cell of diggers knew of the existence of this tunnel—and the others were fighting their way through the American lines. Small pieces of earth fell on to Pham Sang's face. Somebody was trying to open his trapdoor. It could only be an American.

Sang again pulled the pin from one of his grenades and held the weapon in his fist. With the other hand he hung on to the trapdoor lock, a crude stick threaded through the eye of a wire loop. If he lost the silent struggle and the trapdoor flew open, or the wire broke, he would fling the grenade. Drenched in sweat, his fingers bleeding from the increasingly unequal struggle, which was now continued for the best part of fifteen minutes, Sang withdrew his hand and allowed the trapdoor to fly open. As he prepared to hurl the grenade a voice said in Vietnamese, "It's me, it's me, Uncle Pham." It was one of the young guerrillas who had been ordered to stay behind and defend the rear. He had seen Pham Sang enter the tunnel and now asked for shelter, too—for himself and no less than eight of his comrades.

Sang's little tunnel could hold only four at most, and only with extreme difficulty and discomfort. If the trapdoor was closed they would all suffocate; if it was left open and the American infantry arrived and saw it, they would be captured or die. Somebody would have to stay awake all night and guard the open trapdoor, allowing the young guerrillas to survive underground. Sang told the men: "We are in a difficult situation. I'll give you my shelter, but I will guard the trapdoor. I will not let anyone else guard it. I will stay on the ground and let you sleep. If the enemy come I'll pull the trapdoor down. Even if you suffocate and die under me, you will have to keep quiet. If any of you scream, I will explode a hand grenade and we will all die." The soldiers agreed. It was a small gesture but for Pham Sang it was a brave one. The bluster and the revolutionary rhetoric that sounded so impressive on the stage was displaced by the earthy reality of trying to survive.

Next morning, as the sun rose over the battlefield and the men wearily came up from the tunnel, Sang joined them to search for and identify the many bodies of the dead and wounded. For several hours this work preoccupied him, so much so that he did not realize that the Americans were leaving. The battle was over. His song-and-dance troupe, who had managed to slip out of the American noose with less difficulty than he, assumed he'd been killed. They even sent an ox and cart with a local driver especially to find and return Pham Sang's body from the battlefield. Instead, their leader, having refused to travel in the undertaker's cart sent for his corpse, walked back to the base at Phu My Hung. When he was reunited with the ensemble, they wept at seeing him alive. Pham Sang cried a little, too.

In 1972, all Pham Sang's sketches, song sheets, and scripts were lost when the box containing them was buried in a tunnel, following a direct hit during a B-52 strike. Misfortune continued to dog him when he came back from the war in 1975. His wife had taken a lover who was a "puppet," a police informer. The man was arrested by the victorious Communists but subsequently freed. He then married Sang's wife.

By 1979, Pham Sang was working at the Ho Chi Minh City Cultural and Information Department. But that seed of independence and stubbornness that had been sown at Suoi Loi refused to wither away. He was not so naïve as to imagine that peace would bring the solution to all Vietnam's problems, but there were pertinent questions to be asked about the direction of the new united nation. As differences of opinion grew between Pham Sang and his superiors, he asked to be released from the Cultural and Information Department. He was out of show business.

Since then most of his entertainers have died or dispersed; the excitement of the war has, inevitably, been replaced by the anticlimax of peace. Besides, Hanoi today needs different writers to achieve different aims, to mobilize the people against new enemies of the state. Peace has not brought cultural freedom, but Pham Sang remains optimistic.

Pham Sang has turned his back on all theater. He has learned too much about the real world to believe in the stage any more.

He has remarried and is a tax inspector in Binh Thanh district.

14

Operation Cedar Falls

BY 1967 THE AMERICANS were clearly having difficulties with the tunnels in Cu Chi. The Viet Cong had so organized their local and regional forces that not only did bases like Cu Chi face attack, but the security of Saigon itself was threatened. General Westmoreland had to address this growing problem. Most of Cu Chi district was under ARVN or American control by day, but the Viet Cong dominated it by night. The guerrillas did not come from empty air—they had to have shelter, food, and weapons facilities. Many of these needs were supplied in the area adjoining Cu Chi, the large VC base nearest to Saigon, which rejoiced in the menacing name, the Iron Triangle. For two years the Americans treated the Triangle with respect and caution, but in 1967 Westmoreland decided to mount the largest and most destructive operation of the war. He planned to take out the Iron Triangle and its tunnels, to relieve the pressure on Saigon and the surrounding bases, such as Cu Chi.

The Triangle was a forty-square-mile natural citadel of jungle and briar, beneath which was a honeycomb of Viet Cong tunnels and bunkers. Its apex was the junction of the Saigon and Thi Tinh rivers, which formed two of its sides. The third was an imaginary line running from the village of Ben Suc

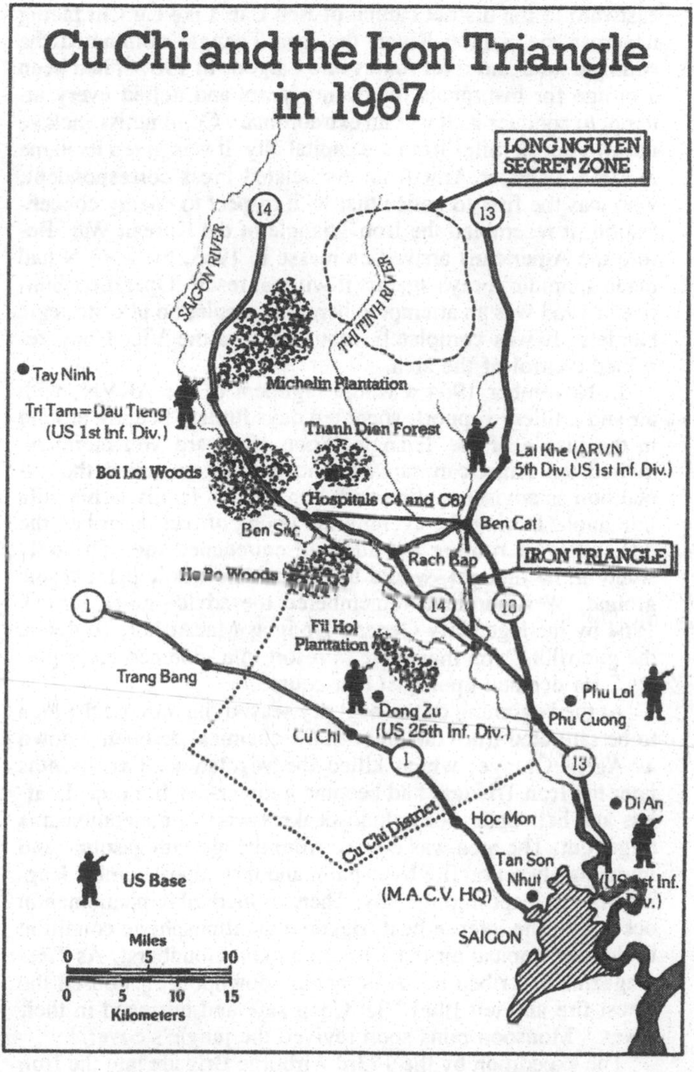
Cu Chi and the Iron Triangle in 1967
LONG NGUYEN SECRET ZONE
14
13
SAIGON RIVER
THI TINH RIVER
Tay Ninh
Michelin Plantation
Tri Tam=Dau Tieng (US 1st Inf. Div.)
Thanh Dien Forest
Lai Khe (ARVN 5th Div. US 1st Inf. Div.)
Boi Loi Woods
(Hospitals C4 and C8)
Ben Cat
Ben Suc
Rach Bap
IRON TRIANGLE
Ho Bo Woods
1
14
16
Fil Hol Plantation
Trang Bang
Phu Loi
Dong Zu (US 25th Inf. Div.)
Phu Cuong
Cu Chi
1
13
Di An
Cu Chi District
Hoc Mon
Tan Son Nhut
(M.A.C.V. HQ)
US Base
SAIGON
Miles
0 5 10
0 5 10 15
Kilometers

eastward to the district capital of Ben Cat. Like Cu Chi facing it across the Saigon River, the Iron Triangle dominated the strategic land and river routes into Saigon. In 1967 it had been a refuge for insurgents for twenty years and defied every attempt to conquer it. It was an extraordinary Communist enclave not two dozen miles from the capital city. It was given its name in 1963 by Peter Arnett, an Associated Press correspondent, who was the first to notice that with respect to enemy concentration, it resembled the Iron Triangle of the Korean War. Before the Americans arrived en masse in 1965, the ARVN had made sporadic forays against it without result. Operation Sunrise in 1963 was an attempt to herd the population into strategic hamlets. It was completely rebuffed, and the Viet Cong resumed control of the area.

In November 1964 a whole regiment of the ARVN, with air and artillery support, spent ten days futilely beating around in the jungle of the Triangle. Soon afterward Westmoreland invited the American captain who had accompanied the expedition as adviser to dine with him and his family at his villa in Saigon. During the evening the young officer described the difficulties of rooting out such an entrenched foe. The only solution, he thought, would be to burn the whole place to the ground. Westmoreland remembered the advice given him in 1964 by the legendary General Douglas MacArthur: To defeat the guerrilla, "you may have to resort to a scorched-earth policy." He decided upon just that course.

At the beginning of the next dry season, he ordered the area to be saturated from the air with the chemical defoliant known as Agent Orange, which killed the vegetation. Two months later the Iron Triangle had become a tinder-dry fire trap. Leaflets and helicopter-borne loudspeakers warned noncombatants to get out. The area was doused from the air with gasoline and immediately set on fire by napalm and incendiary bombs. Raging flames leapt into the sky. Then an incredible phenomenon occurred. The intense heat triggered an atmospheric condition in the wet tropical air that created a giant cloudburst. As *Time* magazine described it: "A drenching downpour . . . doused the forest fire and left [the] Viet Cong safe and unsinged in their caves." Monsoon rains soon revived the jungle's cover.

The expedition by the 173rd Airborne Brigade into the Iron Triangle in late 1965 did some damage but demonstrated yet again the extreme difficulty of denying insurgents the use of the fastness. From then on U.S. units stayed well away from the area. When it became clear to Westmoreland that the Iron Triangle still functioned as Communist preserve, he resolved to mount a final assault so powerful that it could not fail to eliminate the fortress. It was to be a textbook example of the controversial strategy of search and destroy.

"It was unfortunate," wrote Westmoreland, "that American strategy in Vietnam came to be known as search-and-destroy strategy." Perhaps because the term became synonymous in the public mind with aimless thrashing about in the jungle and the purposeless destruction of property, Westmoreland later substituted other expressions, such as "offensive sweep" and "reconnaissance in force." But the object remained the same. A large mechanized body of troops would seek out opponents to fight, installations to destroy, or both. Afterward the American forces would move on or return to their bases. There could be no territorial acquisition, so the only measure of success was attrition: maximizing the number of enemy killed while keeping one's own casualties to a minimum. Hence the size of the units of troops deployed on sweeps in the III Corps Tactical Zone, and the statistical obsession with the body count of supposed Viet Cong dead. In the war of attrition that Westmoreland found himself waging, there was no other way.

Search-and-destroy operations were usually named after American towns and cities, such as Attleboro and Junction City. Troops would be flown, or driven in APCs, to an area of suspected Viet Cong presence. The infantry would fan out and look for the enemy, while the senior officers hovered overhead in their helicopters, directing proceedings on their radios.

Brigadier General Joseph A. McChristian was Westmoreland's assistant chief of staff for intelligence. During 1966, he assiduously compiled and computerized every kind of intelligence tidbit available, from sampan traffic counts on the Saigon River to checking the amount of wood sent to an area for making coffins. Such "pattern activity analysis," along with the more orthodox interrogation of prisoners and defectors, persuaded him that urgent action was needed in the Iron Triangle. In *The Role of Military Intelligence 1965–1967* he wrote: "While Vietnam provided many examples of the role of intelligence in support of operations, Cedar Falls was a classic. I conceived the operation and recommended it to General Westmoreland." McChristian knew that the Viet Cong's Military Region IV (the Saigon area) headquarters moved frequently to avoid detection. But he formed the impression that it was in the Trapezoid, as the Americans called the Thanh Dien forest on the northern side of the Triangle. (He was mistaken: It was usually across the Saigon River in Cu Chi district.) He believed that an urgent search-and-destroy operation against the Trapezoid and the Iron Triangle would uncover and disrupt the Viet Cong's imminent designs upon Saigon itself. In 1966 their saboteurs had seemed able to strike almost at will in the capital; there were more terrorist incidents in Saigon that year than ever before.

Cedar Falls (named after a town in Iowa) was set for 8 January 1967. Its objects were savage and uncompromising. First of all, the village of Ben Suc was to be emptied of people and razed; all the other villages in the Triangle would be treated likewise. The chief aim of the operation was to locate the tunnel headquarters of MR IV, explore it, and then destroy it, along with any other tunnels that were found. Once the civilian population had been cleared out of the Iron Triangle, it was to be stripped of vegetation and declared a free strike zone.

A week's softening-up bombing missions by B-52s preceded the operation. The Vietnam War had begun as a counterinsurgency war—stalking guerrillas in the jungle. Cedar Falls, however, was a multidivisional operation involving over 30,000 U.S. troops, the largest in Vietnam to date.

On 8 January 1967 the village of Ben Suc—former population about 3,500—was wiped off the face of the earth. Its subsequent survival and rebirth testify to the importance of the tunnels in frustrating America's aims in Operation Cedar Falls, and in the Vietnam War as a whole. So long as the tunnels were not eliminated, neither were the spirit and effectiveness of the guerrillas.

Ben Suc was strategically situated at the crossing point of the Saigon River, on the northern bank facing Phu My Hung in Cu Chi district; it was the western point of the Iron Triangle. It had been a prosperous village. Most of the villagers were peasant farmers, raising crops like melons, grapefruit, and cashew nuts. Because a market was held there each day, the place could boast many shops, a pharmacy, and some primitive restaurants. When the National Liberation Front had gone on the offensive back in 1960, they terrorized a small ARVN post in Ben Suc into handing over its weapons. The movement's local leader was Pham Van Chinh, then twenty-three. Today, in his sixties, he is the village Communist party secretary, the local boss—a reward for fifteen years of tunnel existence leading the local guerrillas. He looks only about forty-five, with a mouthful of gold teeth, green-framed thick glasses, and a relaxed and authoritative manner. He recalled that in late 1964 the reinforced ARVN post was driven out altogether by the Viet Cong, who murdered the government-appointed village chief and set up their own administration. As inhabitants of a "liberated zone," the people were obliged to help the Front: they were required to join party associations, such as those for youths and women, and compelled to pay Viet Cong taxes and perform such duties as digging tunnels. Young men were recruited as guerrillas; young girls became nurses, or set booby traps and warned the villagers of their location.

As the war intensified in 1965, Ben Suc was bombed for the first time, and several buildings were destroyed—this despite the Viet Cong's mockingly flying the South Vietnamese flag in the village center in the hope of winning immunity from bombing. Thereafter people dug bomb shelters under their homes, and even shelters for their farm animals. As air-raid-shelter life became more customary, connecting tunnels were dug between homes and between parts of the village. The population of Ben Suc was increasingly swollen by bombed-out refugees from other villages, like Phu My Hung across the river. Pham Van Chinh admitted that Ben Suc was "the gateway to Saigon" and that main-force Viet Cong units were constantly passing through. Chinh himself had sixty-five local guerrillas under his command, and two hundred more scattered through adjoining hamlets, who, like minutemen, kept rifles in their homes ready for action. He also had hundreds of meters of real tunnels. They ran from the river crossing point back underneath the village toward the Viet Cong sanctuaries farther north in the Thanh Dien forest and the "Long Nguyen Secret Zone."

Late in 1966 the Viet Cong high command at COSVN received advance intelligence of Cedar Falls. As usual, the choice of whether or not to do battle rested with the local Viet Cong commander, Colonel Tran Hai Phung of Military Region IV.

Forewarned, he sensibly withdrew the largest main-force unit in the area, the 272nd Regiment, back to sanctuary nearer Cambodia. Meanwhile the local guerrillas were ordered to stay *in situ*—to "cling to the land." Pham Van Chinh said he was not given the exact date of Cedar Falls but was warned that an operation was imminent, and that Ben Suc would bear the brunt of it.

Because the Americans assumed that approaches to Ben Suc would be mined and booby-trapped, and that a battalion of Viet Cong would be defending the village, a new form of attack was planned. An entire battalion, five hundred men of the 1st/26th Infantry, the "Blue Spaders," commanded by a future secretary of state, Lieutenant Colonel Alexander M. Haig, were airlifted into the middle of the village by sixty UH-1 helicopters. This was the largest number of helicopters ever used for such an attack. This great sky-blackening armada, resembling nothing so much as a throbbing and malevolent cloud of giant locusts, lifted off from Dau Tieng base at 7:30 a.m. Flying in two parallel lines of thirty, the "slicks" clattered across the hazy morning countryside and into what the apprehensive GIs aboard imagined would be a hot landing zone and the battle for Ben Suc. It was a rocky ride, as each helicopter created a turbulent wake for the one following. They flew at safe height, but after an hour swooped down to treetop level and flew *away* from Ben Suc, to confuse enemy observers on the ground. Then there was a sudden U-turn as sixty ear-splitting machines startled peasants and their water buffaloes, and charged low across the paddyfields and into the center of the village. There the battalion swiftly unloaded and ran to take up defensive positions. As the soldiers landed in the village, preplanned artillery and air strikes exploded in the Thanh Dien forest to the north, to cut off any escape route. Soon afterward, helicopters carrying loudspeakers and South Vietnamese announcers circled the village. In Vietnamese they made this proclamation: "Attention people of Ben Suc! You are surrounded by Republic of Vietnam and Allied forces. Do not run away or you will be shot as VC. Stay in your homes and wait for further instructions."

There was no significant resistance in Ben Suc; the only American casualties were caused by booby-trap mines. The village was sealed and secured, and in a short while a battalion of the ARVN was helicoptered in to search the village and interrogate the inhabitants. It was the same ARVN unit as had been driven out of Ben Suc three years earlier. The ARVN interrogators sorted through about 6,000 men, women, and children from the village and surrounding hamlets, who had been ordered to gather in an old school building. Of these they concluded twenty-eight might be Viet Cong. The ARVN troops used their habitually rigorous methods of questioning—beating up those whose answers were not those desired. A reporter, Jonathan Schell, witnessed the ARVN soldiers administering water torture to a villager, choking him with a soaked rag and pouring water down his nose. That same day, all the men in the village between fifteen and forty-five were flown out in Chinooks for further interrogation at the provincial police headquarters. Those thought not to be Viet Cong would be inducted into the South Vietnamese army.

Major General William Depuy, commander of the Big Red One, was helicoptered into Ben Suc soon after Haig and his men. "I had no doubt," he said, "that there were a lot of agencies of the VC in there. When Al Haig's battalion went into Ben Suc, we picked up two chaps who were in charge of the education of the Viet Cong youth. They both spoke Russian and had been trained in Moscow. They were very intelligent men. I spoke some Russian, and was able to talk to them."

The next day, all the remaining villagers were shipped out, with whatever belongings they could carry and such animals as they could round up. They were transported in trucks, World War II landing craft, or Chinook transport helicopters. Even General Bernard Rogers (then an assistant divisional commander of the Big Red One) in an army-sponsored and rose-tinted account of Cedar Falls, was moved to call this mass removal of the population a "pathetic and pitiful" sight. "It was to be expected," he wrote in 1973, "that uprooting these villagers would evoke resentment, and it did."

The forced depopulation of Ben Suc was the precursor of similar clearances all over South Vietnam, which emptied the countryside of people who might have succored the guerrillas and NVA, and ended the cultivation of food that might have fed them. A large refugee population was created around Saigon and other towns. General Westmoreland, in his memoir *A Soldier Reports,* tried to dispel the "misunderstanding" that this policy caused at home in the United States. He wrote:

> So closely entwined were some populated localities with the tentacles of the VC base area, in some cases actually integrated into the defenses, and so sympathetic were some of the people to the VC that the only way to establish control short of constant combat operations among the people was to remove the people and destroy the village. . . . That it was infinitely better in some cases to move people from areas long sympathetic to the Viet Cong was amply demonstrated later by events that occurred when the discipline of an American company broke down at a place called My Lai.

At My Lai in March 1968 hundreds of noncombatant villagers were mown down in cold blood by a company of the 23rd (Americal) Division on a search-and-destroy operation. Westmoreland's brutal logic points up the frustrating fact about the Vietnam War that was such a source of pride to the Communists It was a people's war: the Viet Cong were inextricably mixed in with the civilians, and American boys from cities and farms found it impossible to distinguish between them.

When the last truckload of people and boatload of animals had left Ben Suc, the demolition teams moved in. The grass-roofed houses were soaked in gasoline and razed, leaving spindly black frames, charred furniture, and the entrances to the ubiquitous bomb shelters. Then the bulldozers went to work, flattening all the more solid buildings, fences, and graveyards. Afterward 1st Division engineers stacked ten thousand pounds of explosives and a thousand gallons of napalm in a crater in the center of the ruined village, covered them with earth, and tamped it all down with bulldozers. A chemical fuse triggered the five-ton explosion; it was hoped that it would blast any undiscovered tunnels in the vicinity. "One of the major objectives of Cedar Falls had been achieved," wrote Rogers. "The village of Ben Suc no longer existed."

But that was just the overture to Cedar Falls. The bulk of the American troops were to be thrown into the rest of the Iron Triangle. By the end of the first day, an entire American corps had moved into position along its sides. East of the Thi Tinh River were Depuy's 1st Infantry Division and the 173rd Airborne Brigade. West of the Saigon River in Cu Chi district were Weyand's 25th Infantry Division and Knowles's 196th Light Infantry Brigade. In the imagery of the overall commander, Lieutenant General "Jack" Seaman, the "hammer" of the eastern forces was poised to strike the "anvil" of the blocking forces west of the Saigon River, and crush any Viet Cong caught in between. Air cavalry screened the whole area from above. At dawn on 9 January, this mighty leviathan stirred and rolled into action.

As the operation began, the 196th swept through the tunnel-riddled Ho Bo woods in Cu Chi. At first all they achieved was "the uncovering of a small quantity of enemy supplies." Brigadier General Richard T. Knowles realized that he had to devise a way of finding well-camouflaged tunnel entrances as a matter of urgency; tunnel detection would be vital to the conduct of Cedar Falls. He had a bright idea. He had vehicles, such as APCs, drag whole trees behind them through the woods, creating avenues of swept dust as clear as virgin snow. "Then in the morning," he said, "we could see where the VC had come out of their holes, and how they got back. You could see where they crawled, then where they stood up and ran. One thing led to another and we found the openings." These early tunnel finds would lead to more substantial success later in the three-week operation.

Other units, too, were finding tunnels. After the occupation of Ben Suc, 1st Infantry Division engineers began flattening the nearby jungle with bulldozers. Their commanding officer, Lieutenant Colonel Joseph M. Kiernan (who was to die in a helicopter crash in June 1967) recalled at the time: "I guess it was about twenty acres of scrub jungle. . . . The place was so infested with tunnels that as my dozers would knock over the stumps of trees, the VC would pop out from behind the dozers. We captured about . . . six or eight VC one morning. They just popped out of the tunnels and we picked them up."

Other Big Red One battalions were helicopter-lifted into the Thanh Dien forest north of Ben Suc. The Thanh Dien was known as a Viet Cong rest-and-resupply area, but most of the guerrillas had wisely melted away and there was little resistance. Indeed, some troops reported seeing "an unknown number of Viet Cong escaping to the south on bicycles." Tunnels, bunkers, and rice caches were uncovered, and a significant find was made by the 1st Battalion, 28th Infantry. After coming under fire from a Viet Cong unit that killed four GIs and wounded four, Company B of the battalion came across a huge underground medical complex, containing over a ton of medicine, much of it bought in Saigon. The defenders had held off the "Black Lions" until all the wounded guerrillas could be evacuated. The fighters had in fact been a scratch squad of pharmacists commanded by a doctor, Vo Hoang Le. They, too, melted back into the jungle. Dr Le was later decorated for that episode, and given charge of all the Viet Cong medical facilities in the Cu Chi and Iron Triangle areas.

Meanwhile, the tanks of the 11th Armored Cavalry had begun crashing right across the Iron Triangle from Ben Cat to the Saigon River. There was hardly any enemy contact. First, the tracked vehicles turned right and plowed northward through the tangled thickets to join up with the airlanded infantrymen in the ghost town of Ben Suc. Then the tanks turned back southward and battered their way to the far point of the Triangle at the junction of the two rivers. So, in theory at least, the Triangle had been overrun and conquered. Engineers and infantry swept along behind, making sporadic contact with those few Viet Cong local guerrillas who had been ordered to remain there. But an uncomfortable fact was by now becoming clear to the American commanders. Most of the unprecedented array of military might and technology might as well have stayed in its bases. It was not to be needed in battle, for the Viet Cong chose not to fight. Although all the Vietnamese people who were killed were counted as VC, and hundreds of others took the sensible course of "rallying," or seeming to defect to the government side, the larger Communist units that normally frequented the Cedar Falls operational area just vanished away; we now know how.

The experience of the 173rd Airborne was typical, as described in its after-action report:

> The enemy encountered was at no time larger than squad size and normally consisted of two- to three-man elements. Initially, the enemy encountered were primarily small work parties of about three-man size who were living along the tree-lined canals with the probable mission of harvesting as much rice as possible from the surrounding rice paddies.... Few weapons were cap-

> tured, and where possible the enemy fled without prolonged fire fight. Contact seldom lasted more than two to five minutes.

It had been the same pattern in Operation Crimp the year before.

There was one exception. The Tropic Lightning Division's second brigade was airlifted from Cu Chi base up to the western bank of the Saigon River at the village of Phu Hoa Dong. This was the first time that the army had operated outside its bases on both sides of the river simultaneously. Hitherto, Viet Cong units had easily evaded search by crossing from Cu Chi district into the Iron Triangle and vice versa. Despite repeated preliminary air strikes and artillery barrages, a trapped battalion of Viet Cong in Phu Hoa Dong decided to put up some resistance. As the 25th's after-action report said: "This was the only incident during the entire operation in which the Viet Cong elected to fight."

The army came closest to the real objective of Cedar Falls on 18 January, ten days after the operation began. Tunnel rats from the 1st/5th Infantry—the "Bobcats"—under Captain Bill Pelfrey discovered an extensive tunnel complex beside the Rach Son stream, which flows into the Saigon River from the middle of Cu Chi district. The tunnels were beneath the narrow strip of open land between the Fil Hol plantation to the south and the Ho Bo woods. Thousands of documents were discovered, which were taken away in sacks by helicopter. The rats spent four days exploring the winding galleries of the system.

For the 196th, the haul was impressive. In addition to the sacks of documents, there was a typewriter, furniture, women's clothing (including brassieres and *ao dais*, traditional costume), Viet Cong flags, and other indications that the tunnels were part of a headquarters. The half million documents, once translated, yielded information that led Lieutenant General Jonathan Seaman to call the find "the biggest intelligence breakthrough of the war." Among other discoveries there was some "crypto-material"—coded messages that could help unlock other intelligence intercepts. There were detailed maps of the Saigon area and Tan Son Nhut air base, including the plans for an unsuccessful Viet Cong attack that had taken place a month earlier. Brigadier General Richard Knowles hurried to the scene of the discovery. He remembered that the document "showed how they moved squads down from Cambodia into the Cu Chi area, and then down to Tan Son Nhut. It showed where they stayed in the tunnels during the daylight, and where they collected their weapons. They had the parking places of all our aircraft laid out in detail. Even the symbols for the aircraft looked like the real things. Everything was numbered in logical sequence: when each gun was to fire, how many mortar rounds, how many rockets—a classic! In addition to that we found a map with considerable detail, showing where they'd planned to ambush and kill Secretary of Defense Robert McNamara in the middle of Saigon." (The plot, in mid 1966, had been frustrated by a change in the target's schedule; the intended assassin, Nguyen Van Troi, was arrested and executed.) In the same pile of documents were lists of addresses of prominent Americans in Saigon, including General Westmoreland. Bill Pelfrey, who led the exploration, said: "The biggest part was tax receipts dating back twenty years. There were lists of their sympathizers—who needed political training, or punishment or whatever. They had American technical manuals translated into Vietnamese." This was the haul that provided a list of Viet Cong sympathizers including all the barbers working at Cu Chi base.

Because the find was regarded as such a major coup, General Westmoreland himself was helicoptered into the area to talk with the tunnel rats, accompanied by other VIPs, reporters, and television crews—even though there were still booby traps in the tunnels, and some VC hiding in recesses in the system. The tunnel rats pursued them, but gave up after crawling over a thousand yards. The senior NCO on the team, Sergeant James Lindsay, was killed underground by an explosive booby trap. Once Pelfrey decided that no more of the system was worth exploring, it was filled with CS gas, then blasted with explosives.

No official conclusion was reached as to what the tunnel complex the 196th Light Infantry had stumbled across actually was. Because of the volume of documents discovered, General Bernard Rogers believed that "this discovery probably uncovered the headquarters of Military Region IV, or at least a significant part of it." In fact, Cedar Falls missed that target, and the political headquarters of the Viet Cong for the Saigon area as well; they were both slightly farther north in the Ho Bo woods. The area of the tunnel that had been found and destroyed is today clearly marked on maps and records at the Ho Chi Minh City military headquarters. It was the Viet Cong's headquarters for the Cu Chi district only. Escape tunnels are shown to have burrowed away from it southward.

For most of the three weeks in which the army stayed in the Cedar Falls operational area, its main task was to make the Iron Triangle unusable as a sanctuary for Viet Cong forces ever again. Two specialized arms of the engineers were entrusted this task: the bulldozer teams and the tunnel rats. No fewer than fifty-eight bulldozers of various kinds were employed in Operation Cedar Falls, including tankdozers and four Rome plow tractors. The tankdozer was an M-48 medium tank, fitted with a bulldozer blade. The armor protected the crew from mines and snipers; infantry would follow along to search and destroy. This 'dozer-infantry team was the leading edge of the ground assault on the Iron Triangle, putting engineers where they were unaccustomed to being—in the vanguard of the army. The Rome plow tractor, nicknamed "hogjaws," was a formidable land-clearing machine: a sixty-ton tracked vehicle, the D7E, was fitted with a specially curved bulldozer blade with a sharp, protruding lower edge of hardened steel that could splinter trees of up to three feet in diameter. The blade was named after its town of manufacture, Rome, Georgia. A "headache bar" over the driver's seat protected him from falling debris, and a heavy-duty protective cab guarded him from attack. Teams of bulldozers stripped great eighty-yard-wide avenues across the length and breadth of the Iron Triangle so that anyone moving about the free strike zone in the future could be seen and shot at from the air.

The engineers of the 1st Infantry Division left their signature on the smoldering countryside. With their bulldozers they carved out huge clearings on the jungle floor in the shape of both the insignia of the division—a giant figure one—and the badge of the engineers, a three-towered castle. In all, eleven square kilometers of jungle were flattened, about a quarter of the Triangle. As one reporter concluded, toward the end of the operation: "If the United States has its way, even a crow flying across the Triangle will have to carry lunch from now on."

By the time of Cedar Falls, the tunnel rats in various units were refining techniques of exploration and destruction. The problem in that operation was that because tunnels were discovered so often, too many untrained and inexperienced men went underground. Consequently, there were mishaps that resulted in "noncombat" deaths. A private in the 4th/503rd Infantry, for example, suffocated to death on 22 January because an earlier grenade explosion had burned up all the oxygen in a tunnel. Several ad hoc tunnel rats lost their bearings and came up to the surface completely lost. On one occasion two separate tunnel teams were exploring the same system independently and only good luck prevented their shooting at each other underground. Cedar Falls had the effect of establishing tunnel-ratting as a skilled specialty, and the rats would be better organized in the future.

When the operation ended, and the troops quit the operational area to return to their bases, their commanders assessed what they had achieved. As usual in Vietnam, the brightest possible picture was painted in the after-action reports. There could be no disputing the scale of destruction. Hundreds of bunkers, tunnels, and "structures" (buildings) were reported destroyed; the area was apparently depopulated. There was an impressive haul of captured Viet Cong matériel: hundreds of weapons and mines, over 7,000 uniforms, and nearly 4,000 tons of rice—enough to feed 13,000 guerrillas for a year. There were the half million pages of documents. The 750 dead Vietnamese were listed as "confirmed enemy," and 280 suspected Viet Cong prisoners were taken. The statistic that gave the army most pride was the 576 "Chieu Hoi ralliers"—supposed VC induced to change sides by psychological warfare techniques. All turned out to be either local guerrillas—not main force—or "combat support elements," in other words ordinary farmers and peasants. Seventy-two Americans had been killed, and 337 wounded; the ARVN casualties were eleven and eight respectively. Lieutenant General Seaman reported at the time: "In nineteen days, II Field Force Vietnam converted the Iron Triangle from a safe haven to a deathtrap, and then to a military desert. Years of work spent tunneling and hoarding supplies were nullified. . . . A strategic enemy base was decisively engaged and destroyed." Unfortunately, this was just wishful thinking.

General Westmoreland reached a more modest and realistic verdict. He called Cedar Falls "very disruptive . . . for the enemy in the Iron Triangle area." The evidence suggests that this was the limit of its success—temporary disruption. At the provincial headquarters of the newly created province of Song Be, which covers what was the Iron Triangle, the authors were shown a hitherto secret Vietnamese army report entitled "Lessons of the War." The U.S. Army claimed 525 tunnels destroyed during Cedar Falls. But Major Nguyen Quot, who was assigned by the commander of Viet Cong Military Region IV to assess the damage, said: "After the operation I inspected the tunnels and did not find any length more than fifty meters that had been discovered or damaged by the Americans. They had destroyed only about a hundred tunnels with explosives, and a lot of civilians' bomb shelters." Every house in Ben Suc, for example, had an underground shelter connected by tunnel to other shelters. Naturally, most of these were collapsed, inflating the statistics of tunnels destroyed. But bombs and mechanized infantry sweeps in the operational area *had* knocked out all of the Viet Cong's medical facilities.

The jungle had supposedly been stripped away, baring the area for future surveillance. General Rogers was enthusiastic about the engineers' ability, with their tankdozers and Rome plows, to "change the face of Vietnam." The clearance of the Iron Triangle, he wrote, was "particularly impressive. However, the discouraging aspect of such operations is that it takes but a short time for the jungle to grow again." So it proved. As with so many other parts of Cedar Falls' program, the defoliation of the area would have to be repeated over again.

Worse still, just two days after Cedar Falls, General Rogers witnessed the failure of one of the operation's main objectives: denying the area to the enemy. "It was not long before there was evidence of the enemy's return. Only two days after the termination of Cedar Falls, I was checking out the Iron Triangle by helicopter and saw many persons who appeared to be Viet Cong riding bicycles or wandering round on foot. . . . During the cease-fire for Tet, 8–12 February, the Iron Triangle was again literally crawling with what appeared to be Viet Cong. They could be seen riding into, out of, and within the Triangle."

Even the depopulation of Ben Suc had failed. Incredibly, Pham Van Chinh and many of his guerrillas remained clinging to the land as they had been ordered. They hid in part of the village's 1,700-meter tunnel system, much of which had survived despite the discovery and destruction of three of its entrances during Cedar Falls. Acetylene gas and water from the river had been pumped into the tunnels, but they were complex and multileveled enough to ensure the safety of those guerrillas who had not fallen victim to the first wave of the assault. "When the people were taken away," said Chinh, "it was difficult for us. The people had been supporting the guerrillas, their sons and brothers. The destruction of the people's houses caused my bitter hatred. The enemy turned the land into a desert. There was not a tree left. But I could still count on over 200 men to fight beside me during the Cedar Falls operation." Chinh's orders were to lie low and wait for the Americans' inevitable departure before repairing the tunnel system. Through Viet Cong couriers, he made contact with the displaced villagers. Although Ben Suc and the rest of the Triangle was henceforth a free strike zone, with bombs and shells regularly falling upon it, and therefore no house could be rebuilt, the villagers began to trickle back to their ancestral land. By the end of the year, over a thousand villagers had drifted back to Ben Suc. As the guerrillas reconstructed the tunnels so necessary for bringing main-force Viet Cong from Cambodia down to the Iron Triangle, Cu Chi, and Saigon itself, so the returning villagers lived in their old bomb shelters or dug new chambers and tunnels, some shared by families. Grass grew on top of these refuges, concealing them from view.

Just four months after Cedar Falls, Sergeant Bill Wilson of the Black Lions battalion led a six-man ambush patrol into the ruins of Ben Suc from the Big Red One's base at Lai Khe. It was night, and the drenching monsoon rain was falling. They took up positions in a ruined house. Suddenly there was a flash of lightning and Wilson saw an entire battalion of the North Vietnamese army marching down the main street of the old village, on their way to the river and Cu Chi. They had handcarts and heavy weapons. The men in Wilson's patrol were so petrified they dared not fire a shot and reveal themselves. They waited till all the NVA had gone, then sheepishly radioed the artillery to fire in the general direction they had taken. Ben Suc had not been denied to the enemy. It was still a key transit point for them. Its guerrillas were still in the tunnels, tunnels that had protected them from the onslaught of Cedar Falls and defeated its aim.

But the most conclusive demonstration of the ineffectiveness of Cedar Falls and search-and-destroy operations like it came almost exactly one year later. The Tet lunar new year festival of 1968 would see a countrywide series of Viet Cong attacks on bases and towns, including Saigon, that threw the Americans off balance and marked the beginning of the end of their involvement in Vietnam. And the most damaging thrust—that against Saigon itself—would come straight from the Iron Triangle.

15

Dr Vo Hoang Le—Tunnel Surgeon

WHILE THE FEARFUL destruction of Operation Cedar Falls devastated the landscape above ground, below in the tunnels Viet Cong surgeons operated against the clock to save Vietnamese lives. One of them became a legend and a national hero. This is his story.

Dr Vo Hoang Le was one of the most remarkable men to emerge from the Vietnam War on the Communist side. From 1967 on he was chief of the medical section of the Viet Cong's Military Region IV, which covered Cu Chi and the Iron Triangle. He ran the makeshift hospitals in underground tunnels that treated the influx of wounded Viet Cong after the most devastating battles, and was himself a front-line surgeon, expertly improvising surgical techniques in the most hostile conditions of war and shortage. He performed brain surgery with a mechanic's drill, and amputations without the use of anesthetics. He was grievously wounded in the chest, and lost half of his right hand. Today, the colonel-doctor heads the military hospital in Ho Chi Minh City. A square-jawed, open-faced man, he talks with animation and candor rare among the higher echelons of Vietnam's Communists. He is a Hero of the Revolution and an admired and respected figure; he can hold a roomful of seasoned Viet Cong veterans spellbound by his experiences.

He was born in the Mekong delta province of Ben Tre in 1933, one of eleven children, of whom four would die in the war. His father was a Viet Minh fighter who was caught and executed by the French authorities. The young Le was first a messenger and then a courier with the Viet Minh. After their success in 1954, Viet Minh in the South—including Le and his brother—"regrouped" to North Vietnam. Their mother was imprisoned by the Diem regime as a former resistance member, was tortured, and died two years after her release in 1962. In North Vietnam, Le was trained as a guerrilla medic. He returned to the South in 1961. He met his wife, also a Communist, in the Iron Triangle, and married her on 3 November 1962, at a ceremony consisting of just a public declaration. Nguyen Thi Tham was from Saigon and had qualified as a pharmacist. They stayed together for one week; then she was reassigned to do espionage and subversion work for the NLF in Saigon. They were reunited in 1963 when the Saigon secret organization was broken up. They had four children in all; two of them were born in the jungle and later killed by shells and bombing.

Le qualified as a doctor without a formal education. In the Viet Cong he became a "physician's assistant," picking up what he could from the surgeons he worked beside. "I learned from doctors, from friends, and from books," he said. "For example, I had a friend who was expert on abdomens, and I went to discuss the subject and practice with him. Our school was everywhere: in the tunnels, in the forests, beside a patient's bed." In the words of Dr Bruce Mazat, medical intelligence officer for the U.S. Army in Saigon in 1969, Le was an "on-the-job-trained doctor." The first injection he ever gave was to a senior officer who was to command all the Viet Cong, General Tran Van Tra. He encouraged Le to continue his training. Le spent more time studying in the North and became a Bac Si, or MD, in 1966. He was assigned to rejoin the medical section of Military Region IV at a recovery hospital in Ben Cat district, just north of the Iron Triangle, code-named C4. He arrived just in time for Operation Cedar Falls.

The tunnel hospitals in which Dr Le worked astonished the Americans whenever they discovered them. Sergeant Bill Wilson was the tunnel rat of Company B, the 2nd/28th Infantry, the

Quakers aiding the V.C.

Black Lions. He used to put a sweatband round his head, take a switchblade stiletto and his company commander's revolver, and go down into the earthy darkness alone. In April 1967 his battalion took part in Operation Lam Son (meaning pacification) '67, a sweep south of Phu Loi and only nine miles north of Saigon itself. At Lai Thieu they found a tunnel entrance. "I struck my flashlight in there and saw a big room about eight feet high, piled with linen. There was a doorway the other side, and there was a long corridor, approximately three hundred yards long, with beds down the side of it, with these rolled-open mattresses. It was a vast underground hospital. At the far end I could see candles burning. There were operating rooms. We found all kinds of medicine: medicine donated by the Quakers in Pennsylvania; most of the supplies and medication were French. There were two operating rooms down there with oxygen tanks." One operating theater was, he noticed, ventilated by an ingenious air hole with a candle positioned at its base. This had the effect of sucking the hot stale air up into the shaft. Seriously wounded Viet Cong were lowered onto the operating table by a primitive elevator, a door-shaped board that was lowered fifteen feet down from the surface to slide the patient onto the table. Wilson noticed canvas bags containing parts of human bodies. In all, he found eight hospital wards underground. It was one of a succession of underground hospitals that the tunnel rats discovered over the years in Vietnam.

Typically, there were two kinds of Viet Cong hospital. One was a forward aid station near the battlefield for emergency treatment, sometimes called a dispensary. It was normally located in a tunnel complex and manned by a semiqualified physician's assistant, nurses, and male aides. The full-scale regimental or district hospital would be back in a safer area, made up of bamboo-walled bunkers with camouflaged palm-leaf roofs, and with connecting tunnels and bomb shelters underground. There a surgeon would operate in a fully equipped theater with an assistant and an anesthetist. The aid station could accommodate about thirty patients, the hospital one hundred or more. As ever, Viet Cong medics stole their enemies' equipment or cannibalized their enemies' products whenever possible. The walls of their underground operating theaters were lined with parachute nylon. Surgical instruments were made with the metal from downed helicopters (tunnel rat Harold

Roper once found an aero-engine in a tunnel, in the process of disassembly). The plastic tube that coated the electric wire that detonated a claymore mine was used for blood transfusions, instead of polythene hoses.

Electric power, a constant problem in the tunnels, was supplied at best by Honda motorcycle engines used as generators, at worst by adapted bicycles. Such luxuries as X-ray machines were found only in the safest rear areas near Cambodia. For operations, surgeons wore gowns but had no rubber gloves. They wore lamps like miners' lamps on their heads. Their instruments were sterilized in pressure cookers. Like their American counterparts, when battle raged above them, they worked to the point of exhaustion to save lives. Vo Hoang Le performed more than eighty operations over three days and nights in the aftermath of Operation Cedar Falls, snatching a few minutes' sleep between each one.

The majority of Viet Cong who were wounded suffered fragment wounds from bombing or long-range artillery, and the majority of those wounded in the chest or abdomen died before receiving treatment. There were three reasons why so many guerrillas died of their wounds. One was the lack of any intravenous fluid on the battlefield, which resulted in deaths from bleeding and shock. The second was the length of time it took to carry a wounded man to the nearest aid station, in a hammock slung between the two ends of a pole borne by two men. Evacuation could take several hours, and this delay was often fatal to the seriously injured. The third was the minimal surgical care available at the tunnel aid station itself. The consoling fact was that nearly all the VC or NVA who did manage to get to hospital then survived.

Even at regimental hospitals there were few proper facilities for blood transfusion. Blood could not be kept without refrigerators, and these were a rarity, usually run on kerosene. Dr Vo Hoang Le invented his own system. "We managed to do blood transfusion," he said, "by returning his own blood to the patient. For example, if a comrade had a belly wound and was bleeding, but his intestines were not punctured, we collected his blood, filtered it, put it in a bottle and returned it to his arteries; at the front we did blood transfusion like that. All our military medical staff had their blood groups checked. And we analyzed the blood of a patient who was brought to us. If I happened to have the same blood group, I gave him my blood."

The Viet Cong's tunnel hospitals did not just cater for the wounded. Malaria was the second largest cause of death and loss of effectiveness, the Viet Cong's chief medical problem after battlefield wounds. (The Americans suffered exactly the same problem.) The commonest strain of the mosquito-borne fever in Vietnam in 1969 was falciparum, which is resistant to the standard antimalarial drugs. Captured documents indicate that nearly half of any Viet Cong unit had malaria at any given time, and half of those would need treatment in the hospital. There they would rave and sweat in delirious agony until the fever abated. The political cadres were urgently instructed to enforce preventive measures, like the use of mosquito nets, antimalarial drugs when available, and insect repellents. Other frequent illnesses among the guerrillas were the inevitable results of their unsanitary existence in sewerlike underground holes: amoebic dysentery, fungal skin infections, such as eczema, and intestinal parasites. "Out of all the people we examined in the prisoner-of-war camps for Viet Cong and NVA," said Dr Bruce Mazat, "where we had the ability to do stool sampling, we found one hundred percent of them had intestinal parasites of significance—hookworm, roundworm, tapeworm, that kind of stuff. These parasites actually suck blood from the intestine, and it's a very common cause of chronic anemia." The Viet Cong Military Region IV's Medical Plan for 1966–67 said: "The crucial area in preventive medicine is in resolving problems regarding water and excrement." The poor food supplies caused vitamin-deficiency diseases such as beriberi. Above all, the cycle of debility was compounded, as Dr Mazat observed, by a general anemia among Vietnamese men—a low red-blood-cell count with a consequent reduced capacity to carry oxygen to the body. This was caused by both the protein-deficient diet and malaria; it also made the onset of malaria more probable and undermined the body's ability to withstand the effects of shrapnel and bullet wounds.

The NLF prided itself on producing its own drugs, many—such as the antidote to the bite of the bamboo viper—based on ancient Oriental formulae and herbal remedies. But in practice the bulk of their medication was bought or stolen from South Vietnamese sources. Antibiotics like penicillin deteriorated quickly when stored in tunnel or jungle caches. The NLF had great public-health responsibilities because of the number of villages and districts in which it was the sole effective authority; a large part of its medical organization was given over to providing clinics for the villagers in the countryside. But the medical section of Military Region IV existed only to serve the guerrillas in the front line. The section was created in 1963. Its area of responsibility covered the whole of Cu Chi and Ben Cat districts and northward into Tay Ninh province as far as Nui Ba Den mountain. Half of its members were female. By 1966 it had two full surgical teams (called C3 and C5), a pharmaceutical platoon (C6), a dental platoon, an administrative staff, and six more or less mobile forward aid-station teams (all called C, plus a number). Both surgical teams were located in Cu Chi district: C5 was at the Cu Chi district military hospital at the hamlet of Ho Bo, less than two kilometers from the Americans' Cu Chi base camp; C3 was at Phu My Hung, next to the Viet Cong military and political headquarters of Colonel Tran Hai Phung and Mai Chi Tho. Every single one of the medical section's vulnerable bases was hit during Operation Cedar Falls in January 1967.

Hospital C3 was damaged beyond repair in the softening-up B-52 bombing raids that preceded Cedar Falls. The chief surgeon was killed and his assistant, Dr Vo Van Chuyen, took charge. Dr Chuyen was a native of Cu Chi who had qualified in Hanoi and returned to the South in 1962. He ordered all the patients and equipment to be moved from Phu My Hung across the Saigon River to the recovery area called C4 in the Tranh Dien forest northwest of Ben Cat. Local people were coopted to carry the wounded in hammocks. The newly qualified Dr Vo Hoang Le had just been assigned to C4; his wife, Nguyen Thi Tham, belonged to pharmaceutical platoon C6, then located a few hundred yards to the south. There was a huge cache of medicines at C6. A new tunnel hospital was quickly established at C4. Dr Le took charge when Dr Chuyen returned to Cu Chi to try to pull together what remained of the medical services there.

On 9 January 1967, the 1st Battalion of the 28th Infantry, part of the Big Red One, was helicoptered into Ben Suc, two kilometers south of C6 and C4. It was the first time the Americans had come into the area, and the Viet Cong knew that a sweep northward through the hitherto untouched sanctuary of the Thanh Dien forest was a probability. Although a doctor, Vo Hoang Le found himself the highest-ranking officer in the two medical units. They were supposedly noncombatant and had few weapons. The pharmacy team numbered seven, including Le's wife; their spider holes would be the first encountered by the Americans advancing northward. They had just four old K-44 Russian rifles, one carbine, and a Thompson submachine gun. Dr Le had his officer's .45 revolver. He called a meeting and discussed the options. C6 was a major medical storehouse and C4 contained sixty wounded patients. But the medics had never fought the Americans, and most of them favored prompt withdrawal. Dr Le had to persuade them otherwise.

"After organizing our fighting positions," he recalled, "I called a meeting of all my staff members and we passed a resolution: The liberation fighters would not surrender. There was no alternative to fighting and dying. We could not let the enemy capture us." Le was in a quandary. Other Viet Cong units had orders to save their lives and fighting capacity by melting away through the tunnels. Le saw his duty as primarily to his patients; naïvely, perhaps, he decided to try to defend them. Each member of the pharmacy squad was given a spider hole from which to snipe at the oncoming Americans. They settled down for the night with foreboding about the next day's battle. Dr Le remembered his feelings. "While packing up the unit's supplies of medicine, my wife and I opened a machine-gun case which contained our personal effects. We found a photograph of our only child, who had been looked after by my family since he had been born. We missed him very much. We had intended to go and see him after the B-52 raids ended; we did not realize the enemy was going to launch a big operation. After looking at our child's picture, my wife said that perhaps we would never see him again. But she comforted herself by saying that some of our comrades might survive the next day's battle, and would tell our son that his parents had fought courageously and sacrificed their lives. He would be proud to have had such parents.

"We chatted while we lay in our hammocks. I said: 'In

tomorrow's battle, perhaps one of us will die. I may be killed, or wounded, or taken prisoner. If you could choose one of these alternatives, which would it be?' My wife thought for a while, then answered: 'I would rather not choose any of these alternatives. But if I had to choose, I would prefer you to die. Our son and I would be very unhappy, but I would take him to visit your grave and tell him the story of your life; we would live with the image of you. I do not want you to be captured, because the enemy would have inhuman means to torture and interrogate you, or would corrupt you. You would not be able to resist; you would give them information and become a traitor. Once you had betrayed our side, the enemy would spare your life. You would be reunited with me and our son, who would have to live all his life with the shame of having a traitor for a father; he would be unhappy and not respect you. As for me, if I had to live with a traitorous husband, I would reluctantly endure it because of our vows, but I would not be happy. I would rather choose your death.'

"So, before the battle, my wife strengthened my determination. At dawn, I went to inspect our positions, then returned to our bunker. My wife broke off a ball of rice, sprinkled some sugar on it, and told me to eat it because once the fighting started there would be no time to eat. I had just taken one bite when I heard footsteps crackling the twigs. I looked up and saw three Americans advancing. They were big, strong, and frightening. I signaled to the others and said, 'The Americans are coming!' To tell the truth, seeing that the Americans were so big, and not having seen them before, I was a little frightened. When they came to within five meters I fired three bullets and all three fell. The others behind them immediately pulled back and responded by firing all kinds of weapons: machine guns, grenade launchers, everything they had. They fired continuously for about fifteen minutes. When they stopped, I raised my head; about five meters away the three Americans were dead. I told my wife and comrades who were in the bunker that it was not difficult to shoot and kill Americans; I told them to come up and see the bodies. My wife noticed there were three guns, and told me to give her covering fire while she was in the open collecting them. She ran out the short distance and came back with three M-16 automatic rifles, plus some ammunition. An American crawled forward and tried to pull away one of the dead Americans by his legs. I shot at him and he lay there."

The after-action report of the 3rd Brigade of the U.S. 1st Infantry Division on that incident on 10 January reads:

> At 1230 hours, Company B of the 1st/28th Infantry located an extensive base camp in the vicinity of map reference 619379, and were engaged by an unknown member of Viet Cong, resulting in four U.S. killed in action and four U.S. wounded in action.

Dr Le's account continued: "Their retreat had been followed by intense bombing and shelling. Our position was showered with napalm bombs and the acrid smell of the burning American bodies invaded our bunkers. Burning napalm trickled down into the tunnel and we had to use sticks of wood to push it aside. Twice they failed to advance to our position, but I reckoned that if we continued fighting we would run out of ammunition and be captured. So I decided to pull back to C4. I suggested that one of us should volunteer to go to C4 to get them to fire at the enemy and create a diversion while we ran up to join them. There was no connecting tunnel; it was open ground. At first there were no volunteers, but finally my wife offered. I was shocked, but since I had asked the others I could not refuse to let her go. I was sure she would be killed. I gave her an M-16, and she said good-bye to us all. I told her to climb out of the bunker and run after I had counted to three. When she went I was surprised not to hear anyone shooting at her.

"Half an hour later I heard C4 start to attack the enemy at their rear, and the pharmacy squad and I left along the only path where they hadn't planted mines. On our way I picked up an American satchel which contained a map. It showed the positions of C6 and C4 with arrows pointing at them. So we knew that the enemy did not encounter us by chance, but had advance intelligence and aimed to wipe us out. I reorganized the defense of the hospital, and gave a weapon to any wounded soldier who could still fight. We repulsed three enemy assaults on C4's position between 2:00 and 4:00 p.m., but by 5:00 p.m. the enemy had occupied C6's position and started pouring down shells and bombs on us; not a single tunnel shelter was left intact.

"That night I raised the question of withdrawing. Some of my comrades were against the idea. They asked: In what direction can we go? How do we know where the enemy troops are? How can we carry all the wounded? I told them that if we stayed, we would not be able to withstand the next day's assault. Even a well-armed battalion would not be able to defend our base against the next attack, never mind a bunch of medics. So we made preparations to go. We left six of the wounded behind in secret tunnels; they had lost legs, or had head wounds and could not walk. Two nurses stayed to look after them. I decided to withdraw northward through the forest. The enemy was shelling it, and some comrades said we would be killed. I agreed that some of us might, but it would be a success if half of us survived, or even two or three of us. If we stayed, the enemy would kill or capture all of us. So we left, with fifty-four wounded soldiers. We went through the shellfire; anyone killed would be left temporarily in a bomb crater, to be buried properly later. Anyone wounded would be bandaged up and helped to continue their journey. In the event, two men were wounded during the journey, but none was killed."

By the time the troops of the Big Red One overran the second of the two medical bases the next day, Dr Le and most of the staff and patients had vanished into the jungle. The pharmacy section had had to abandon a ton of medicine, including 500,000 ampoules of penicillin; there were medical books and journals belonging to Dr Le, and sets of surgical instruments. Major General William Depuy himself, the divisional commander, helicoptered in to inspect the haul. He called it "one ginormous medical depot."

Both of Military Region IV's surgical teams had been put out of action by Cedar Falls. C5 was knocked out by heavy artillery fire. Four of its staff were killed, one surgeon wounded, the rest vanished. All its equipment and medicines were lost when they were discovered by men of the 2nd/22nd Mechanized Infantry, part of the Tropic Lightning Division, at the Ho Bo site on 13 January.

Vo Hoang Le and his party, having left C4, made their way northward through the Thanh Dien forest. "Soon after Bau Tran we ran into advance scouts of our regional military headquarters. We were talking among ourselves as we walked through the shellfire, for there would be no enemy patrols where they were shelling. At about three in the morning we reached the headquarters of Military Region IV. They were happy to see us. We had with us a memento of battle: a shoulder-flash of the Big Red One. I was startled when I realized whom we had been fighting. Hai Thanh, the director of logistics, told me he'd written us off for dead." Colonel Tran Hai Phung, the regional military commander, personally congratulated Le and his wife. Pharmacy unit C6 was awarded a "Killer of Americans" banner, and Le's wife was given the title American-Killer Heroine. Honors were also heaped upon the doctor.

The next day the regional headquarters suffered a B-52 raid. Dr Le said: "My wife was with two comrades in an underground shelter that was hit. After the bombing it took us forty minutes to locate the shelter and dig up the victims. Two were dead. My wife was seriously wounded; blood was oozing from her nose and ears and she had stopped breathing. I gave her the kiss of life. Then I discovered that her left lung was punctured and the pressure had pushed her heart to the right side of her chest. We did not have the equipment to operate on her chest where we were." Nguyen Thi Tham was taken away to be treated for four months at the hospital at COSVN. When she recovered, she was sent back to her native Saigon to take part in secret preparations for the Tet offensive of January 1968. But it was from the effects of the wounds received in that air raid that she was to die in 1982.

Meanwhile, in January 1967, after her evacuation, Dr Le was ordered back to the Cu Chi area to try to reconstitute the remnants of the medical section. He began the process of reorganization. In April he became the overall director of medical services. By May, four months after Cedar Falls (and one month after Operation Manhattan, which also covered the Tranh Dien forest, and in which the empty C6 and C4 were discovered anew by the 2nd/28th Infantry), Dr Le was able to report that all his medical units had returned to their pre-Cedar Falls locations and were functioning again. The surgical hospital C5 was completely reconstructed and restaffed. This achievement highlights two key facts about the Vietnam War: One was the energy and speed with which the Viet Cong rebuilt its often-damaged tunnel installations; the other was the futility of the army's sweeping through an area for a short time, only to allow the Viet Cong to move back in and resume their activities.

Dr Le's official report of this period was captured and translated in October 1967; it was declassified in Washington in 1984. It reveals that Cedar Falls was undoubtedly a complete disaster at the time for Viet Cong tunnel-based support units like his; the medical section was made almost totally inoperative. But the members' response to this appalling setback was positive and constructive. "After the battle and subsequent defeat of the American aggressors of C6," reads the translated report, "the entire Party and Party headquarters realized our new potentiality for self-defense." Henceforth, each of the Cs in the medical section was no longer noncombatant, but was armed with modern weapons and doubled as a guerrilla squad, including the girls. Secondly, Le and the other doctors embarked on a soul-searching program of self-criticism, picking on even the smallest oversights, to lick the shattered medical section back into shape. Surgeons had been too proud of their successes, and had failed to analyze the reasons why some patients had died. Medics had treated the wounded casually or roughly—one, Patton-like, had slapped a wounded soldier. The overstretched air stations were criticized for sending wounded men from one dispensary to another. The pressure on the Communists' medical system is vividly illustrated by this story from the report:

> Comrade Thieu's leg was injured by shell fragments. Blood flowed from his artery, so we tied a tourniquet round his leg and sent him to Cu Chi military hospital [C5] for treatment. They refused to admit him. He was then sent to C3, which was crowded with the wounded from the Cay Trac battle [during Operation Cedar Falls]. He was later evacuated to the public health unit, which did not accept him either. Finally, he was sent back to C5. Due to the length of time prior to his treatment, his leg was amputated. In C3, many medical officers and medics refused to examine his case, in order to avoid facing problems. Comrade Thieu was so angry that he burst out with the following words: "I would rather die than be evacuated from one place to another. I hope that you shoot me and finish off my life." The amputation

of Comrade Thieu's leg was due to the fact that his leg had been constricted by a tourniquet for more than ten hours. His leg should have been amputated at C3, but not at C5. The Military Region Field-Grade Political Officer informed the Medical Section Party Committee Secretary of the incident and ordered him to conduct a criticism session, to draw a lesson for medical units. Comrade Thieu said: "An ordinary doctor in a bourgeois country is better than a Communist doctor, because he has a professional conscience." This was a painful lesson that should constantly remind our party headquarters not to neglect the indoctrination of our medical cadre.

Vo Hoang Le returned to the Thanh Dien forest, just north of the Iron Triangle. It was April 1967, and the Americans were just launching their follow-up operation, Manhattan, into some of the places already devastated by Cedar Falls. Defending a hospital area against advancing American armor, Le was hit in the right hand by a sniper's bullet. "My little finger was attached to the rest of my hand by just a little strip of skin. I was bleeding a lot, so I tore the finger off. We always carried some bandaging, so I bandaged myself up. But I went on bleeding. I took the rubber thong from my sandal and made a tourniquet. As soon as I could, I left the area of fighting and was operated on by a comrade at a hospital. My hand was unusable, so I started to write with my left hand; now I can write with both. I had to learn to hold a scalpel, forceps, or needle with my left hand. After a year of practice I returned to surgery, operating on the brain or the abdomen, using my left hand."

Le's attitude to his work was realistic and pragmatic. He knew that the conditions were so poor that many of his patients would die. For example, a wounded Viet Cong could easily become infected with gangrene. "Gangrene can spread two or three centimeters in an hour; left alone it is fatal. We had to amputate arms and legs, even when we were out of general or local anesthetics; otherwise the patients would have died. If the patient could not endure the pain, he might die of shock, but we had to take that 50/50 chance: if we amputated, he had a 50 percent chance of survival; if we didn't, he was certain to die. When we had it, we would use fifty cubic centimeters of Novocaine for amputation; normally you'd need a liter to deaden the nerve ends. But in fact, the operation was practically like sawing raw flesh. The patient would faint with pain, and we'd revive him later. When we succeeded it was not just thanks to our techniques, but to the patients' spirit, their will and determination to live for revenge.

"When the enemy attacked the Dat Thit plantation, our surgery team was working behind the Quyet Thang regiment [of regional VC troops]. We were operating on a soldier wounded in the stomach when the enemy tanks arrived. We took off our gowns, put the patient in a hammock, grabbed our equipment and ran. We made it to the next village, where the guerrillas held off the tanks with mines. We halted to continue the operation in the hammock. The instruments were filthy by this time, so we sterilized them by burning alcohol. We sewed up the punctures in his intestines and stitched up his abdomen with nylon threads taken from enemy parachutes. The wounded soldier survived.

"We were short of instruments for brain surgery. I bought a drill that mechanics use for drilling steel, with 10 mm to 12 mm bits, and used it to trepan the skulls of wounded soldiers. I once operated on the skull of the second-in-command of the Thai My village platoon in Cu Chi district. He was wounded by a mortar fragment that penetrated three centimeters into his head. I thought at first it was a simple wound and let another doctor operate on him. But when the fragment was taken out, the doctor realized it had cut through the vein that runs from front to back inside the skull, known as the sagittal sinus. Once perforated it bleeds a lot, and if the bleeding isn't stopped, the patient will die in five to ten minutes. The blood spurted out and could not be stopped. You cannot stop a hemorrhage inside the skull with a plug, as you can a flesh wound. If you want to pinch or sew a vein inside the skull, you have to open the skull. When my colleague could not stop the bleeding, he sent for me. When I arrived I stuck my little finger inside the wound to staunch the bleeding, then used a gouge—pliers for cutting bone—to gnaw away at the bone on both sides and expose the vein to tie it up. We had to operate quickly. The enemy were all around us, and we had to finish by four in the morning to move the patient to a safe hiding place.

"The vein turned out to be broken and it was impossible to

pinch it closed. Left as it was, the patient would have died. I thought of a new idea. I twisted a long piece of gauze into a plug and soaked it in Thrombin Roussel, a solution that stops hemorrhage, and pressed it onto the vein temporarily to stop the bleeding. Then we carried the patient away and hid him. We put up his hammock in the middle of an open field and concealed him with grass; we hid in the tunnels. The enemy attacked the area that morning. That evening I operated on him a second time. In the end I could not find any way of tying up the vein. I changed the plug, again soaking it in Thrombin Roussel to stop the bleeding temporarily. Then we took the patient to the tunnel hospital C5 at Ho Bo to be cared for there. I suggested that he be taken to the big hospital in the COSVN area, where a specialist could see him, but there was so much enemy activity in the Ho Bo area that it was impossible to move him. Twenty days later I went back to C5 and was surprised to learn that the patient was leaving the hospital. I had left instructions for the plug to be changed after fifteen days, and the procedure to be repeated if the bleeding restarted. I was told that when the plug was removed the vein had not bled, the patient was well and was returning to his unit. I asked Dr Trong Quang Trung, who had been my teacher, whether such a treatment had been done before. He said it had never happened, it was a new technique—one which Dr Hoi Nam, an army doctor and friend of mine, used to save many people.

"After the Tet offensive of 1968, we had surgical teams who followed the units that had mounted attacks inside Saigon. We were in Hoc Mon, on the northern outskirts of Saigon, and many kilometers from the nearest tunnel aid station or hospital. The enemy counterattacked and sent their troops scouring the area. How were we to treat the wounded? We could not stay among the people in the villages. We were forced to operate at night in the middle of flooded fields. We tied a small sampan to four posts to prevent it from rocking, and put a plank over it for an operating table. To work, I stood up to my waist in water. The enemy's helicopters passed overhead, shining searchlights. If we had worn white gowns they would have been conspicuous and we would have been shot at. For camouflage we built a frame over the sampan and covered it with marsh vegetation. I operated by the light of a small electric torch, with the reflector covered, leaving only a small pinpoint of light. The nurse who held the torch had to follow the surgeon's scalpel and the movement of his hands. In the daytime, the wounded were hidden in specially made concrete shelters, semisubmerged in the waterlogged fields. The medical teams hid wherever they could, in bushes and bamboo clumps. If we could, we moved the patients at night by boat, but when the enemy cut off our routes along the Hoc Mon canal and the Saigon River, we were forced to leave the wounded in the care of the local people. Our nurses hid drugs in boats, and traveled by water to treat the wounded in their hiding places."

In July 1969, in the Thai Thanh woods, Le, accompanied by two guerrilla bodyguards, was ambushed by an American patrol. The bodyguards fired back, but a hand grenade fell in front of Dr Le. "I saw a flash of light in front of me and heard the explosion. I fell, and felt pains all over my body. I was bleeding, did not know where the wounds were, but had to get away from the scene of the ambush. I ran on, but felt blood escaping from a wound in my chest, air blowing through it when I breathed. I realized my lung was punctured and used one hand to stop the air entering through the wound. I kept running, but was soon exhausted and could run no farther. I asked my companions to bandage the wound with the piece of nylon sheet we used to shelter from the monsoon rain. I simply could not walk, so they made a hammock and slung it from a pole they made from the branch of a tree. But it became impossible for them to move through the forest carrying the hammock. I told them to support me and help me walk; every few meters we stopped, for me to catch my breath. Finally, we reached an old hospital tunnel complex that we had abandoned when the 11th Armored Cavalry had overrun the area. There was no one there. I asked my companions if they had a needle for stitching up clothes and told them to sew up my wound. They thought I would die of the pain, for there was no anesthetic, but I assured them I would die if they *didn't* stitch it up; so they did.

"The wound has healed, but the scar is somewhat irregular; it wasn't stitched according to strict surgical methods. I survived, but became increasingly breathless because blood was filling my wounded lung. I had a needle and syringe with me, and told one of my companions to plunge the needle into my chest to extract the blood—regardless of the unsterile needle.

He took out some of the blood, and I could breathe better. We repeated this procedure every time I felt breathless. We stayed in the tunnel for some days. We sterilized the needle and syringe by boiling it in an old American C-ration tin. I had an ampoule of the antibiotic streptomycin, and in the evenings told them to carry me outside and inject me with it. I also had a pot of honey, which I applied to the wound. After fifteen days, my wound healed." Honey was known by generations of Vietnamese to be an antiseptic; as it acidifies, it kills bacteria. It was typical of the practical folk medicine that necessity drove Dr Le and his colleagues to employ, and it saved his life.

The atmosphere of a Viet Cong tunnel hospital during the war, like the bloodstained surgery of one of Nelson's ships, was nightmarish. Even the efficient and sterile operating rooms of U.S. bases like Cu Chi had their share of horrors and agony, of terribly mutilated bodies and shattered young lives. For the Viet Cong, there were multiple privations: not only the lack of medicines and equipment, but chiefly the need to work in holes in the ground to avoid bombing and artillery. Vo Hoang Le has what he most admired in his patients, who suffered amputations without anesthetics and bore the pain with fortitude. It is an aggressive spirit. "Military doctors in Vietnam," he said, "are trained to fight, and take command in battle. You should not be surprised that we doctors fought in the war. People have asked me: A doctor's profession is to save life; did not fighting and killing take away your humanity? This is how I see humanity. When enemies come to your country, destroy the countryside and your village, kill your countrymen, your comrades and the defenseless wounded, you have to kill them and defend your compatriots; that is true humanity."

16

Psychological Operations

OPERATION CEDAR FALLS netted 576 Chieu Hoi ralliers, or defectors from the Viet Cong. The Chieu Hoi reception center for Binh Duong province (which covered Ben Cat and the Iron Triangle) took in more of these men during Cedar Falls than in the whole of the previous year, and almost half were former guerrillas. Their defection was the product of American PSYOPS—psychological operations—which were an increasingly potent weapon against the Viet Cong in the tunnels, and were a constant factor in their lives. PSYOPS were a success in Vietnam, undermining morale among the Communist guerrillas and troops. Revealingly, one of the first demands of the North Vietnamese at the Paris peace talks, which began in 1968, was that the United States end their leaflet drops and cease all psychological operations in Vietnam. It was an acknowledgment of the sophistication that PSYOPS had reached.

Even Captain Nguyen Thanh Linh, who steadfastly endured the horrors and privations of five years in Cu Chi's tunnels, singled out helicopter-borne loudspeakers as a serious threat. He recalled: "The most common form of psychological warfare was to threaten us—with B-52s, with tanks and modern weapons. But against us Vietnamese, who have been fighting invaders for centuries, such threats were ineffective. But we had our weakness: We missed our wives and families. We fought the French and the Americans for twenty years. I was away from my wife for five years; I had never seen my second child. We missed the gentleness of life. Sometimes we were hungry for six or seven months. Four men would share a tin of rice soup; we'd look for plants in bomb craters to boil. Then at night when we came out of the tunnels, American loudspeakers would broadcast children's voices, crying in our language: 'Mummy cannot sleep, she loves you and cries for you!' Or an actress's voice would say: 'Dear husband, why are you away so long? Your mother is crying her eyes out.' Sometimes they even knew our names, and sometimes said our wives had taken other men. It went on all night. Can you imagine it, for a soldier in a tunnel away from his family for years at a time? It certainly had a psychological effect on the fighters' spirits."

Captain Phan Van On belonged to the regional guerrilla force in Cu Chi; he too was separated from his family for years. He lives in Nhuan Duc village, adjacent to the former Cu Chi base. Surprisingly, he admitted with frankness that from time to time in the war, young guerrillas ran away and surrendered to the South Vietnamese. They lacked "a sound point of view"; they did not have enough "strong conviction." The cohesive party discipline had a breaking point, and life in the tunnels, under the bombs and gas, was enough to tax any man's will to go on fighting. For some Vietnamese country boys, especially those press-ganged into the guerrillas' ranks, defection with a guarantee of clemency and financial aid was too hard to resist.

Chieu Hoi means "open arms"; the concept was introduced under President Ngo Dinh Diem on 17 April 1963, at the same time as the strategic hamlet program. As with so many schemes in South Vietnam, the program was not conceived by the Vietnamese but suggested to the Saigon government by American and British advisers, like Sir Robert Thompson. Those induced to defect were called Hoi Chanh—in English, ralliers or returnees. In the event, hardly any important Communists defected during the war. But thousands of rank-and-file guerrillas decided—as a Big Red One report put it—"they would rather switch than fight." What were the PSYOPS techniques used to effect this apparent change of heart?

"Never in the history of the United States have we practiced a more extensive use of psychological warfare tactics than in Vietnam," boasted Captain Andris Endrijonas, PYSOPS officer of the 25th Infantry Division at Cu Chi base in July 1968. "Last month we dropped approximately 22 million leaflets over the division's area of operations, and ninety-eight hours of loudspeaker broadcasts were logged." It was the art of aerial loudspeaker broadcasts that was to be perfected as the war went on. Speakers of up to 1,000 watts' power were mounted on observation helicopters or gunships, to play specially recorded Vietnamese tapes over areas where the Viet Cong were thought to be hiding. It was found that broadcasting conditions were better at night; night broadcasts also harassed any Viet Cong (or anyone else) who wanted to sleep. Captain Lee Robinson from Fort Pierce, Florida, another PSYOPS officer, served as G-5—PSYOPS and civil affairs officer—of the 1st Infantry Division. Interviewed at Lai Khe base during the war, he described his work: "One of the best themes we've found is the 'family appeal broadcast.' This is basically a nostalgic theme that will make our audience think of home and the family they may have left behind. We also use a harassment theme called the Wandering Soul. This is a recording of eerie sounds intended to represent the souls of enemy dead who have not found peace. The enemy is supposedly very superstitious about being buried in an unmarked grave, with his soul not able to rest with his body because he was not buried properly. Superstition goes a long way—it's conscious but also subconscious. The enemy realizes these sounds are coming from a tape recorder on a chopper, but that still doesn't help to suppress the fear they evidently have of their souls some day wailing and moaning."

There were other even more cunning uses of loudspeakers than Operation Wandering Soul. If a Viet Cong was induced to desert and become a Hoi Chanh, his defection was exploited for propaganda purposes as early as possible. He was made to record a taped message to his former comrades, to talk them out of their tunnel hideouts. This procedure was streamlined still further with the invention of the Early Word system by Big Red One officers. This eliminated the need for the Hoi Chanh to tape-record a message. Instead he could be told to coax his former comrades to join him in real time straight after his reception by American or South Vietnamese troops—even in the heat of battle. If the Hoi Chanh could point to the general vicinity where he thought the Viet Cong or North Vietnamese soldiers might be located, he was handed a PRC-25 field radio set and told to ask his former friends, by name, to surrender. The ground transmission was picked up by a receiver in the loudspeaker helicopter hovering overhead and broadcast live to the enemy below. The system was automatic and required only a pilot in the helicopter.

Whenever an area or village was swept by American or South Vietnamese troops, all the men between fifteen and forty-five were taken into custody and sent to the provincial headquarters of the national police for interrogation. Of the hundreds of detainees, invariably some were found to be Viet Cong suspects, and others draft-dodgers or deserters from the ARVN. Any thought to be high-ranking Viet Cong were sent on to the Combined Military Interrogation Center. The rest usually went to Chieu Hoi centers, before being inducted into the South Vietnamese armed forces. Whatever their former existence had actually been, their numbers swelled and probably distorted the Chieu Hoi statistics, which for most of the war averaged over 20,000 a year. At Chieu Hoi centers, conditions were reasonably comfortable and the regime easygoing; this special treatment was designed to win defectors' cooperation. There were about forty such centers in all South Vietnam, and the Hoi Chanhs spent about eight weeks being "reeducated." Afterward, if possible, they were sent back to their home villages, often in NLF territory, to talk round their families and friends. But most were drafted into the ARVN; others joined the South Vietnamese armed propaganda teams touring the countryside, or volunteered to become scouts for the American army.

American infantry platoons came increasingly to depend upon Hoi Chanh Kit Carson scouts, named after the hero of the Old West who guided the U.S. Cavalry through hostile Indian country. These Vietnamese scouts could instinctively assess dangerous situations that young, green, and annually rotated GIs would have stumbled into and discovered the hard way. They had local knowledge, spoke the language, and were intimately familiar with Viet Cong methods. They could communicate with prisoners, villagers, and the ARVN troops. Trained as soldiers, and properly fed and looked after, they added to the strength of American rifle platoons, depleted by soldiers going sick, being wounded, or taking rest and recreation.

The tunnel rats were particular beneficiaries of the Chieu Hoi program. Rat teams always included Kit Carson scouts, who had often worked in the tunnels in their Viet Cong days. They knew the probable layout of any tunnel system and the likely location of booby traps. They undertook the task of coaxing cornered VC or NVA out. They were full-time and served continuously. As a result, any one of them soon acquired more experience of tunnel warfare from the *American* side than the members of the teams they assisted, where the personnel changed constantly with the annual rotation system. But they were never completely trusted.

An official American report, *Sharpening the Combat Edge*, acknowledged that Kit Carson scouts were under-used, owing to "a certain subconscious uneasiness at having Communist defectors in front-line units." The ARVN regarded them with suspicion and contempt. "All ralliers are untrustworthy and a waste of time," said one ARVN officer to his American opposite number, Colonel Stuart Herrington. After all, in following the Communists and then defecting to the South Vietnamese government, a Hoi Chanh had been a traitor twice. Or possibly more than twice. American military analyst "Cincinattus" wrote in his book *Self Destruction:*

> Cynics believed—with some evidence for their position supplied by VC defectors—that insurgents surrendered whenever they had been in the jungle long enough to warrant a time of rest and recuperation. Since the VC had no facilities of their own, they simply rallied to the GVN under the terms of the Chieu Hoi program, got out of the fighting long enough to eat good food and rebuild their endurance. When they had restored themselves, they once more disappeared into the jungle fronds to rejoin their own comrades. There were indications that with decent and circumspect intervals, some VC changed sides as many as five times.

Even so, the existence of hundreds of defectors was a constant worry to the National Liberation Front, and contributed to its gradual disintegration.

At Trung Lap village in Cu Chi district lives former Viet Cong commander Pham Van Nhanh. Now in his late forties, with six children, he has a shock of upright black hair, gold teeth, and, oddly and distinctively, two thumbs on his left hand. During the war, he and a squad of fellow guerrillas were hiding in a tunnel near Trung Lap that was betrayed to the South Vietnamese special branch by a Chieu Hoi defector called Bay, a former member of his own unit. (In fact, most of the special police were Hoi Chanhs.) Bay's special skill was locating and dismantling the Viet Cong mines and booby traps, some of which he had formerly made and set himself. He was able to lead the police squad straight to Pham Van Nhanh's trapdoor and disarm the mines around it.

Why had former guerrilla Bay defected and betrayed his former comrades? "He surrendered because he could not endure the fierce bombing, shelling, and toxic chemicals anymore," said Pham Van Nhanh. "He could no longer bear the hardship and danger. Once he had defected from the fight against the Americans, he tried to perform difficult tasks like mine-disposal to redeem his past." What happened to Bay? He vanished after the Communist victory in 1975; he probably got out of the country. Pham Van Nhanh grudgingly admitted that the Chieu Hoi ralliers were a formidable problem for the Viet Cong and were the Americans' strongest card. They knew where to lead the troops and where the mines and traps were; they set up cruel conflicts of loyalty among their families and other villagers who succored the guerrillas. And Hoi Chanhs were central to the intelligence campaign called the Phoenix program that aimed to identify Communist cadres.

After the fall of Saigon in 1975, the Communists were able to seize all the records of the Chieu Hoi program intact. They forced all those identified as genuine defectors to return to their original units to be dealt with by their former comrades. Their fate can be imagined.

17

Fighting Science

EVEN BEFORE THE ground war in Vietnam had begun to settle down into one of grinding attrition—a strategy that is proof of a lack of strategy—the Americans had already begun to rely heavily on their overwhelming superiority in weapons technology. It was, after all, the most shattering high-technology weapon of all that had abruptly ended World War II in Japan. There remained in the American collective military consciousness a strong awareness of the advantages that could be reaped from the use of the most advanced weapons.

But in the guerrilla war in Vietnam this dependence produced serious difficulties. If the enemy could not fight that kind of war, but was unsporting enough to resort to primitive tactics, then the crutch of high-tech weapons might prove extremely unsupportive. This is what happened in the tunnels war.

At first, the Americans were somewhat bemused at the idea of finding themselves in conflict with a bunch of little guys living in holes in the ground. A MACV instructional manual, "Hole Huntin'," took a patronizing and jocular view of this kind of combat: "Find, fix, and finish" was the sum of the author's suggested tactics for dealing with the Viet Cong in the tunnels. It represented the early and simplistic attitude that technological inferiority, poverty, and stupidity somehow went together inside the black tunnels.

It was a view held by the commander in chief himself. Senator William Fulbright, then chairman of the Senate Foreign Relations Committee, recalled that President Johnson "believed that with the primitive society the Vietnamese had, they couldn't possibly prevail against the United States with its unlimited power."

There was also a prevailing view among senior commanders that because Vietnam was not a full-fledged war but rather an extended police action, it was not necessary to endure the usual hardships of war. Unlike the conflict in Korea, which had sometimes been unbearably difficult for the United Nations forces, the war in Vietnam was made easier and more comfortable for the troops by the deliberate will of the senior commanders. For every grunt who hunkered down in a grubby bunker in some remote and dangerous firebase out in the jungle, another four or five slept snugly between sheets, often in air-conditioned rooms, in the relative security of a huge base.

As we have already shown, the tunnel rat was one of a handful of outstanding exceptions to the overlong ranks of those who chose, or had chosen for them, a reasonably easy rotation in Vietnam. With his knife, handgun, and flashlight, the rat looked and behaved like a warrior. His consuming interest in physical fitness, mental alertness, and the mechanics of his humble fighting tools made him more of a professional soldier—a samurai—than the typical overequipped and overfed GI of the 1960s.

There is little evidence to show that unit commanders fully understood the long-term significance of the tunnels of Cu Chi, or precisely how to deal with them. Consequently, the comfortable reliance upon technological solutions—ones without too risky a human investment—never lost its appeal. Vietnam became the laboratory and testing ground for many new weapons systems. Some worked well; others were laughably ineffective. Even if their intention was to make the GIs' lives safer, many turned out to be incompatible with the extraordinary war that was being fought underground.

Sometimes it seemed as if the only winners from this cornucopia of new weaponry were the eager young scientists back home, from whom the financial leash had been slipped. Research and development funds cascaded through the government laboratories and the offices of the major industrial contractors, eager for a piece of the war action. Out of this flood were washed weapons and equipment, some useful, some just nasty, some more than a little cranky.

There were 1,000-pound parcel bombs that opened in the air, spewing out hundreds of lethal little antipersonnel bombs (some disguised as oranges, which exploded when picked up). Mobile radar units could spot infiltrators at a thousand yards. There was the "daisy cutter," a 15,000-pound monster bomb, which would blow a hole 300 feet in diameter on a hilltop, to create an instant fire support base. There was the dreadful "earthquake bomb," the CBU-55, which sucked all air from its huge explosion area. There was "spooky," a propeller-driven plane carrying enough flares to floodlight an area with a mile radius at night, while firing 6,000 rounds a minute. Whatever new military problem might be troubling the high-technology-conscious general, some scientist somewhere would come up with the answer, regardless of cost.

If the scientists thought they could seal the South from the North (and for a while they did), then detecting and destroying the tunnels of Cu Chi should surely have proved to be a minor operation. So they embarked on projects that would have made Heath Robinson and Rube Goldberg pale with jealousy. Firstly, the scientists reasoned, since it was difficult to find a man underground, the thing to do was wait until he surfaced and then find and destroy him. So they came up with the People Sniffer—officially, the Olfractronic Personnel Detector. This heliborne contraption was used in the "detection of humans by acquisition and sensing of natural human exudates and effluvia, either vaporous or particulate." In other words, it smelled people through the ammonia and methane gas they or their excrement and urine gave off. The General Electric Company was awarded the Pentagon contract, which was initially designated the XM2 Concealed Personnel Detector—Aircraft Mounted. Strapped to a helicopter, the People Sniffer was flown over areas where tunnel dwellers were likely to come up for air. It was not a complete triumph. It broke down a lot and was unable to distinguish between the good guys and the bad guys. As most above-ground VC gatherings tended to disperse hastily on hearing any helicopter at all, it was difficult to find and attack the enemy. Because the People Sniffer got excited about any bad air, the Viet Cong began laying false trails for it, including—rather unsportingly—rigging up bags of buffalo urine along the likely path of Sniffer helicopter patrols. The urine fetched retaliatory air strikes like flies. General Westmoreland's closest military adviser, Major General William Depuy, had the last word: "They were never very successful. The fact we don't have them today may be sufficient evidence that they weren't."

Another advanced device in the war against the tunnels was ADSID—the Air Delivered Seismic Intruder Device. The Communists called it the Tropical Tree. This was a small device, three feet high and six inches broad, which looked like a bomb. When it was dropped from a plane, it buried itself in the ground and threw up a four-foot antenna, which was camouflaged like jungle foliage. It transmitted seismic intelligence—footsteps, truck rumblings, and so on—and had a battery life of about one month. The coded transmissions were relayed through aircraft in the area to the signals reception base. The local commander, on hearing activity in a suspected area, could then order an artillery or air strike against the Communists who had strayed noisily above ground.

Captain Linh said that both the Tropical Tree and an earlier American personnel detector *had* caused problems for the men in the tunnels. "The Americans took advantage of our weaknesses," he said. "We often gathered together outside the tunnels to sing; it was a characteristic of the revolutionaries. We did not have salary, only high spirit. We thought we would be safe at night, but it was not so." At first the Americans used a primitive Mark One version, claimed Captain Linh, a boxlike radio transmitter dropped by red-and-blue parachutes. But it had a short battery life and was easy to spot and destroy. The Tropical Tree, however, because of its camouflage and long battery life, was a problem at first. On one rice-collecting mission, one of Linh's tunnel squad, having picked up the rice, loitered by a surface well to wash and lark around a bit in the fresh air. Within minutes, he came under heavy and accurate artillery fire. The man escaped, but the area was devastated. "I couldn't understand why this had happened, and I left the place alone for several weeks after that," said Linh.

The next time the Viet Cong returned to that spot, Linh personally led his men, creeping slowly through the jungle, quietly clearing new paths. The mission was a success. It was dusk, and once again it seemed perfectly safe to relax for an hour or so. The men boiled some water for tea and talked loudly and laughed while they drank. Almost at once an American spotter plane flew over, followed within minutes by an airborne attack. Linh and his squad raced to the nearest tunnel entrance; he was last in, and within moments, a bomb fell on the tunnel above his head. Linh lost consciousness, but because the bomb failed to penetrate, he didn't lose his life. When he was revived, he took his men through the tunnels to a spot about one kilometer away and they watched the air strike continue for several hours. When it was over, they went back to inspect the damage and found their first cluster of Tropical Trees—old ones uprooted in the bombing strike, and mostly inactivated because of it.

Linh took the devices back to Phu My Hung, where they were examined to see how they worked. The Viet Cong figured out that if the Tropical Trees could be quietly approached, and the four or five sprouting aerials tied together, this rendered the transmitter ineffective. This is how they were eventually neutralized—but only if the bombwatchers, who also looked out for unexploded ordnance, were sufficiently adroit to spot where the ADSIDs fell.

The Americans did play one tactical trump card in this game. As described by tunnel rat Lieutenant David Sullivan: "It worked rather well. We pretended to 'lose' PRC-25 radios from helicopters as they were taking off with a dust-off or whatever. VC trail-watchers inevitably saw them falling out. In fact, these radios were deliberately thrown out and they had specially bugged antennae. Often the VC would take the bugged radios back to the tunnels—and this led to several tunnel discoveries."

But this was the height of technical sophistication compared with some of the other gadgets—gizmos, as the Americans called them—that came from the crowded test-benches of laboratories in the United States. Project Bedbug, sponsored by the Limited War Laboratory (LWL) in Maryland, only just failed to take off. This involved the tactical use of bedbugs (or "man-seeking anthropods," as LWL called them) to warn infantrymen of approaching VC guerrillas. William Beecher of the *New York Times*, who visited LWL, described the project as follows: Since bedbugs "let out a yowl of excitement when they sense the presence of food, specifically including human flesh, the lab created a bedbug carrier fitted with a sound amplification device. . . . when a bug-bearing patrol approached an enemy ambush, the members of the patrol would be forewarned by the happy cries of the animals upon sensing a meal up ahead." The project collapsed when it was discovered that the bedbugs couldn't control their excitement. They became so deliriously happy at just being carried about by GIs that they were too busy "swooning with delight" to warn their patrons of any approaching Communist ambush.

By 1967, there were so many tunnels in the Cu Chi area that any thorough search was bound to find new entrances. Lieutenant Jerry Sinn, who led one of the two tunnel rat squads in the Big Red One, calculated that during Cedar Falls the Rome plows were turning up thirty to forty tunnel entrances in every square kilometer of the Iron Triangle. But this did not deter the scientists back in Maryland from inventing something brand-new. They now came up with the Tunnel Cache Detector—the Portable Differential Magnetometer. During tests in the United States it seemed to work well. It was rather like a metal detector and allegedly spotted the soil characteristics where tunnels had been dug. The sensor then gave an aural warning to the operator. Theoretically, all you had to do was carry the pack around, set it up, stick the sensor in the ground, wait for a reading—and bingo. At least that was the intention.

However, the more the tunnel rats began to understand tunnels, the less they needed equipment. Nevertheless, the Portable Differential Magnetometer (PDM) arrived in Cu Chi for evaluation, weighing 106 pounds. It was brought by NETT, the LWL New Equipment Training Team, comprising two NCOs from Maryland and one representative of the manufacturer. Training started in the old VC tunnels on Cu Chi base, and all the trainees said they understood how to work the PDM after twelve hours. Next came operational training. Some problems developed. The weight and physical awkwardness of the PDM made it extremely difficult to get through undergrowth. One operator who tried carrying it in typically heavy vegetation became exhausted and collapsed and was left behind by his own men.

In other combat tests the unfortunate operators found it took so long for the cumbersome machine to be set up, tested, and then operated that the supporting infantry squad, whose job it was to provide security for the operator, simply moved on and out, reluctant as ever to loiter in VC-controlled territory. Once left alone without infantry cover, the operator tended to end the test prematurely and run after his bodyguards. As testing continued, the use of PDM decreased so dramatically that it averaged less than one operation per unit per week. In the whole of its evaluation trials, the PDM discovered precisely one tunnel—just ten feet long, and abandoned. And it found this only because the unit had originally spotted, with their eyes, a nearby important tunnel complex. It was during this operation that the operator encountered many false signals on his PDM from fragments of metal embedded in the soil (as they were all over Vietnam). The many canals, ditches, and rice paddy fields in the Cu Chi area further restricted the size and shape of any attempted search pattern. Five of the eight PDMs broke down, and the crucial sensor heads and rotating joints "continually became loose." Unit commanders and tunnel rats pointed out that most tunnels really *were* spotted by the old-fashioned eyeball, and the LWL team went home. The PDM never was deployed in Vietnam.

Undeterred, the scientists back home next came up with the Seismic Tunnel Detector (ACB-35/68M)(U). Here was yet another method, this time using the sonar principle of sound detection, to do electronically what the tunnel rats were doing with their eyes and by touch. The STD made even the PDM look like a diviner's twig. It needed two operators to cart it around, one to handle the probes that were stuck into the ground, and one to act as mulepack for the heavy electronic gear that went with it. Once again, initial training began at the 25th's Tunnels, Mines, and Booby-Traps School, inside Cu Chi base. Once again, it was taken out on a combat evaluation.

The evaluators, flown in from Washington, discovered that in dry soil it took one full hour to poke around just one fifty-square-foot area. Time and again the coupling between the gizmo and the ground either failed or took so long that the infantry unit accompanying the evaluators prudently took to their heels, rather than wait as sitting targets for tunnel snipers. Left on their own, the two-man crew had "difficulty" in rushing through the jungle, given the size and weight of the—so far—useless machine. The Seismic Tunnel Detector never made it back to Vietnam either.

Tunnel detection was to remain an overrated problem while tunnel destruction was consistently underrated. It is ironical that in the one field in which high technology really *was* needed in order to secure tactical military victory in the tunnels war, it was never seriously applied. There was little scientific investigation of the tunnels structure or comprehension of the vital role of the interlevel trapdoors, which acted as efficiently as the conning-tower hatch does for the submarine. There was a reluctance by units to stay on the ground overnight, unless on a major military operation like Cedar Falls, in order to complete the work of tunnel destruction. And ultimately there was a misunderstanding at the highest command level of the true role of the tunnels of Cu Chi. All these factors allowed the Communists to keep their tunnels virtually intact for a long time.

Lieutenant Colonel James Bushong, the chemical officer with the 25th Infantry, admitted that they never discovered any effective way to destroy the tunnels or even deny their use to the Communists. He still does not know how he would do the job today, without using banned chemical weapons. Brigadier General Richard Knowles, who agreed that the importance of the Cu Chi tunnels system was underestimated, felt the nature of the war itself precluded the kind of planning that would have led to their destruction. He was the commander of the 196th Light Infantry Brigade, and he directed and fought a highly mobile war, much of it using the ubiquitous helicopter. "One of the problems with exploring these tunnels was the fact that you'd park all this sophisticated equipment and leave a highly exciting and fast-moving situation to go into a dark tunnel that was quiet and took a lot of time and patience and was very tedious, and that's just not in the American character, to take to that sort of thing naturally. Commanders like to do the things that are exciting, that the men like, and you get recognition. You couldn't get reporters to go down those holes, and it just wasn't of interest to most Americans.

"After Cedar Falls I was fully aware of the tunnels, but certainly not of the significance of the VC and NVA effort in South Vietnam. . . . I'd like to feel that we appreciated the full significance of the tunnels at that time, although the technology wasn't available [for their destruction] . . . I'm convinced we could have done it. But we didn't have the patience, the time; there appeared to be too many other things that were lucrative that drew us away."

Because of the relative proximity of the Saigon River to many of the tunnel systems, flooding was thought to be an easy and convenient method of tunnel destruction. In fact, it turned out to be an expensive, time-consuming failure. On 3 December 1967, the 1st Battalion, 277th Infantry, was assigned the task of destroying a large complex that had been uncovered eleven days earlier. Flooding was the chosen method, after water sources relatively close to the main tunnel entrance had been located. Firstly, a bulldozer had to clear a path through the jungle from the tunnel mouth to the water source. Because of a shortage of flexible hose it became necessary to lengthen the canal, which was being used as the water source. That being done, a ditch had to be constructed, again with the bulldozer, from the tunnel entrance to the end of the (still short) flexible hose. At the water source end, because of the sheer toughness of the soil, the extra ditch had to be blown out, using bangalore torpedoes (five-foot-long torpedo-shaped explosive charges). Two hundred and fifty meters of ditch had to be blown out this way.

Next, two large water pumps and a further 3,000 feet of flexible hose had to be flown in by helicopter from the Cu Chi base. As the installation of the pumps and the hose presented further problems, the 1st Platoon, A Company, of the 65th Engineering Battalion had to be flown in to help. By now, the area was beginning to resemble the foundation-laying of the Boulder Dam. The bulldozer was used to lay the extra hose along the ditch it had previously cut. Finally, the pumping began, and for the next thirty-eight hours, 800 gallons of water were pumped every minute into this one single tunnel complex. However, the pumping completely failed to destroy it—the water just drained away. So in desperation, cratering charges were floated in and detonated. Even then, only some of the tunnel was destroyed.

Captain Herbert Thornton found flooding tunnels a complete waste of time. "Even if we'd diverted the entire Saigon River or a complete rice paddy into the tunnels, it wouldn't have worked," he explained. "The problem was the clay laterite absorbed the water in the dry season. In the wet season it didn't matter, because those trapdoors held fast anyway." Colonel Thomas Ware, a former battalion commander in the 25th, also found flooding was useless. "It maybe inconvenienced them for a while, but the tight locks worked. Charlie always came back."

The militarily romantic but technically inept gesture of hurling grenades into tunnels in the belief that they somehow made them collapse was also primarily an exercise in naïveté. But the system was frequently used by non–tunnel rats who had no wish to be involved in tunnel exploration, or by soldiers in a hurry to move on and out. Grenades made a lot of noise and dust and were effective killing instruments at close quarters, but trying to destroy tunnels with them was like scooping out a river with a teaspoon. Cratering charges, C4 charges, and Shape explosive charges were also commonly used. Tunnel "denial" was often assumed after these explosions, but there was insufficient postexplosive investigation to establish the true extent of the damage.

Sergeant Bill Wilson, the tunnel rat in the 1st Infantry, used to examine tunnels after they'd been "destroyed" by explosives. "They were putting crates of the stuff down there and setting it off—it didn't do anything. All it did was put cracks in the walls, made a hole here or there, but it didn't do anything to the major structure of it." Tunnel rat Bernard Justen has kept the photographs of the "damage" done by 40-pound cratering charges. They show walls that failed to collapse, because the laterite clay had set so hard, it was like concrete. In fact, many tunnel rats originally were convinced that concrete had been used in tunnel construction, whereas it was merely the rock-hard clay. Gilbert Lindsay, the Japanese-American rat with the 25th, said that the use of grenades simply "shuffled the dirt." A little more scientifically, his squad tried a mixture of explosives, digging holes and planting many explosives, sawing through wooden support beams with chainsaws, and carefully "imploding" strategic tunnel sections. (They would then retire at night because it was unsafe to stay on the site.) To their dismay, from the relative safety of their nearby Fire Support Base, they could hear the Viet Cong reconstructing the tunnels.

"They were very ingenious little people. They don't say no."

Brigadier General Ellis W. Williamson, commander of the 173rd Airborne during Operation Crimp, expressed his feelings about the impossibility of tunnel destruction in a vulgar but succinct way: "It's almost like trying to fertilize a forty-acre field with a fart, or fill the Grand Canyon with a pitchfork. You just work and work and work, and blow up and blast and work more, and the tunnel system's still there. They were so vast and so deep, and there were so many of them, it became a physical impracticality." The general was still angry about this failure. The reason for it was not only technological failure by the Americans (who, after all, used more bombs in Vietnam than were used throughout all of World War II), but also the fact that the tunnels were an ingrained part of Vietnamese culture, a fabric that they were able to draw round their bodies like clothing. It is a metaphor with which Ho Chi Minh would not have disagreed.

Not surprisingly, indeed on cue, to counteract the growing despair about tunnel destruction, the scientists began to return to the center of the stage. This time they'd come up with the ultimate bang—a new liquid explosive for destroying tunnels. On 5 October 1968, a Big Red One tunnel rat squad under Lieutenant Earl H. Culp was flown to a 300-meter "test" tunnel, one that had been uncovered a year earlier and abandoned by the VC. The rats, long since inured to the eccentricities of the enthusiastic young scientists, were ordered to cooperate. They flew in at eleven in the morning and by one-thirty had charted the tunnel and set standby explosive charges of C4 in a smaller tunnel, adjacent to the main one. They'd been told the scientists with the new liquid explosive would be on site by three-thirty. But by dusk no one had turned up. In some annoyance at having their time wasted in this way, the rats spent the night at a nearby 11th Armored Cavalry night defense position, returning to the tunnel the next morning. Eventually the men from the Concept team USARV (United States Army in Vietnam) turned up, together with the new invention. The rats graciously allowed them to do the work. By eleven-fifteen the system was set up and the liquid explosive was pumped into the tunnel entrance. After exactly two minutes, the hose became twisted and pumping had to stop. Subsequently, the hose repeatedly snarled and fouled. The rats sat by, smoking, sunbathing, or snoozing. Increasingly nervous, unaccustomed to the midday heat, and dubious about their equipment, the Concept team decided to call it a day and blow whatever explosive had already been pumped into the tunnel. Unfortunately, when they tried this, the booster charge went off but the main charge failed. The Concept team now gently asked the rat squad for a little help. Could they explore the tunnel and find out—in the cause of science—what had now gone wrong? The rats pointed out that the tunnel was polluted by the booster charge. There was a long wait until gas masks were flown in. A check of the system showed that the hose and the firing wires had become hopelessly entangled inside the tunnel. It took the rats an hour to untangle the twists and repair the hose, and that being accomplished, the Concept team, now somewhat revived and emboldened, decided to go for another test shot. The rats were unhappy about this but were overruled. When the Concept team detonated the test shot, the entire tunnel system exploded, injuring three members of the tunnel rat squad. A fistfight between the rats and the scientists was narrowly averted. The rat squad, carrying their injured, were airlifted back to Lai Khe. The Concept team went back to their offices, and the revolutionary new liquid explosive was withdrawn.

The use of gas to destroy or pollute tunnel sections achieved some degree of success. The most popular was acetylene. "Mighty mite" commercial air blowers pumped the highly volatile gas into the tunnel system from the generators that manufactured it, after attempts had been made to seal all possible tunnel exits and ventilation holes. Then one or two pounds of ordinary explosive would be placed near the tunnel entrance and detonated, causing—with luck—a chain explosion through the tunnel. But there were limitations. The trapdoor seals prevented the gas from spreading very far, gas did "bleed" out of the tunnels, blow-backs sometimes destroyed the generators, and skilled and trained soldiers had to be used to operate the system. Moreover, one double generator provided sufficient gas to destroy only fifty meters of tunnel, at a depth of five to seven feet. In early comparative tunnel-destruction tests by the newly arrived 25th at Cu Chi, explosives were at first thought to be superior. The amount of equipment necessary to destroy just one 500-meter tunnel is instructive:

10 double generators
300 pounds of calcium carbide (which produces acetylene gas when mixed with water)
50 gallons of water, weighing 400 pounds
9 forty-pound cratering charges
4 boxes of military dynamite
665 pounds of explosives

All this was needed for only 500 meters of tunnel, yet there were 150 *miles* of them to be located and destroyed if the Americans were to win the war in the tunnels.

Needless to say, it did not take long for the scientists to get back in on the act. They figured that the problem lay with the size of the generators and mighty mite air blowers; in their minds bigger would be better. After due deliberation, they recommended field trials for three new gasoline-driven air blowers, now grandly renamed Tunnel Flushers. They were the Model K Buffalo Turbine, the Mars Generator, and the Resojet.

The supposedly portable Buffalo Turbine weighed, incredibly, 800 pounds. The Mars weighed 175 pounds, but used six gallons of gasoline every thirty minutes. The Resojet needed two strong soldiers to cart it around and it also had an insatiable thirst, drinking two and a half gallons of gasoline every fifteen minutes. It could not be refueled during operation. The tunnel rats watched the combat field tests with growing amusement. The sight of 800-pound tunnel flushers being manhandled through rice paddies, swamps, and jungle, in temperatures of 100 degrees with saturation humidity created only sympathetic headshaking among the handful of professionals who watched from the sidelines.

The word soon got out, and the grunts found themselves suddenly unwell when it came to handling the grotesquely overweight Buffalo Turbine. Flying it around on helicopters and then humping it onto APCs or jeeps to try to get it near tunnel entrances became so impractical that the turbine was quietly abandoned.

The Resojet fared little better. Smaller, lighter, it was nevertheless ill-adapted to the jungle. When a squad from the South Korean contingent tried it out at an accessible tunnel entrance in a deserted village, it wouldn't start in the heavy rain. The

Mars Generator did at least make first base, but it was suddenly discovered that the products of combustion were blown into the tunnel at a temperature of 1000 degrees Fahrenheit. "This is considered to be unsafe if friendly personnel are in the tunnel," noted an army report dryly. The tunnel rats thought so, too, and pledged to stay well away from it. Although the Mars received a qualified "go" for Vietnam, it was the little "mighty mite" that endured.

In the end it was human—not scientific—ingenuity that proved most effective against the tunnels. The best way of dealing with them was almost certainly worked out by a young marine lieutenant colonel who discovered a few tunnels in his sector near Chu Lai, near the DMZ. Lieutenant Colonel Oliver was a battalion commander with Task Force Oregon, a division-sized force then under the command of Major General Richard Knowles, who told Oliver's story ruefully, and with an acute sense of hindsight.

Colonel Oliver had been chasing a Viet Cong company near Quang Nhai without any success. The company was locally drawn and was causing havoc. Oliver's battalion had spent fruitless weeks hunting the elusive Communists, embarrassed that a company-sized force was able to play cat-and-mouse with a full U.S. battalion. Early one morning, during an extensive sweep, his men found a series of bunkers and tunnels. Oliver concluded, correctly, that this was probably the base for the VC company. There were no tunnel rats with the battalion, nor was anyone with tunnel warfare experience available. Most battalion commanders would probably have called for an artillery or air strike, tossed a few grenades into the holes, and reported the VC company destroyed. Colonel Oliver was not that sort of marine. He embarked on a crash program to teach his men how to identify hidden bunkers, ventilation shafts, tunnel entrances. He instructed his officers to teach the men how to probe for tunnels, using bayonets where appropriate, or metal rods. He carefully mapped the location. He could have turned for help to the scientists, but he ignored them.

Only after the training had been done did he approach his commanding general and ask for permission to conduct the operation. Knowles agreed. The plan was simplicity itself. The entire area would be seized and held for as long as it took. Perimeter security would be established and maintained, come what may. Then the *entire battalion* would cover the ground, inch by inch, like policemen searching for a murder weapon in the undergrowth—only the GIs would be probing and eyeballing for tunnels. In this arduous, time-consuming, and dangerous way, they found all the tunnels. The operation was a complete and unique success. General Knowles claims that nothing like it had ever happened in South Vietnam. The whole VC company was dug out, and in a series of small firefights and subsequent surrenders, eighty-nine out of a company of ninety-two were killed, wounded, or captured. "We know those figures were right," said Knowles, "because we caught the VC company commander and made him go through his own personnel list, which we checked against the dead and the captured, name by name. It was tremendous. I became very enthusiastic about this technique. General Abrams had just been assigned deputy MACV, and we briefed him on it, and he became enthusiastic."

It was now August 1967. The operation generated considerable paperwork, and Colonel Oliver was asked to help establish a Tunnel School, where these simple and effective tactics could be taught. There was, however, no serious tunnels problem in the northern area, the I Corps Tactical Zone. The news of this tactic evidently failed to filter south to the increasingly frustrated commanders of the 1st and 25th Infantry, continuously fighting to pacify the hostile countryside of the III Corps Tactical Zone and defend Saigon, while also trying to consolidate their own base security. Colonel Oliver's work went unrecognized, and in the Cu Chi district the Viet Cong obstinately remained underground.

Major General Charles M. Duke commanded all U.S. Army engineers in Vietnam; his tour of duty ended in May 1968. In his confidential debriefing report for the Chief of Engineers, he wrote: "Counter-tunnel warfare or doctrine is still in its infancy. A number of devices are under development or testing designed to assist in the detection, exploration, and destruction of tunnel complexes. None of these has so far proven to be completely successful. Efforts in that direction should continue . . . Much remains to be done." The U.S. Army had already been in Vietnam for three whole years.

18

Rat Six and Batman

THE SPECIAL IMPORTANCE of the tunnels was acknowledged by the Americans as their military presence in Vietnam reached its peak—to over half a million men by mid 1968. If some lessons in tunnel warfare remained unlearned, Operation Cedar Falls had at least one noticeable result: the decision not to allow untrained men to explore tunnels. There had been too many "noncombat" deaths underground. After that operation, the commander of the only division with an organized tunnel rat team—the Big Red One—transferred that role from his chemical platoon to the engineers, who were expert in demolition explosives. In June 1967 the Tunnel Rat team was formally created as an offshoot of the intelligence and reconnaissance section of the 1st Engineer Battalion. A lieutenant commanded the team, and he was known as Rat Six, "six" being the division's own codeword for a commander. The 1st Engineer Battalion's commander had the code-name Diehard Six, and the team became known as the Diehard Tunnel Rats.

Rat Six was supported by one or two sergeants. Sergeant Robert Batten was assigned to the rats from the outset and then volunteered for two extra tours of duty, staying in Vietnam for three years. Universally known as Batman, he was the most feared and respected of the tunnel rats. He was from New Jersey, a red-haired man in his mid twenties. It was he, not the officers, who was credited with the elite reputation that the rat squad came to enjoy. During his time, the team could boast a body count of over a hundred enemy dead. Like Captain Herbert Thornton before him, he was on the Viet Cong's "ten most wanted" list, after the well-known generals, and was the only NCO on that list. Interrogated Viet Cong prisoners knew his name.

Batten was prejudiced against blacks and would allow none to be appointed a tunnel rat; so none volunteered. There were many Hispanics, though; one officer called them Napoleon types. Most of the men had months of experience in Vietnam before volunteering for the rat squad, and would serve only a year in total. The officers rotated even more frequently; the average Rat Six served four months. The team was about seven or eight men strong, except for the short period in 1969 when there were two tunnel rat teams. The men received an extra fifty dollars a month as hazardous-duty pay. Each team had its own medic and radio operator, and there were two long-serving Kit Carson scouts, Tiep and Hien. Both were teenagers who had experience in the tunnels when they were with the Viet Cong. They were given a limited amount of trust, but never allowed to "go point," or be first man in the tunnel. The rats wore distinctive jungle-fighters' bush hats to distinguish them from their steel-helmeted comrades-in-arms. They were on fifteen-minute standby at Lai Khe base to be helicoptered out to explore any tunnel discovered in the field by one of the division's battalions. The men were trained to "rapell," or slide down ropes from the helicopters. At night they would normally return to Lai Khe base. Even though many tunnel rat missions were cold—there was no contact with the enemy—they were usually justified by the haul of rice, ammunition, explosives, weapons, and documents that were captured from the Viet Cong.

Their most successful operation was from 9 to 11 August 1968. The 11th Armored Cavalry under Colonel George Patton III (son of the World War II general) and the 5th ARVN Division had sealed off the neighboring villages of Bung Dia, Chanh Long, and Bou Dai—all known to be under Viet Cong control. The tunnel rat team was requested. It arrived, commanded only by its sergeant, Robert Batten, Batman. The tunnels were hot. Five guerrillas were flushed out on the first day at Bung Dia and captured by the ARVN. The next day at Chang Long, seven VC were discovered; three were killed in an underground firefight and the rest captured. Fifteen more surrendered when the rats discovered their hiding places in compartments underneath beds and living quarters, and, in one instance, under a manure pile in a pig pen. On the same operation a day later, Batman and his men probed into a tunnel leading from the village of Bau Dai. An enormous number of Viet Cong, 150 in all, filed one by one into captivity as they backed out of the tunnel. Underground contact had been heavy, and three of the rats were wounded. All of them were awarded the Bronze Star, the Batman his third Purple Heart (for a wound received in action). He was wounded going point but continued forward until he collapsed. The other rats pressed forward, forcing the guerrillas backward out of the complex and into the ARVN's guns.

Lieutenant Jack Flowers was Rat Six from February to August 1969. He was a college dropout from Indiana who had been drafted. He was short, tough, and spiky, with an aggressive crewcut and a prominent, jutting lower jaw. Antiwar by temperament, he became obsessed as a student about others getting killed on his behalf, especially his own father, who was in the Reserves. One of his girl friends was a Danish Communist, and he spent a year in Denmark with her. On his return he was called up. Once in the army, he was sent to Officer Candidate School and, after a few short assignments in the United States, he went to Vietnam as a second lieutenant in the Corps of Engineers. He was assigned as a platoon leader to the 1st Engineer Battalion at Lai Khe. This base, a few miles northeast of Ben Cat, was known as rocket city, after the local Viet Cong's propensity for lobbing rockets into it; at one point in 1967 they averaged over a hundred a day.

Flowers's first tasks were supervising the cutting-down of trees and the clearing of landing zones, and similar duties. A few weeks in, he was bitterly stung to be called a "REMF" by a helicopter pilot he had kept waiting, and who taunted him: "I've got to pick up some guys who've been fighting all day." What was a REMF? Another officer explained: a rear-echelon motherfucker, and Flowers knew it applied to him. That was the (usually welcome) fate of the great majority of Americans who served in Vietnam—to be part of the huge tail of logistics and support units that kept a relatively small number of unfortunate grunts in actual combat. Flowers was planning to become a total REMF, an information officer at divisional headquarters at Di An, when unexpectedly he was invited to volunteer to become Rat Six—in his words, "the worst and most dangerous job in the battalion" for an officer. He suddenly saw the war anew. He remembered seeing a dead grunt being dragged messily out of a tunnel two weeks before and felt a surge of militancy. He was being asked to join the war. No one would ever call him a REMF again. To his own amazement, he accepted.

That night he ate dinner with the battalion S-2, or intelligence officer, a captain. Flowers recalled the very words of the briefing: "You're only going to have one problem, Jack, and that's Batman." "Batman? I thought he was the whole key to the rats." "He is. That's the problem. He knows it, too. If he weren't in the army, he'd probably be in jail someplace. On the surface he's like any other NCO, pretty good-natured, keeps his men straight, respects rank and everything else. But he's mean inside. Nobody in his right mind should love being a tunnel rat, but he does. Your biggest job is going to be to learn everything he knows and yet still be in charge. There's a rule with the rats: There is no rank underground. Don't try to be a hero. They know what has to be done, and Batman is very proud of the fact that none of the rats has ever been killed." "How many have been wounded?" The captain laughed. "I think he's proud of that fact, too. Everybody's been wounded at least once."

The next day Flowers was introduced to the formidable Batman, the man who had voluntarily stayed in Vietnam three times longer than necessary. Flowers remembered their conversation, too: Why had the sergeant stayed in-country for so long? "Because I love getting those gooks out of there. They think they have it made down in those holes. Well, they've got it made like a rat's ass when Batman comes after 'em." Wasn't two years of war enough for anybody? "Not if it's the only one you've got." He looked knowingly at the lieutenant. "We'll get along just fine if you stay out of my way. If you don't, I might be dragging you out feet first. Strange things can happen down there. People have been known to be accidentally shot in the back."

"Fragging" was the murder of officers or NCOs by their soldiers, usually a fragmentation grenade rolled into a hut. If a leader was thought dangerously incompetent, the grunts would sometimes get rid of him, especially after 1969, when the decisions of the newly elected President Nixon to withdraw the American troops sapped their morale. Batman's warning to Flowers was no joke. But for Flowers it was less of a threat than a challenge. Flowers had to accept that he knew nothing about tunnels and would at first be utterly reliant on Batman's unrivaled expertise. But unlike some of his predecessors, this Rat Six wanted to lead his squad underground himself, and never ask an enlisted man to do anything he would not do. In other words, he intended to command the tunnel rats in fact as well as theory, to take over the role that had hitherto been Sergeant Batten's. He decided that Batman could remain the indisputed leader of the squad for the next thirty days only. After that, Flowers would have learned enough to take over.

Flowers's relationship with Batman was at the core of his performance as Rat Six. Batman was a decorated hero and a natural tunnel rat—mean, aggressive, as sharp as his wily opponents, at home in the subterranean theater of war where the slightest error could be fatal and battle was reduced to individual combat. He was a tough character, contemptuous of Flowers's college background and pretensions as a drafted junior officer. In Flowers's view, Batman reveled unhealthily in a necessary but unpleasant job, but was at the same time a hardened warrior whom he could only respect and admire. He needed Batman's approval; it was fear of his sergeant's adverse judgment that made Flowers drive himself to succeed in the unpopular task he had volunteered for.

Then he met the rats. They wore clean, pressed uniforms and well-shined boots. Above their breast pockets they wore the tunnel rat badge with its nonsense Latin motto, "Not worth a rat's ass." Flowers was given one of the badges on the strength of having been in a tunnel once since he had been in Vietnam. For most grunts the Vietnam War was an uncomfortable and indecisive business of counting the days of one's year in-country. Flowers sensed immediately that the rats were different. Volunteers for a hazardous assignment, they were well-motivated professionals with codes and rules of their own, which Flowers would have to honor.

Assiduous training then followed for the young officer. One skill to be learned, in a specially constructed culvert, was hand-to-hand fighting on hands and knees. There were rules about operating in tunnels. You would never fire off more than three shots from your revolver in the darkness; fire off six and an enemy would know you were out of ammunition. When you came out of a tunnel you whistled "Dixie" all the way; American troops on the surface were apt to assume muddy figures emerging from tunnels were hostile, and shoot them. Week by week, Flowers began to chalk up tunnel missions and experience. Most were cold; some were hot, necessitating setting demolition charges and entombing (as the rats assumed) the Viet Cong inside.

By March 1969 the enemy was back in the Iron Triangle, and on the twenty-sixth, the tunnel rats were called out again by Colonel George Patton. North Vietnamese army soldiers had been spotted disappearing into a tunnel complex after a fierce battle beside the Saigon River. One of Patton's tank commanders followed them into the tunnel and was immediately killed by a booby trap. When Flowers and the team arrived, Batman took one man with him into the tunnel. Flowers heard shots and grenade explosions down below, and minutes later Batman appeared at the bottom of the entrance shaft, announcing that the other rat was wounded. They dragged the man, bleeding from shrapnel wounds in his arms and legs, up to the surface. Then Batman's head peered out. "The pricks have got us cold," he reported. "They're sitting on top of a trapdoor." Flowers asked the sergeant what he advised, and Batman said they should go back after the NVA. To Batman's slight surprise, Flowers himself insisted on coming down; Batman, in Flowers's view, had won enough medals already, and it was one of Flowers's men who had been wounded.

Flowers entered the tunnel, and followed Batman to the first sealed trapdoor in the roof. Smoke and fumes hung in the air from the grenade that had wounded the first tunnel rat. Batman cautiously pushed the trapdoor upward, then quickly fired three shots into the blackness. Then he took his lamp and put his head through the hole. "Give me your pistol," he commanded Flowers. Flowers passed it up and started reloading Batman's.

One NVA soldier hiding in the tunnel had retreated; it could turn into a long pursuit. Batman went ahead and soon came across another trapdoor leading downward. Flowers followed a few yards behind, the distance beyond which a grenade explosion would not be lethal. Batman approached the new trapdoor in the same way. He lifted it and started firing. Suddenly an automatic weapon lashed out from underneath. Dirt flew everywhere. Batman fell backward. Flowers assumed that he'd been hit. He crawled up to the sergeant. Batman was unhurt, but dirt had been thrown into his face and gone into his eyes. Flowers crawled up to him and Batman indicated the small twelve-by-twelve-inch opening. "Shoot in there," he said. Flowers fired three shots and reloaded as Batman sat rubbing his eyes, talking to himself, psyching himself up for the continued pursuit. "Those pricks. Here they are, trying to kill me again." He tried to move past Flowers. "You've had your two trapdoors," said the lieutenant. (The rule was that the point man would be changed after two trapdoors, so great was the stress and tension.) Batman looked at him groggily, six inches from his face, and conceded. Flowers edged past Batman, and went down through the trapdoor.

He fired three more shots as he crawled down to the lower level, and three more from Batman's pistol as he approached a curve in the tunnel on his knees, flashlight in one hand, gun in the other. Batman came down behind him. The tunnel straightened out then went another ten yards and stopped at a wall. A little dirt fell from the ceiling at the end, betraying the existence of a rectangular trapdoor to another level up. Flowers held his lamp steadily on the door.

The NVA soldier was evidently lying just over the trapdoor. Batman moved up beside Flowers and made to push upward on it. But Flowers prevented him. Flowers was Rat Six, and the point man; he insisted upon dealing with the situation by himself. Batman crawled back a few yards. Flowers tensed in apprehension; sweat was running into his eyes. He edged up to the wall and sat under the trapdoor about twelve inches above his head. He placed a lamp between his legs, shining upward. Then he put his hand under the door and exerted a small amount of pressure. Batman cocked his pistol; Flowers gripped his. Flowers took a deep breath of the dank air and pushed up on the door. It yielded. He twisted it and set it down crosswise on its beveled frame. Then he paused, planning to slide it away and start firing into the void.

A foot above Flowers's glistening and grimy face, the trapdoor was quietly turned round and slotted back into its frame. Flowers froze; the gook was right there. Suddenly the door moved again. Something dropped into Flowers's lap, right in front of his eyes. He watched it fall, momentarily transfixed; then the danger to his life overwhelmed him as he screamed "Grenade!"

The American M-26 grenade has a steel casing over a coil of pressed steel. The coil is designed to burst into over seven hundred pieces, and the case into chunks of shrapnel. It is fatal at up to five meters. It is detonated when the pin is pulled that releases a handle igniting the fuse. The acid fuse burns for five to seven seconds before the detonator sets off the pound of high explosive.

In his nightmares for years afterward, Jack Flowers saw that grenade falling as a series of still frames in a slowed-up reel of film, dropping jerkily, hypnotically . . .

Flowers did not know how far he had crawled when the explosion ripped through the tunnel. There was a tremendous ringing in his ears and his legs were bleeding, but he was still crawling. Batman too was moving away when Flowers reached him. He shone his lamp on Flowers's torn and bloody fatigues. Flowers was suddenly preoccupied about having dropped his pistol. Batman advised him to forget it and keep moving. Another explosion rocked the tunnel. The NVA soldier was trying to make sure that the tunnel rats were dead, even pursuing them. Flowers blindly scrambled back through the different levels. When at last he saw daylight, and reached for the hands of the men above, he collapsed. When he came round, medics were taking shrapnel out of wounds in his legs. Colonel George Patton III was standing over him.

The exit to the tunnel was under one of Patton's tanks; the NVA had been trapped. But Flowers decided against further pursuit. Tiep, the Hoi Chanh, tried to talk the NVA soldiers out, without success. Charges were set at each tunnel entrance timed to go off simultaneously and cave in the whole structure. Batman, like Flowers, already had a ruptured eardrum from the earlier grenade explosions. As the dust-off helicopter took them off to hospital, the tunnel collapsed; the enemy was smothered to death. Next day Colonel Patton ordered the bodies to be dug up for the body count.

Flowers recalled his thoughts in the hospital bed. "If it had been John Wayne, he would have picked up the grenade, lifted up the trapdoor, and thrown it back at the bastards. If it had been Audie Murphy, he would have thrown his body over the grenade to save Batman's life, and his mother would have received his posthumous Medal of Honor. But since it was Jack Flowers, I started crawling like hell." In fact, both men received the Bronze Star (V) from the division's commanding general. For all his self-preservation instinct, Flowers had been blooded underground. At last he was Batman's equal.

Within a few weeks, early in April, Flowers and the tunnel rats were back in the Iron Triangle, this time training a platoon of ARVN engineers in the science of tunnel exploration and demolition; Vietnamization had begun. The ARVN used TNT to destroy tunnels; it was more bulky and less sophisticated than the C4 plastic explosive used by the Americans. On the second day out, an old but recently renovated tunnel was discovered and Flowers decided it would be an ideal training location for his South Vietnamese counterparts. The TNT charges were lowered into the access shaft and stacked at the tunnel opening. Batman was contemptuous of the ARVN: "These goddam little monkeys will never make tunnel rats."

Flowers descended the access shaft to supervise the demolition; there were notches in the sides for knees and elbows. Tiep, the Kit Carson scout, was supervising the ARVN soldiers carrying the TNT from the stack into the tunnel. Flowers looked up at the circle of sky. An ARVN soldier was looking down, carrying a box of detonating caps that were needed for the charges. At that moment there was a tremendous explosion above ground, and the next thing Flowers saw was a shower of thin silver cylinders falling down on him. He covered his head. He was sitting on fifty pounds of TNT.

Detonating caps can easily explode, and careless soldiers over the years have lost fingers and eyesight from accidents with them. They are never carried in the same pack as explosives. A cap dropped onto concrete will explode, as will a cap squeezed in a vice. And a cap will set off any other explosive material nearby. Flowers was sitting on high explosive with a box of them scattered around him. "Batman!" he screamed.

Then he ordered the terrified Tiep and the ARVN soldiers to retreat down the tunnel and send for a tunnel rat called Morton who was up ahead. Batman appeared at the top. It seemed that the Viet Cong had fired a rocket into an ARVN APC, and there was a firefight going on above ground. But Flowers dared not move. Morton appeared from the tunnel and, wide-eyed, gingerly began to pick up the caps. Batman meanwhile had found the ARVN soldier who had dropped them. It had been a brand-new box of fifty; seven were still in the box. That left forty-three. Morton was carefully picking up as many caps as he could see. Thirty-two. Flowers had still not moved. Then Morton shifted the sticks of TNT that were free of Flowers's weight. He found three more caps; five were unaccounted for. Batman looked down and decided to string a rope round Flowers to pull him up. That way Morton could move the rest of the TNT. A rope was lowered. Slowly Flowers was hoisted clear of the explosive. A cap fell from his lap and Morton quickly picked it up. As Flowers reached a standing position, three more caps were revealed. That just left one. Batman continued pulling Flowers up to the surface. As he neared the top, Batman stopped: "Son of a bitch!" He reached down and Flowers felt his hand on his head. The last of the detonating caps was lodged in Flowers's bush hat.

Flowers was to lose Morton's services. Some weeks later, they were exploring a tunnel system in the "Catcher's Mitt," a VC base area east of Lai Khe shaped like a baseball glove. Morton, going point, reached a trapdoor leading upward and went through it. Then he let out a piercing scream. Denny Morton was from Cleveland, Ohio. He was nineteen years old and had joined the army on his eighteenth birthday. He had volunteered for Vietnam, and for the tunnel rats. He was only five feet four, slender and wiry—the ideal size for a rat. He had already received a Bronze Star and a Purple Heart; now he would receive another.

After the scream, the next thing Flowers heard was three shots, followed by Batman calling him. When Flowers reached the trapdoor, Batman was standing in it. Morton was rolling on the tunnel floor, his hands covering his face. Blood was flowing freely through his fingers. "The son-of-a-bitch knifed him," said Batman. "I think he got it in the eye." Batman was shooting as Flowers began working Morton back down the tunnel. Morton moaned as they hauled him along, a few feet at a time. He was unconscious when they got him out. His face was covered with coagulated blood and dirt. There was a great gash starting at his hairline and running across the bridge of his nose, down through his left cheek. Flowers couldn't tell whether Morton still had his right eye when the dust-off helicopter ferried him away.

Fifteen May 1969 was Sergeant Robert Batten's DEROS—date of estimated return from overseas. He was not allowed to extend, or take another tour. He wanted to carry on killing gooks, but the decision was taken at division level to send him home. He had been wounded four times, and twice was the normal limit. Flowers sat drinking with Batman for some hours a few days before the sergeant left Vietnam. Batman delivered his verdict on the lieutenant. Flowers had been determined to emulate the sergeant's toughness and courage. Batman was not deceived; he made a scornful prediction. "You're not a killer, Six, and that's your problem. You're pretty good, the best Six I ever had, but you'll fuck up somewhere. Charlie hasn't killed a rat for quite a time. And you'll either let him get you, or what's worse, you'll get yourself."

Flowers heard that Batman left the army when his final request to return to Vietnam was turned down; he returned to New Jersey to work on construction sites. The new sergeant was Peter Schultz. He was a good NCO and demolitions man, but solidly built and over six feet tall—the wrong physique for a rat. He was reliant on Flowers's tunnel knowledge. Without Batman, Flowers was exposed; it was as if he had lost his right arm, the ultimate source of tunnel wisdom and know-how. Increased work and responsibility weighed upon Flowers. He led mission after mission, but fatigue began to infect him, and with it, fear. In one tunnel the enemy set off a large mine that completely buried him. It took Sergeant Schultz five minutes to dig him out, unconscious.

The end came in late July 1969. Flowers and the rats were on a mission in the Iron Triangle that discovered a Viet Cong base camp in the course of construction, with woven baskets and long bamboo poles to hoist the earth from the tunnels. The rats explored a succession of holes into which Viet Cong or NVA had run to hide when the 1st/4th Cavalry had arrived in the area. All proved to be cold. At length only one hole remained. And all the soldiers in the tunnel rat squad knew that at least one enemy had to be down there. Flowers realized that every member of the squad had been down a tunnel that day except him. Sergeant Schultz offered to take one of the Kit Carson scouts and explore the last hole. But Flowers knew that as the officer in charge, he had to take the most dangerous job himself. As usual, a grenade was dropped down the shaft first, but all the rats were aware that this was little more than a noisy warning gesture. The Viet Cong had years of experience ducking round corners in tunnels to avoid the very limited range of a grenade.

The hole was about fifteen feet deep and curved away to one side at the bottom. Flowers knew that it was not connected to any of the other holes, so if his theory was right, the Viet Cong had to be down there, waiting for him. He sent for a Swiss seat, a cradle of straps in which he could be lowered into a hole. The two strongest men would pay out the rope to lower Flowers to a point three feet from the bottom, then at a signal suddenly drop him, to surprise the waiting Viet Cong. It could take thirty seconds to get down. Flowers assessed the situation coolly: The only question to be answered was survival at the other end. It would be a confrontation that he had long anticipated. The rest of his squad looked at him grimly. As Flowers went over the side of the hole, the two Kit Carson scouts were almost tearful, the newer tunnel rats appalled by the ordeal. Schultz offered the lieutenant a second pistol. Flowers declined it, but ordered that it be ready loaded to drop down to him. If they heard anything other than his pistol firing, they were to pull him up.

Flowers began his suspended descent. Fear gripped him, the fear that knows no ranks and possesses every young man who faces the reality that his life might be stolen from him in a few, fleeting seconds. As Lieutenant Flowers thought back over his life, the image of Batman kept reappearing to him, saying, "You'll fuck up, you'll fuck up." His feet and elbows rubbed against the sides of the shaft, dislodging clods of earth that would tell the Viet Cong below that he was coming down. Flowers pictured the enemy down there on his knees, leaning against the side of the tunnel with his AK-47 set on full automatic fire. In an aperture about four feet in diameter it would be hard to miss. Twenty rounds would cut through Flowers in four seconds. So Flowers knew that the first shot from his pistol would have to kill the VC. He would aim straight at the VC's face; a shot to the body would not disable him enough to prevent him firing the AK-47. Flowers swung sideways, with his left arm over his chest and his right shoulder hunched to protect his temple, to minimize the wounds he was bound to take. He was three feet from the tunnel floor. He signaled to Schultz to release the rope. The moment had come.

Flowers hit the floor with his pistol firing; the first shot went through the VC's forehead, the second his cheek, the third his throat, the fourth, fifth and sixth pounded into his body. Blood racing to his brain, Flowers kept pulling the trigger, clicking on the empty chambers of his revolver. Schultz heard the firing and instantly hurled the loaded pistol down to his Rat Six. The gun clattered down the shaft.

Cordite smoke lingered in the dank tunnel air.

Flowers stared dumbly in front of him, disbelieving what his mind had created. There was no enemy soldier there, no adversary with a rifle, just a blank wall with six holes neatly grouped in the earth. Six. And the time-honored law of the tunnel rats said no more than three. Sergeant Schultz and the others peered down at their leader. The Rat Six had faced his enemy. Somewhere inside Flowers's head, Batman laughed.

Two days later at Lai Khe the battalion's executive officer relieved Flowers of his tunnel rat command, and told him to go home. "Don't make me tell you what you already know. You're finished. You've fought your war. Stay out of sight for three weeks, then forget all about Vietnam and the tunnel rats."

After they had pulled Flowers out of the hole and had been told there was nobody down there, nothing was said—but they all knew. Flowers's own strict rules would have to be applied to him as ruthlessly as to any other tunnel rat. Sergeant Schultz had gone to the executive officer and told him what had happened: The men's confidence in their leader was shaken; he might be a danger to them. The tunnel rats were sent out on a mission and Flowers was not told about it till they had gone. For the sake of their morale he was quickly shipped out of Lai Khe to Di An, where he was drunk for a week; then to Bien Hoa and home. He had just vanished; there were no farewells, no handovers.

In 1984, in the penthouse restaurant of the Philadelphia

skyscraper where he worked as a stockbroker, Jack Flowers ruminated on the end of his war. "Rat Six was dead. He died in some tunnel in the Iron Triangle. Batman had been right. Charlie didn't get me; I'd gotten myself."

19

Vo Thi Mo—The Girl Guerrilla

SHE HAS A SMALL handsome face with perfect white teeth that miraculously survived the calcium deficiency of the tunnel diet. Her skin is silk-soft, its texture belying her thirty-eight years. The malaria has left a tendency to early fatigue, as if she were aware before others of the rising heat of the day. The other scars remain mercifully invisible beneath her simple blue cotton work suit—the leg wound, the scar on the chest (both the least and the most painful to a woman), and the bullet fragment embedded forever in the top of her right arm, like all shrapnel wounds, an aching reminder of temperature changes. She is a truly reluctant heroine who needs help remembering the names of her medals. She has killed many tunnel rats. Her name is Vo Thi Mo.

In fact, there is nothing new about Vietnamese heroines. They have long occupied a cherished place of honor in the nation's history. Trung Trac led the first major Vietnamese insurrection against the Chinese in 40 A.D., together with her sister, Trung Nhi, and a third titled lady, Phung Thi Chinh, who supposedly gave birth to a baby in the middle of the battle and continued with the infant strapped to her back. When the Chinese counterattacked two years later, the women committed suicide by drowning. Two centuries after that, an even more famous heroine, Trieu Au, a sort of Vietnamese Joan of Arc, also launched a revolt against the Chinese conquerors. Gloriously defeated, she too killed herself at the age of twenty-three, implementing the by now traditional policy of defeat before surrender.

Vo Thi Mo was never forced to make the choice, but at the time she took to the tunnels of Cu Chi to fight the Americans, she was the inheritor of a uniquely Vietnamese feminist tradition, one of advanced emancipation by Asian or European standards. Vietnamese women can inherit land, share their husband's property, take charge of most financial matters relating to business and home, and of course, fight in war.

Even before the Americans came, the National Liberation Front created special women's associations, particularly in the safer Communist-dominated villages and hamlets—including naturally the fiercely nationalistic Cu Chi district. The women helped families whose sons had joined the regional forces. They took care of guerrillas who needed help, organized health education classes, and set up small maternity clinics and medical dispensaries. Others were carefully trained by the district party officials to proselytize uncommitted young men and even the ARVN troops.

One of the people credited with actually beginning the guerrilla war against the Saigon government, on 17 January 1960, was Nguyen Thi Dinh, a peasant woman from Ben Tre province. She was to become deputy commander in chief of the National Liberation Front's armed forces.

The elite members of the women's associations in Cu Chi became a fighting force in 1963. There was nothing very new about young women joining battle, fighting together with the men; what *was* original was a decision to create an exclusively female guerrilla fighting force. By 1965 a special company—C3—had been formed under the command of Tran Thi Gung. Her leadership was praised by her contemporaries as being bold, imaginative, and utterly ruthless. She died of illness in 1973, when a new female company commander, codenamed Trong, was appointed.

An early photograph shows two members of C3 posing rather rakishly in their uniforms—black pajamas, webbing belt, linen hat, and the distinctive black-and-white check scarf slung round the neck and tied with a huge knot. The rest of the equipment was VC standard issue, including Ho Chi Minh sandals and, in the early days, "Red Butt" K-44 carbine rifles.

Within a year of C3's formation, the women scored their first significant combat success by overwhelming the small ARVN guard post at Phu My Hung and killing the commander. The unit was so respected that it was offered, and accepted, training with a detachment of the Viet Cong's F-100 Special Forces group. By the time Vo Thi Mo had become a deputy platoon leader within C3, the women had learned, and applied with considerable enthusiasm, the techniques of small-unit infantry fighting, the use of sidearms and rifles, the application of hand-grenade throwing, the wiring and detonation of mines, and assassination.

Vo Thi Mo was hardly a surprise candidate for officer status in C3. Her father had been a Viet Minh and fought the French with an old World War II rifle, and when that simply fell apart, he fought them with bamboo spears. Resistance against foreigners who occupied their land was endemic in the Mo household; it grew with the maize and the peanuts in their smallholding. She had a sister and nine brothers, of whom the sixth, the eighth, and the ninth all died in the war against the Americans. She was fifteen and still helping with the housework when her home was obliterated by bombs at five in the morning of the first day of Operation Crimp. Her parents had been warned the day before of the impending American assault and had taken the precaution of getting up before dawn and taking themselves and their daughter into the tunnel shelter their home, like nearly every other home in the hamlet, possessed.

"It had been a prosperous area, there were many fruit trees, many cattle; life had not been easy but we had lived well enough by our honest endeavors. When the Americans came, they devastated the area. They bombed and shelled until ten in the morning, and then their troops landed at the Go Lap, An Phu, and Dat Thit plantations."

Reasonably safe inside the tunnel, the fifteen-year-old contemplated the destruction of her home, her family's land, their cows, their ancestral graves, and their way of life. All this was being done by a country of which she knew only one thing: its name. From where she crouched, there were no larger concepts than her own small and insignificant existence; the slow turning of the land's fruitful cycle. Even if she had believed the notion that the defense of the "free world" began here, and in this way, it would not have stopped the tears and the pain. It was no consolation that her father revealed a secret—their tunnel shelter was in fact connected with another tunnel and another, and they could make their way out of this hell, safely and silently, to a place where there was no death. It was no consolation that he told her that there were stores of cooked rice, rice mixed with sugar, and clean water to drink. The fifteen-year-old's pain as her childhood was obliterated ended only when a sharper emotion enveloped her. The hatred of the American soldier that was born in the flames of her burning home grew into her bones. For many months it was a comfort, a pillow to the cheek, a reason to stay alive. Within a year, she would be leading other women—widows, the orphaned, the homeless—in a long and painful battle to regain their heritage. They would be based inside the tunnels of Cu Chi.

Ironically, it took a man to describe some of the hardships the women fighters faced while living in the tunnels. There is a strong sense of modesty among the Vietnamese, shared by both sexes, which runs to the point of prudery by Western standards. However, Major Nguyen Quot, who spent nearly a decade in the Cu Chi tunnels, explained that life inside for women was particularly hard and unpleasant. "Women who had their periods had considerable difficulty in keeping themselves clean. If there were water shortages, and that happened frequently, or if the women had to stay down because of the fighting above, then personal washing problems were very great. Women often sacrificed water for cooking, to wash their clothes, but then of course it was almost impossible to dry them underground, so they would wear damp clothes until body heat dried them. In the early days we did have toilets—the large jars—but as life became more arduous because of the bombing and shelling, the jars became a luxury. There were times of great personal hardship."

Vo Thi Mo found it possible in the early days to go above ground and wash in water-filled bomb craters during the predictable shelling lulls. Fortunately, the heavy field artillery from Cu Chi base and the batteries at Trung Hoa worked to a timetable. In 1966 there were still usable wells, although after a time, these were deliberately polluted by the enemy with bodies of dead animals. There were times when conditions for a woman inside the tunnels were so unpleasant that she considered herself lucky to be able, as a guerrilla, to leave the underground caverns to go up and fight. Sometimes it meant the chance of fresh water from inside the strategic hamlets, or as a treat, some soap, or even a change of clothing.

Vo Thi Mo's first real battle took place at Xom Bung hamlet in the village of Cay Diep. She was already second in command of the village guerrilla platoon and was nominated at a meeting to lead an all-female hamlet guerrilla squad. A reconnaissance-in-force infantry unit from the 25th Infantry Division base at Cu Chi was advancing toward Bu Lap hamlet. They were attacked by her platoon; a helicopter brought reinforcements and, following a short and inconclusive firefight, the Americans withdrew and Vo Thi Mo took her squad into a tunnel to rest while she kept guard above. Within a couple of hours she heard the ominous rumble of tanks, approaching from the Rach Son bridge. They were rolling down Road Number 15, which had already been carefully mined and booby-trapped with iron spikes and punji stakes. Vo Thi Mo brought her girls back up to prepare for the tank battle. It was a textbook guerrilla warfare confrontation. On the one side, a heavily armed M-48 medium tank—the mainstay of U.S. armor in Vietnam—"versus a handful of teenaged guerillas, carrying obsolete Red Butt K-44 carbines and a few hand grenades, fighting from a road mined with homemade explosives and spiked with bamboo traps.

"I saw the tank when it was about 500 meters away," explained Vo Thi Mo, "and I called my squad to their positions. The girls were very nervous and some had never seen such a huge tank, and so near, and coming nearer. The mine that blew it up had been planted by the hero To Van Duc (the man who invented the cane-pressure mine, which brought down helicopters). The tank stopped immediately, and was quite badly damaged. It stopped by a small hut where we had been staying. The enemy fired their guns fiercely while they tried to repair it. They worked on the tank from eleven until four in the afternoon, but they could not repair it. We had been firing our rifles at the Americans, but we hit no one."

The Americans sent a second tank to help the first, and it too hit a mine, which brought it shuddering to a halt. Vo Thi

Mo's squad found themselves fighting both broken-down tanks from trench positions between them. When they ran out of magazines for their rifles, they hurled grenades at both tanks. Slowly, inch by inch, and only by using their massive self-defense machine guns and personal weapons, the Americans managed to repair one tank, inch it toward the other (which was too badly damaged for local repair), and eventually tow it away. It was, like most battles, one that produced no victors or losers, although the Americans might have drawn some early and ominous after-action conclusions from achieving only a standoff in a skirmish between two M-48s and a handful of girl guerrillas and one ten-year-old messenger boy.

The district committee was not enthusiastic about allowing units from the C3 female company to come into close contact or hand-to-hand fighting with the Americans. Curiously, the committee did not object to the women's fighting the ARVN soldiers at close quarters, but generally they were persuaded away from the kind of combat that might lead to capture by the GIs. It was not a golden rule, it was effectively unspoken, but it was almost certainly based on cultural and racial prejudice rather than battle experience. Vo Thi Mo was consequently discouraged from fighting the American tunnel rats when they followed in hot pursuit during a battle. However, from what she saw, she was not always impressed by their performance. "Once after a battle we withdrew into the tunnel, went down into a lower level, moved along a bit and emerged to the upper level again. A tunnel rat was not far behind us. American people were big and could not get through all the trapdoors. This one got through to the lower level but when he came up again, he could not pass through the opening. I was with Uta, an old guerrilla, who is now dead. He was guarding the second trapdoor. When the American tried to pull himself through, he became stuck. The old man stabbed him and he died. We left him there."

In fact, deliberately luring tunnel rats to their deaths inside the holes was an early Viet Cong tactic and often involved a particularly unpleasant way of killing them. Two or three tunnel rats would be encouraged to proceed without hindrance down one level, as Vo Thi Mo has described. Even the Viet Cong could not predict the girth of the lead tunnel rat, but what was inevitable was that he would have considerable difficulty when trying to wriggle up through the narrow trapdoor that led back to ground level. He had to come up head first. There was no choice.

Originally, this one dreadful moment of weakness was exploited by the tunnel defenders by shooting the man as he emerged. But soon they refined a more practical technique. As the unfortunate point man cautiously put his arms and head through the hole, a guerrilla would wait with a sharpened bamboo or even an iron spear, which he would plunge through the GI's throat with tremendous two-handed force. The soldier remained impaled, his body wedged in the trapdoor, a grotesque human cork in a bottle, held in place by the spear resting on both sides of the shaft. The tunnel rats below could neither throw grenades up nor pull their dead point man back down. Their only option was to return the way they had come. Naturally, the Viet Cong had made appropriate plans for their perilous return journey.

Vo Thi Mo recalled the Americans' fury when their comrades died in this way. They would respond by hurling satchel charges or grenades down the tunnels, but of course this did not cause much structural damage. "When they used gas it was more of a problem for us," she explained, "but we started to isolate the gas by keeping specially shaped rubber-tree trunks in the tunnels and then using them as plugs in the narrowest part of the tunnel, to prevent gas passing through. It worked well and sealed the tunnel, but we did run out of rubber trees after the Americans began using Agent Orange to poison our land."

She stayed close to the Cu Chi base in the belt, and with her girls organized the first of the spy rings that riddled the 25th Infantry's base. Next she led sniper attacks on the GIs foolish enough to snatch midday dips in the water-filled bomb craters, just outside the perimeter wire. Using the tunnels dug under the rice fields that flanked the Ben Muong bridge, Vo Thi Mo's girls were able to use spider holes only 500 meters away from the base. The GIs had to learn through bitter experience that swimming-hole trips, even just outside the wire, were potentially fatal.

Late in 1967, Vo Thi Mo was in charge of a twenty-four-woman platoon of guerrillas ordered to combine with a male VC company to attack a large ARVN military post at Thai My, to the west of Cu Chi town. Her platoon was part of the second strike force, which included a male platoon. She was also second in command of that force.

ARVN military posts in the Cu Chi district usually had short and exciting lives. In an area that remained unpacified throughout the war and was the center for Viet Cong activity near Saigon, it was difficult to maintain even a nominal government presence. The ARVN soldiers had long since reached an accommodation with their Communist countrymen to stay out of all tunnel activity—that dangerous chore was left mainly to the Amercians. The South Vietnamese soldiers were poorly paid, they were for the most part draftees who had not been able to bribe their way out of service, and they were often commanded by corrupt officers. With a handful of heroic exceptions, the ARVN was an unreliable fighting force, the more so in Cu Chi, where it was perpetually surrounded by a hostile population. Not surprisingly, the Thai My military post was ringed by no less than eleven fences, four of which were barbed wire. The post had one perimeter guard post standing just inside the extensive wire protection, while several hundred yards from that stood the main ARVN HQ block, where the majority of the defenders had their fighting and sleeping positions. To attack the post successfully required either very heavy munitions, which the guerrillas did not then possess, or the deft use of what explosives they had, together with the commando-style ability to scale those eleven fences.

The plan was for the attackers to make full use of the moonlight, poke DH-10 claymore mines through the wire barriers, and blast a path through the formidable protection and into the guard post as quickly as possible. When the assault began, the main group managed to explode their way through only five fences. Vo Thi Mo's girls had torn through a full nine when the assault ground to a halt. Several of the mines had been kept in the tunnels and had been ruined by damp and failed to detonate. The attack flopped. The entire plan was reset for the following month, to coincide with the best moonlight. And this time, because of her previous success, Vo Thi Mo was promoted to second in command of the primary assault group. It comprised two of her girls and one man. Each carried two DH-10 claymores, properly checked for damp this time. At first everything went successfully. All the mines exploded as planned, the group vaulted over tangled barbed wire, crawled over and under each new obstacle, blasted with explosives where the body couldn't go. Within five minutes they had reached the perimeter guard tower. So far, so good—except that Vo Thi Mo had left her trousers on the barbed wire. She stood somewhat awkwardly, carrying her new AK-47, wearing the black pajama top and briefs. But the fighting had to continue.

The perimeter guard tower put up little resistance, and Vo Thi Mo sent her messenger boy (the same ten-year-old she had used during the tank battle) to return through the wire to ask permission from the VC command outside to take the main post. Because Viet Cong guerrillas were subject to strong and disciplined central control, even in the very heat of battle, the messenger had to run through fire again and again to take action reports *to* the command, and new orders *from* the command back to the front. Vo Thi Mo was cleared to attack the main post and ordered to bring back prisoners if possible. As she fought her way as far as the ARVN HQ, she found two soldiers hiding in an underground shelter. She ordered them to surrender, which they did, and as she reached for the electric wire in her pocket to tie their hands together, she realized she had no trousers and no wire. The ARVN prisoners simply gaped at the unusual battle dress of this extremely attractive seventeen-year-old.

It was at this moment that a rather illogical thought seized her. She became obsessed with tying her prisoners up. Normally, she would have used the black-and-white scarf that she wore, but she had discarded it for this raid because the white squares would show up in the moonlight. The luckless messenger boy was again instructed to pick his way through the narrow path blown through the eleven fences and ask command for a couple of scarves.

But by now, the main ARVN guard post had begun a counterattack. Vo Thi Mo was momentarily frozen with two prisoners. One tried to escape and she shot him on the spot, the other took the force of a hand grenade thrown by one of his own comrades from the tower. Vo Thi Mo looked round and saw that the second strike unit was still having problems reaching the ARVN HQ, too. For several dangerous minutes the Viet Cong attackers were pinned down. Then the boy messenger returned, without the scarf, but with the order to retreat.

She took her badly wounded prisoner back through the wire and returned safely to her own base. The operation, in which several ARVN soldiers were killed—the remainder were subsequently evacuated to Phuco Hiep—was regarded (with little real justification) as an unqualified success.

Shortly after this attack, the Communists began their Tet offensive of 1968. Vo Thi Mo was wounded during Tet and while in the hospital received a personal telegram from Mme Nguyen Thi Binh (who was then a member of the Central Committee of the NLF), announcing the award of the Victory Medal Class Three (the highest class) to the entire female platoon, specifically for its conduct during the two assaults on Thai My.

In the two years that she fought with all-female C3 company, Vo Thi Mo's hatred for the Americans grew. She was once in a tunnel when a direct bomb strike killed a pregnant woman who was within days of delivery, and another who was breastfeeding her child at the time of the strike. "The first time I killed an American, I felt enthusiasm and more hatred. I thought I would like to kill all the Americans to see my country peaceful again. Many people in my village were killed by bombs and shells. In one shelter, over ten of my friends were killed by napalm bombs. You know how napalm burns. When we pulled the bodies out, they had only burned and crooked limbs. These battles kindled my hatred. I did not think of myself, I did not think of the hardship. The Americans considered the Vietnamese animals; they wanted to exterminate us all and destroy everything we had."

It is in the light of this emotion that her last Cu Chi action remains a paradox, unless one can hold to the comforting view that a woman's innate compassion and tenderness may overcome even her blind hatred. In a curious incident that might not have taken place had the protagonist been a man, Vo Thi Mo, the American-killer, ended her military service in Cu Chi.

The action took place at Cay Diep later that year. There had been a series of battles with the Americans at two different locations. The women's platoon was temporarily integrated with a larger mixed Viet Cong company. During the first encounter with the U.S. infantry patrols, the Communists had suffered sufficient casualties to be forced to withdraw to a rear tunnel base. As usual, Vo Thi Mo allowed her platoon to go below for water and rest while she maintained guard at the spider hole. With her was her faithful messenger boy. She had been there only about twenty minutes when two GIs walked straight out of the undergrowth and sat down just ten meters away from her rifle muzzle. A few minutes later they were joined by a third. Vo Thi Mo could hardly believe her good fortune. The men were unprotected, seemed to have sprung from nowhere, had taken not the slightest defensive measure, and were now sitting targets in front of her heavily camouflaged spider hole. It would take just three bullets and the Americans wouldn't even be able to reach for their M-16s, carelessly flung by their knees. She tightened her grip on the AK-47; she was already lying down, spread-eagled. All she had to do now was hold her breath and squeeze the trigger.

The three Americans sat in a small triangle. They took out some letters and photographs and showed the photographs to each other. Vo Thi Mo, consumed with curiosity at this first human action she had ever observed of the enemy, held her fire. The men read the letters to themselves and then to each other. She watched, transfixed. What they were doing was what soldiers everywhere do. Having sentenced them to death, she was inclined to give the victims a few more seconds alone with their thoughts of their loved ones. Her small guerrilla companion looked sideways at her and raised an eyebrow.

The Americans took out some cookies and sweets. They talked to each other, and ate. Then after a while they began to cry. One took his handkerchief and wiped the other's eyes, then his own. Vo Thi Mo remained baffled. Were these three really sadistic killers, pillagers of the land? Or were they unwilling conscripts forced to come to Vietnam, now broken men, missing their loved ones, yearning only to return home? For the first time since she had watched her home destroyed by American bombs, Vo Thi Mo allowed a grain of doubt to enter her mind. What she was a silent witness to was so remarkable and so eloquent that language was not necessary.

At that time, the Front had decreed that anyone who killed three Americans would automatically receive the Military Victory Medal Class One (for six, you earned a Class Two, and for nine Americans killed, you would receive a treasured Class Three—-body counts were not uniquely American). She was a finger squeeze away from the award.

After the three had wept for some time, the GIs tore up the letters and photographs and put the remaining food with them in a small heap in the center of the triangle. The messenger boy, who was also armed with a Red Butt rifle, quietly lifted his weapon in an obvious move. Vo Thi Mo placed her hand on his arm and shook her head. The moment had long since passed. The line between duty and murder had been crossed. She understood that. Whatever she felt, it was something that neither the Front nor her own training could suppress. No amount of hatred could lead her to destroy these three young men, only a little older than she, who cried in secret just like the Vietnamese. When the three got up, she let them walk away.

There was a short party inquest. The messenger boy was ordered to give evidence, but he loved Vo Thi Mo and spoke only for her. The district headquarters political commissar was angry but listened carefully to her explanation. Whatever he may have felt as he heard this seventeen-year-old girl explaining why she had pardoned the three GIs, he suspended judgment, pending an on-the-spot investigation. In all solemnity, a small political team, together with the girl and the little messenger boy, returned to the place outside the spider hole. In the dirt, just as Vo Thi Mo had explained, they found the letters and the torn photographs and the sweets and cookies. They were as baffled as she had been. There was no formal verdict. Suddenly, the Communists started laughing and teasing. In a good-natured way, they jeered: "You have become kind and human to the Americans. The American killer has become the American lover." It was the end of the matter.

There is no logical explanation for this strange behavior by the three Americans. The letters and photographs may have belonged to comrades killed during earlier fights that day, or they may have been from their own families. There is one possible answer. As American infantry losses rose during the war, more and more American troops, when sent out on patrols, sweeps, on search-and-destroy missions, began to develop their own special kind of search-and-avoid tactics. They would leave base, strike off on their own into the jungle, find a secure area, and simply goof off for the time allotted to their mission. Sometimes they established their own perimeter security, and then they would sleep, write letters, smoke, eat their rations, and let the hours pass. They would then pack up and return to base, reporting negative contact with the enemy. Vo Thi Mo's description of their behavior could also suggest that the three soldiers had been smoking marijuana, which was widely used by GIs, even in the field. The symptoms of smoking are excessive emotional reactions, including laughing or crying, and sudden food cravings. Some of the more sophisticated search-and-avoid missions involved taking unregistered previously captured Viet Cong weapons and turning them in as evidence of an engagement with the enemy. If it was indeed such a mission that Vo Thi Mo refused to fire at, then it was, if nothing else, a small victory for natural justice.

Vo Thi Mo stayed with the C3 Women's Company until the end of the war. Just one year earlier she had married an irrigation engineer in a simple party ceremony in a forest near the Cambodian border. After the war she returned to Cu Chi. Miraculously, both her parents had survived. All three went to the site of their ancestral home. There were so many bomb craters, and still are, that it was impossible to reconstruct a house there, and will remain so. Reluctantly, a new family home was taken in Tay Ninh, where Vo Thi Mo's husband now works. They have three sons and one daughter.

20

Tunnel Rat Squad

BY 1969, AS FAR AS THE Big Red One was concerned, tunnel rat strategy had been honed down to a sharp edge. The old days of on-the-job training and the vagaries of combat experience were giving way to organization and professionalism. There was real divisional enthusiasm and support for the tunnel rats of the engineer battalion that had taken over responsibility for the job from the original chemical detachment.

At the Cu Chi base of the 25th Infantry Division, tunnel rats were less organized. They were still drawn from the infantry platoons who could be expected to discover tunnels, or from the 65th Engineer Battalion, who had a broader responsibility for destroying the Viet Cong tunnels. Their approach included the use of Rome plows (used extensively during the Cedar Falls operation) to tear up the earth above tunnel complexes, a tactic that lacked the finesse of the small, mobile, and trained tunnel rat squad. The 25th Infantry's Operation Kole Kole, which ran from May until December of 1967, found 577 tunnels, but the copious after-action reports scarcely mention tunnel rats. Unlike the Big Red One, farther north across the Saigon River at Lai Khe, the 25th Infantry did not give priority to detecting and destroying the tunnels. General Fred

LOCATIONS OF MAJOR VC TUNNELS FOUND IN III CORPS TACTICAL ZONE UP TO JANUARY 1968 (Source: Confidential US Army map)

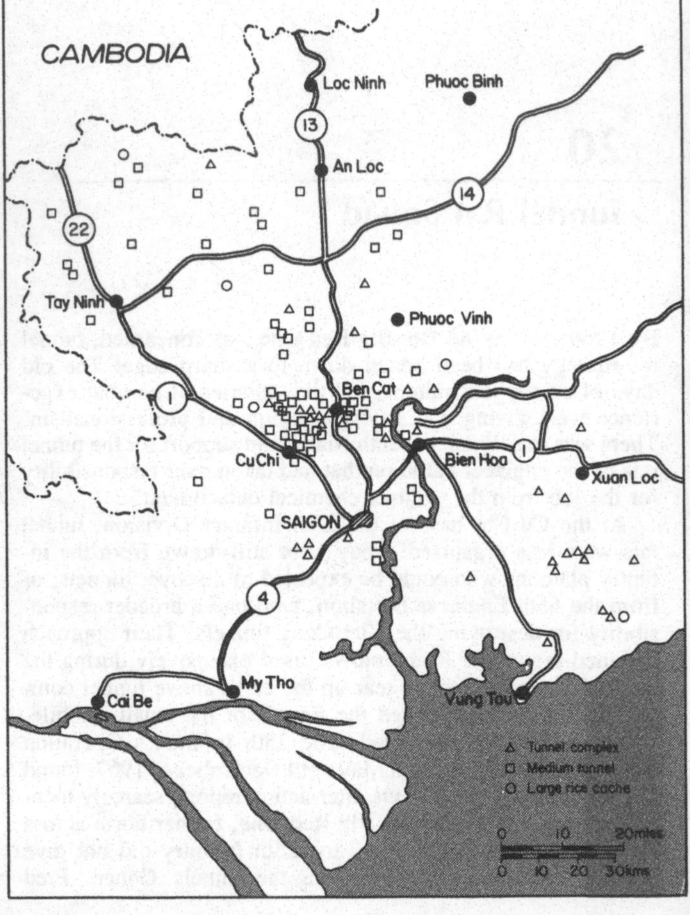

Weyand, who commanded the division when it first arrived, did not feel unduly concerned about their existence. "They were there, they'd always been used by these people to protect themselves and to move about, but I never viewed them as anything that was a major threat to the division. . . . there was no way that you could seal them all up. I suppose if you sealed them up, why, they could dig them out again."

This relaxed view of the military importance of the tunnels was simply not shared by the 1st Infantry Division commanders. Consequently, they formalized the tunnel rat squads, officially christened them, allowed them their own flash and motto, and subtly encouraged the military elitism that went with tunnel-ratting.

Following Jack Flowers's enforced departure from the leadership of the squad, Lieutenant Randolph Ellis became the new Rat Six, and with him came a new team. He commanded Alpha squad, and Lieutenant Jerry Sinn, a fresh-faced, fair-haired arrival in-country, took charge of Bravo squad. The entire tunnel rat section comprised thirteen men, all volunteers, all men who had undergone considerable psychological and physical examination before their applications for the job were accepted. Ellis and Sinn were to develop differing techniques, but the broad management of the "Dirty Thirteen" was coordinated. (In the 25th Division, as a rule, officers did not go down tunnels.) Although individuality was encouraged, Ellis and Sinn ran tight units and each, using basic textbook disciplinary techniques, earned the admiration and respect of their men. The days of the Flowers-Batman "jock" confrontation were over. There were men just as mean as Batman on the squads—Cuban-born Sergeant Pete Rejo was one—but officer authority was never to be so blatantly challenged again.

In fact by 1969 a discernible rat breed had begun to emerge. Each man was wholly individual yet subsumed his individuality by recognizing and working with a team. Many of the qualities found in Britain's Special Air Service or the U.S. Special Forces were evident in the kind of man who volunteered to become a tunnel rat. Physically they were all slim. They were men who could live off the land, taking only enough to stay alive. They tended to reject most of the earthy pleasures available to men in war, especially the Vietnam War. They abhorred drugs, were not obsessed with sex, and did not gamble. Most spoke a foreign language, read copiously, and sought solitude rather than the entertainments of the NCOs' or enlisted men's clubs. They were dangerous men: to the enemy, to barroom loudmouths, to battalion bullies who might be tempted to take advantage of their lack of height. In action they found their way to where it was most dangerous and complex. If there was battlefield indiscipline, it was because of their impatience with officers they considered stupid or uninvolved. This kind of maverick is not unusual in any fighting force—many of the dust-off helicopter pilots in Vietnam were similar—but he is not just the product of the environment of war. Men like that are born, and the shrewd recruiting officer knows how to spot and exploit them.

Lieutenant Randy Ellis knew precisely what kind of man he wanted in his squad. If there were recruiting errors, and there were, draconian use was made of Article 15: Any conviction under military law, no matter how minor the offense, meant instant dismissal from the squad. His tunnel rat procedure followed several basic and rigid rules. No fewer than three men ever entered a tunnel; a full tunnel exploration team was never less than five men, and was usually six. Two men always remained at a tunnel entrance, either to pass supplies forward or help pull a rat in trouble out as quickly as possible. The point man (it was usually Pete Rejo) was never less than five yards ahead of the next rat, so that if he was killed by a grenade, the second man would survive. If the rats came to a Y junction in the tunnel, one man stayed there to help monitor the progress of the others in case they started going round in circles, or in case a VC was luring them into a trap. To deal with the high death rate faced when going through trapdoors, where possible the door was dynamited. Grenades were used only in emergencies, because they destroyed so much oxygen in the tunnel. Even the tricky business of exiting a tunnel by a hitherto undiscovered ground-level trapdoor and risking being shot by one of your own men was solved. All tunnel rats were given red flashlights (in the certain knowledge the VC did not have them) and on emerging, rats would first raise the torch and signal before putting their heads out.

All the Dirty Thirteen maintained their strong contempt for the inventions of military science and stuck faithfully to the basic rat gear: pistol, common wire, bayonet or knife, and flashlight. No gadgets or "miracle" machines were ever adopted.

Randy Ellis's standard operating procedure was to take his squad into each tunnel in a "softly, softly" operation designed to catch as many Viet Cong as might be there. It was a tactic that invited the most dangerous response from an angry, frightened, and desperate guerrilla, trapped by surprise in his own hole. That's precisely what happened on the day Ellis earned his Bronze Star (V).

On 2 February 1970, Alpha squad was ordered into what was undoubtedly a hot hole at the edge of the Michelin rubber plantation. Ellis was the number-three man, Private Virgil Franklin was point, and the NCO in charge, Sergeant Cox, was second. An infantry battalion from the 1st had been dropped in an air-mobile insertion; there had been a firefight in the area and Charlie had, as ever, vanished. Ellis was shown the most likely tunnel entrance. Silently, and according to all the agreed procedures, the three rats slipped into the shaft. Ellis's rules were that no one man in the chain should ever be out of sight of the other, even when crawling through the tightest communication tunnels or turning the sharpest bends. Franklin vanished for an instant as he turned to the right, and just as Ellis began worrying about it, the tunnel erupted with the cacophony of an AK-47, and a stream of green tracers burned, like grotesque fireflies, into the clay above and just ahead of Ellis's left shoulder. Ellis heard Franklin's pistol fire every round—he counted each one—and knew his point man was in serious trouble. Cox crawled the five yards to Franklin, who lay seriously wounded in the stomach, right arm, and shoulder. Ellis had instinctively already passed a fresh .38 magazine to Cox to give to Franklin, but the GI was too badly wounded to move.

Slowly and painfully Cox and Ellis pulled the wounded soldier back. They had less than a hundred feet to go before they were safely at the shaft. Ellis then broke the rules, and after Franklin had been medevaced out, returned alone into the tunnel, crawled to the pool of blood where Franklin had been hit, and lobbed two grenades into the darkness before returning to the tunnel entrance. It was perhaps a foolish and unnecessary action—a conventional ingredient of heroism, after all. But his attempt to drive out, singlehandedly, the guerrillas in the tunnels ended as light fell in the later afternoon. It was of course *the* golden rule that tunnel fighting had to stop with darkness. It would have been impossible to guarantee the capture or death of an enemy flushed up after dark, or to emerge safely from the trapdoors oneself. As he left the tunnel entrance, Ellis sprinkled copious quantities of standard-issue foot powder at the mouth of the shaft and just inside at the bottom. On his return at first light the next day, he would need to know if the Viet Cong had been back to booby-trap the entrance for him. But although the carpet of powder had remained undisturbed, the next morning proved to be a final frustration. Clearly the VC guerrillas had escaped. For his coolness under fire, and his success in evacuating his wounded comrade, Ellis received the Bronze Star (V).

Lieutenant Jerry Sinn's Bravo rat squad had a man of different caliber as leader. More an engineer by temperament than an infantryman (he would command the 1st Engineer Battalion fifteen years later), Sinn believed that tunnel-ratting had tunnel-destruction as its sole aim. Not for him the stealthy entrance, the chance encounter with a cornered VC, the sudden grab of a cache of documents of arms. While following the same basic tunnel rat rules as his friend and comrade Randy Ellis, Jerry Sinn did not believe in stealthy reconnaissance. He believed in giving Charlie ample time to get out before the rats went in. "Any time I moved through a trapdoor or changed locations, I'd run that lantern up there, and stick my pistol up there and fire. And I kept thinking, my mission is to gather as much intelligence as possible and destroy the tunnel complex and to deny its use to the enemy. You're not talking to a hero."

So under Sinn, Bravo squad had no tunnel firefights, took no casualties below ground. But the inquisitive young officer did study, very carefully, the effects of gas and explosives on the tunnels, and was largely responsible for refining the C-4 explosive charges to the point where they did the maximum (but still quite insufficient) damage to the tunnel walls and overburden.

Taken together, this was the most fertile period for the Big Red One's tunnel rats and it is doubtful if under the circumstances they could have done very much more to interdict the tunnels. Techniques, equipment, SOP, and personnel were about right. Under the strict but enthusiastic command of both officers, there emerged an extraordinarily brave and ruthless squad of rats. It was, for example, inevitable that Randy Ellis would pick Staff Sergeant Pete Rejo as his NCO and senior point man. Rejo was a killer of Communists who worked with the kind of quiet and controlled vengeance that any tunnel rat officer longed to harness. Rejo had been around a year before Ellis joined, working as a sort of human mine detector in the Big Red One's area in War Zones C and D. A lanky five-foot-eleven Cuban, he had spent his early teens in Havana, taking pot shots at Castro's men and developing an active dislike for Communism. While most supporters of the dictator Batista were tactfully buying themselves a one-way passage to Florida, the young Rejo took his father's .38 and fired at the bearded revolutionaries. He was lucky to escape with his life then, even luckier when he had gone mine-detecting up Vietnam's Highway 13 in 1968. It was Rejo, his taut cadaverous face never moving a muscle, who first discovered the mines, discovered the grenade booby traps beneath them, and finally discovered the Viet Cong were making homemade jobs out of captured American ordnance.

On three separate occasions Pete Rejo heard the sound of certain death as he stepped on a mine, sprung it—and, incredibly, it did not go off. The handful who have heard the click of a booby-trapped device and lived to talk about it can rarely find words to describe the moment after the sharp metallic announcement of doom. On each occasion that it happened to Rejo, he examined the mine and found it in working order. His comrades used to call him the human probe, and after a time the gibe took on real form. He smelled mines. Even if his squad went over a suspected area time and time again and swore blind it was clean, if Pete Rejo smelled a mine, a mine there was, and he would personally dig it out.

Whatever impulses drove Rejo to mine-detecting soon drove him to become a tunnel rat. He was to spend three years in Vietnam, like many of the rats, three times as long as necessary. What kept him there, and in the tunnels, was that sense of obscene excitement that all men can find in the pit of their souls, but few care to examine. Unlike Ellis, his officer in charge, who wanted prisoners and documents and tunnels destroyed; and unlike Sinn, who wanted to get it all over with, Staff Sergeant Pete Rejo wanted to kill Communists in tunnels. He would try to rationalize it any way he liked. It was part of the eternal fight against Communism, it was for the flag, it was a blow for democracy in Vietnam, Asia, the free world.

It showed his buddies how American he really was, and how efficient the GI could be. The truth is, he needed the juices to flow. For at the climax of each operation, if he was lucky, he would find an enemy soldier, and one took no prisoners in the tunnels. There were then, and remain now, paradoxes in his psyche. "I loved it. The enemy hit us, and then they went down the holes, and I knew we were going to get them down there—what other place were they going to go—deeper? I would have gone deeper, too. I enjoyed it very much. I liked it a lot. In fact, when they told me they had a VC down there, I came unglued. I got over there about a hundred miles an hour. To me it was like going hunting. They told me, 'Hey, we've got a VC down there,' and I got all ready. I wanted to be the first down there. I wanted to get down there right away, I didn't want to mess around no more, I wanted to go after him."

So he killed many men deep down in the holes, where he was on his own even if the squad *was* behind him, this long, thin, lightweight Cuban who stepped on mines and lived, who begged to go point more times than the rules allowed, and who became tense and restless only when he could *not* go down a hot hole. Of course, Ellis was a strict officer. "He had rules, he was very strict, I can't say different. But when you're down there, one on one, there were no rules at all."

His Army Commendation Medal (V) citation is a glowing testament to a man without nerves. It tells of the bravery of a tunnel rat who, despite all the odds, despite the fact that the tunnel might have contained the Viet Cong who had already wounded two of his squad colleagues, instantly volunteered to go in and look for documents and destroy the tunnel. The citation recalls that Rejo entered the hot hole, even though it had already been contaminated by his own men with CS gas; that he refused to wear a gas mask, and with scant regard for his own safety, inched his way through the complex and arranged its destruction with explosive charges. What the citation does not relate, because Rejo's officer Randy Ellis did not know, was that the point man had found an NVA soldier in the tunnel. Driven by the smell of the enemy, just as he had been by the smell of their mines, Rejo had defied the choking, burning CS gas and literally carved his way through a communication tunnel that became so narrow he had to open it up with his knife just to get through. Randy Ellis was well behind, but trying to stay close enough to cover Rejo. They wanted prisoners at the top. The policy on prisoners was to take them only when one could reasonably expect to make the hazardous journey back to the entrance while somehow, in those two-foot-wide holes, maintaining control over a captive. It could be done. But not by Pete Rejo.

He was still widening the tunnel with his knife when he came face to face with the Communist soldier—not a Viet Cong guerrilla, but a northerner, dressed in the distinctive dull-green uniform. He was carrying an AK-47. No one will ever know why the Communist did not fire at the tunnel rat. Why Rejo didn't follow his instinct and kill the soldier may be partially explained by his orders to take prisoners, and by the relative proximity of his disciplinarian officer, Randy Ellis. Rejo, who boasted that there wasn't a tunnel dug that he could not turn around in, did so, crawled toward Ellis, risking a bullet in the back of the head from the NVA soldier, and said, "Elly, order me a shape charge." He told his officer that he could go no farther and that it was time to blow the tunnel. He neglected to mention the NVA soldier crouching in a corner of a small chamber only a few feet away. Why didn't Rejo tell Ellis? "Well, because he knew I was wild. If I would have told him, he would have interfered with what I wanted to do. Randy was a professional. I was a killer. You see what I'm saying?"

Eventually they brought Rejo the 40-pound cratering charge, and he returned to set it. He crawled all the way back to see if he could find his NVA soldier, but he didn't see him. But then, he didn't need to see him. He could still smell him—the sweat and the body odor were unmistakable. As he set the charge, he wondered how many he would kill when the tunnel caved in. He wondered why they didn't open up on him; he was a sitting target. It was like those mines not going off. After the explosion he wanted to go back down, just to confirm that he had killed the NVA soldier. But Ellis stopped him. There was another call for the rat squad.

They gave him ten days off to go to Guam to become an American citizen—his greatest dream ever since leaving Cuba. He would have stayed in the tunnels forever if the American involvement had not been coming to an end. Even then he begged to stay on. As the tunnel squads came to the end of their work, and as the Americans began to withdraw, Rejo implored his superiors to let him join the First Cavalry gunship unit out at Le Quon Loi. They used to fly very low, skimming the jungle, shooting at people on the ground with high-speed machine guns that fired 6,000 rounds a minute. That was for Rejo. But they told him he'd been long enough in Vietnam and needed to come back home.

Even with his hard-won medals and his U.S. citizenship, Rejo has not found peace. He has been married and divorced three times. He never speaks about the days in the tunnels to his friends, nor does he attend the noisy veterans' reunions. But he did buy a shotgun, and a .22, and a big .300, and a .243, and some knives, and began hunting the deer and the elk and the coyote in the hills of Colorado. He hunts alone.

Rick Swofford fought with Ellis's squad, too. Unlike Rejo he was not tortured by the dark and contradictory forces that drive a man. Swofford was a twenty-year-old who somehow drifted into the army and fetched up in Vietnam, filling sandbags with the Engineers. By 1969 the fame of the tunnel rats was such that they had already become a legend to him. Ellis felt he could use the tough, glory-seeking soldier and took him on. Swofford was a demolitions expert, and his precision skill with explosives was just what Alpha squad needed. Too much could be dangerous, too little had no effect, inept handling could threaten everyone down in the hole, and Swofford got it right. Pete Rejo did not like the cocky youngster and needled and pulled rank on him until Swofford began to get angry. The tunnel rats did not use rank in this way, nor did they impose the kind of bullshit pecking order that existed outside their numbers. Swofford challenged Rejo and they fistfought each other to a standstill. After that they became firm friends. Swofford loved the glamour of the squad. Their distinctive flash roused envy every time they walked into the NCOs' club. They talked missions a lot. Anyone outside the squad who was allowed in on the rapping was strictly a guest.

It was Rick Swofford who blew the tunnel after Franklin had been shot in the action in which Ellis won his Bronze Star (V). It had been a tense and difficult time for the whole of Alpha squad. Swofford just went down there with Ellis and twenty-five cases of C-4 explosive, making some 300 pounds in all. They had to haul the stuff, crate by crate, through the long tunnel complex and set them scientifically at the same time. Each case was a foot and a half square, and they were soon physically exhausted. Then they discovered they had not brought enough fuse wire, only a foot and a half, which would be extremely dangerous to use on that amount of explosive. Ellis asked him, "Swofford, is that enough fuse?" and Swofford, who had seen too many Westerns, lit the fuse with a cigarette, and answered, "No, you'd better start running now, Elly." One could not, of course, run down a tunnel, but professionals did perfect an astonishingly fast if undignified crawl, which stripped the skin from the elbows and knees. As the two men shot out of the shaft like a couple of corks, the 300 pounds blew. Swofford was knocked down by the blast. The tunnels exploded as if in slow motion. Hundreds of tons of earth and stone hung suspended in the air. It was an unusual luxury to use 300 pounds of explosives, but it *was* the tunnel in which Virgil Franklin had been hit.

After the earth had settled, they discovered Swofford had set the charges so perfectly that the entire lid of the tunnels maze had been lifted like a scalp from a skull. They saw tunnels they had never even found during the early searches. Ellis forgave Swofford the theatrical gesture. Swofford loved every minute of it.

While the 1st Division tunnel rats were refining their unique military skills, challenging and often winning individual tunnel encounters, the 25th Division down at Cu Chi across the Saigon River was implementing a more laborious approach to the business. Long after the Big Red One tunnel rats had been officially created, the 25th Infantry maintained its policy of engineer involvement, but without the specialization and continuity of their colleagues farther north in the defense ring around Saigon. In May 1968 an operational report analyzing the lessons of Operation Atlanta showed 25th Division infantrymen were still using the Rome plows to expose the subtle intricacies of the Cu Chi tunnels. It was like shaving with a broken bottle. The equipment was massive and expensive, the process was time-consuming, the results lacked precision. It was a loud and crude way of dealing with tunnels.

It is debatable whether full-time tunnel rat squads would have been able to discover and seal the tunnel belt around Cu Chi base. There were frequent American sorties into the holes, but to the embarrassment of the 25th Infantry, they were never fully located and destroyed. This meant that as late as February 1969 the Communists were able to mount their stunningly successful raid on the base, using the old tunnels and some new ones, too. VC prisoners told their interrogators that they had hidden in the tunnel belts around the base camp for three to four days before the attack. In other words, a full three years after arrival, the 25th Infantry headquarters at Cu Chi was still not in control of the land outside its own wire. Not only that, but the base had become a bulky fortress, forced to spend more and more time, energy, and money feeding itself and defending itself. A determined command approach to tunnel destruction might have allowed the division the luxury of more offensive missions. However, where part-time tunnel rat squads did evolve, their training and tactics reflected not the scientific approach of the engineers, but the old gung ho tradition of the infantry.

"The Rock," "Chicago," Jackson, Funchez Wright, and Manifold was such a squad. The Rock was Floro Rivera; he was the sergeant in charge. Neither he nor any of the squad were volunteers. They were all from the elite Wolfhounds, the 2nd Battalion of the 27th Infantry, part of the 25th Division. The Wolfhounds had been created in 1901 in Fort McPherson, Georgia. The canine soubriquet was added late in World War I, when the White Russians compared the unit's ferocity to that of the giant dog.

Flo Rivera would have become a legendary tunnel rat had he been an engineer with the Big Red One. He was, like Thornton or Ellis or Rejo, born to the job. As it was, his ad hoc tunnel rat squad was to lack the fame and recognition earned by his colleagues at Lai Khe. Unlike them, he had no squad officer in charge. His platoon leader did not even go down the holes. So as it became evident that the Wolfhounds needed somebody to cope with the tunnels of Cu Chi on something more than an impoverished basis, they told Rivera he had the job.

He was born in Hawaii of Filippino parents. His mother died when he was a baby, and his father, a humble plantation worker, was left to bring up three sons. Both his elder brothers served in World War II and then got out. He had a stern and hard upbringing. His father taught him never to back off if he believed he was right. He was taught to use his fists and soon became a talented flyweight boxer. If Flo did anything wrong, his father beat the hell out of him. One day when he was still only nine years old, his father gave him a large knife and told him it was his turn to kill a pig. "Don't make a mistake. You seen how I do it," warned his father. "Kill it with one stroke, the first. You get this wrong, I'm gonna whack hell out of you. If you ever use a knife, then be good with it." The pig died instantly, and Flo Rivera grew to use a knife like Davy Crockett.

He greatly loved and feared his father. At twenty, he joined the army for a career. Not backing off and refusing to take orders from dummies soon landed him in the stockade. He was a firm believer in discipline, but he never said please. There were bad NCOs who wanted to break him, but they failed. He had respect only for efficiency and discipline. "A PRC told me to jump, I would jump. A corporal told me to roll over and die—I would." Anyone could have predicted that Rivera would become one of those legendary first-class sergeants destined to lead their men with honor. But for a while his stubbornness placed his career in the balance. During a tour in Germany, his boxing prowess became known to his colonel, who asked him to fight for the unit. Rivera had just promised his new bride he would give up boxing, so he declined with thanks. The colonel gently pointed out that the invitation had just become an order. Rivera did not say please. He saluted and left the office. The colonel arranged for Rivera to be given every dirty job that could be found on base, together with a string of all-night guard duties. Rivera still did not say please, and it was reaching an ugly moment in his military service, when a crafty master sergeant took him to one side and advised him to compromise. "Don't box, become the team coach," he said. Rivera agreed, and the war with his CO ended.

He was a natural for tunnel duty—small, lithe, very strong, and quite fearless. OJT presented no problems to him, but turning his squad into tunnel rats did. Some, like Jackson, a big, slow-moving black, were physically unsuitable. Others had as much desire to go into the holes as they did to hack at their own throats with rusty razor blades. Unlike Ellis, Rivera could not handpick his team, so they simply had to be beaten into shape, an expression the little sergeant did not use as a metaphor. He reached an early agreement with his platoon commander, Captain Gavin, an amiable young officer who left the whole dirty tunnel rat business to Rivera, to handle the men the way he thought fit. NCOs like Rivera were as rare as roses in the desert, and if they blossomed, you left them alone. Rivera was given full platoon authority.

He gathered the squad together inside the Cu Chi base and informed them that with great pride and honor he had accepted their requests to become tunnel rats as and when the occasion arose. There was a brief silence—no one knew at first what he was talking about. Then hands went up. The squad knew all about the tunnels. They had been under fire from VC who had popped up from tunnels, even inside the base. They were Wolfhounds, not terriers. Rivera gave them one further chance to think again. He told them that on every operation he guaranteed he would be down there himself; there was nothing to worry about—he would be there alongside them. A leery silence followed. He could not say please, nor could he trade on his rank any further. He waited for the first refusal and when it came, he simply challenged the man to a fight. It was illegal and immoral. He offered the trembling private the choice of a knife or pistol with one round in it. You did not fight Rivera with a knife unless you wanted overnight repatriation in a body-bag. A one-shot duel with pistols was equally unattractive.

He was to use this technique on several occasions when he felt the platoon's discipline was slipping. It was not a question of personal pride or face—he was far too good a soldier for that; but keeping a bunch of grunts involved in tunnel-ratting was not going to work unless there were sticks and carrots, and Rivera knew all about sticks. No one ever did accept a challenge from the sergeant. And more significantly, no one ever reported that the challenge had been offered. Rivera would, of course, have faced a court martial had he been found out.

Slowly, awkwardly, Rivera's rats began to shape up. "Chicago" was even smaller than Rivera and usually went point. OJT produced the obvious golden rules. No one ever went alone; the tunnel rats' standard equipment was soon adopted. Booby-trap training continued endlessly.

Jackson was a problem. It was not that he was unwilling or even a bad soldier. But he was too big and ungainly. He carried the platoon's machine gun on his broad shoulders, but it was useless as a tunnel-fighting weapon. More often than not he had no tunnel duties other than standing entrance guard duty. He remained, in Rivera's eyes, dangerously uninvolved, and a weak link in the squad. One night, away from the base, the platoon camped out in hostile territory. Once the perimeter had been secured, Rivera detailed the guard and went to sleep. He woke during the night and went on an inspection of the guard, and found Jackson apparently asleep on duty. He took the burly private's M-14 rifle away from him and, as he did so, Jackson woke up and tried to pull his bayonet on Rivera. Rivera's knife was out in a second, and he cut the soldier's neck. At dawn, Rivera ordered the private to make his own formal report of the incident to the company commander, Captain Gavin. Both men were clearly guilty of serious court martial offenses. As Jackson walked over to the officer's tent, Rivera called Gavin on the field phone and told him exactly what had happened. The captain told Rivera not to worry, then told Jackson he was lucky to be alive. The incident was closed.

But tension between Rivera and Jackson remained. He still posed a threat in the sergeant's eyes to platoon discipline. Shortly afterward, when the platoon was living in bunkers on the perimeter of Cu Chi base, the Viet Cong began making extensive use of the tunnel belt around the headquarters to attack the men inside. Rivera's squad suddenly found itself under sniper attack every single day. At almost precisely the same time, a few minutes before their lunch, a sniper, using the same Red Butt K-44, would take a few pot shots at the platoon, and the platoon would spray the rubber plantation back in impotent rage, but always without success. Rivera began to study one particular tree in the undergrowth and fastened on it as the possible source of the sniper attacks. But what he could not begin to understand was how the sniper got into the tree, given that the surrounding area belonged to and was fully occupied by the squad.

Not for the first time Sergeant Flo Rivera committed a serious offense, punishable by court martial. He called Jackson over and ordered him to walk, fairly quickly, past the tree and to make that walk just before lunch time. "Don't stop," Rivera warned the private. "You stop, you're gonna get zapped. When he fires, don't stop." Jackson, who no longer argued with his NCO in charge, took the long walk as planned. Rivera had set up two machine guns. One pointed at the top of the tree and one at the bottom. Jackson was about a hundred yards from the tree when the sniper opened fire. The big GI fainted. Rivera opened up simultaneously with both machine guns on the tree. Leaves, splinters, and one riddled body fell to the ground. They revived Jackson with water and went on to inspect the tree. The inside had been hollowed out and a rope hung there, falling down into a tunnel that had been dug below the tree. The sniper had been able to get up the tree through the *inside*, which was why he had remained invisible. Jackson asked the sergeant, nicely, not to use him as human bait again. The sergeant agreed and they called it quits.

Rather like Ellis over at Lai Khe, Rivera sensibly worked out what he called a buddy system of cover inside the tunnels. Nobody went in alone, nobody wandered too far ahead without cover. Before each tunnel investigation, Rivera began to rehearse his squad down to the finest detail: who would go point, who would cover, how far would they go, who would guard the entrance. The squad was beginning to synchronize, and Rivera grew proud of the men. They even began to gain a small reputation inside the base, although they were only one group of part-time tunnel rats among many.

There were no great heroic firefights in the holes. The policy of the 25th Infantry was to investigate and destroy if possible, but there were no particular tunnel imperatives. Rivera's squad had its moments. They found an underground conference room bedecked with a handsome hammer-and-sickle flag, and they frequently found documents, rice stores, and a few weapons. They also discovered the danger of leaving tunnels by newly explored ground-level trapdoors, and risking being shot at by their own side. Rivera did not invent a version of Ellis's subtle red flashlight system, but he did protect his men the hard way. After a couple of scares, he decided only *his* squad would stay in the vicinity of a tunnel while he had men down there. If other Wolfhounds came into that sacred area, they were quickly ordered out by the little sergeant. Most complied. Those who did not were bawled out and they then usually left. Those who did not respond to that invitation found themselves facing a half-maddened NCO with a drawn .38. Then they quit. He was reported for this kind of behavior so many times, it ceased to be news. His platoon commander never let him down, and never let a written complaint go up. None of the squad was ever killed or wounded in the tunnels. With luck and judgment, Rivera kept the compact he made with them when he volunteered their services. They understood that he had kept his end of the bargain. In return, despite the frustrations of too many cold tunnels, they fought their hearts out above ground. Every member of the squad, including Jackson and Captain Gavin, was wounded.

Rivera was to receive two Silver Stars, three Bronze Stars, and the Army Commendation Medal. He left the 25th Infantry and Cu Chi for reassignment as a special U.S. adviser to the ARVN. After that he was sent to Korea, but the lack of action there bored him. He eventually returned to Hawaii to work, as a civilian, within a hundred yards of an army base.

21

Winners and Losers

THE TET OFFENSIVE of January 1968 was the climax of the tunnels' existence. The coordinated series of damaging attacks by the Viet Cong on the capital city, Saigon, was planned and prepared in tunnels in Cu Chi and the Iron Triangle a mere twenty miles away, and at a time when MACV was telling the American public that the war was going its way. Such was the psychological impact of the Tet offensive that it became the turning point of the war, the beginning of the end. "Without the tunnels," said Lieutenant General Robert Knowles, "you wouldn't have had the Tet offensive." After it, as the decimated guerrillas were increasingly replaced in the fighting by the regular army of North Vietnam, the tunnels' role diminished correspondingly. But in 1968 they were crucial.

Among those they sheltered were the elite of the South Vietnamese guerrillas, the Dac Cong. They were the sappers, or commandos, who carried out the most daring raids and acts of sabotage. Sometimes as few as three of them would penetrate huge U.S. or ARVN bases and create havoc. Today the Dac Cong is an element of Vietnam's army like the Special Forces or Britain's SAS. During the war they were organized in battalions, and the most important of these was F-100. Set up in

1965, it was based in tunnels at An Tinh village next to Cu Chi district. Its members were recruited from inside Saigon itself and trained for urban guerrilla warfare. Most of them wore city clothes and led apparently regular, legal lives "integrated with the enemy." F-100 came under the personal command of the military head of the Communists' Military Region IV, Colonel Tran Hai Phung. His encrypted orders were communicated to the base by radio; girl couriers connected the headquarters with its agents in Saigon. No other Viet Cong knew the location of the battalion's secret base. It had a long history of rocket attacks and terror bombings in Saigon, including the one at the American embassy in 1967, and a regular succession of similar attacks on police stations, nightclubs, and restaurants, which made the capital a jumpy and dangerous place. But at Vietnam's sacred holiday period, the lunar new year festival on 31 January 1968, F-100 would spearhead a wholehearted military offensive inside the capital city.

The decision to mount the nationwide Tet offensive of 1968 was taken at the highest levels of the Lao Dong party in Hanoi. In July 1967 the funeral of General Nguyen Chi Thanh took place in the northern capital. He was the erstwhile military commander of COSVN, who died of cancer. The occasion was the opportunity for a conference of political and military leaders from all over Vietnam. At General Giap's urging they agreed to break the stalemate with a general offensive and general uprising at the next lunar new year festival. This would be almost sacrilegious, and cause deep resentment among ordinary Vietnamese. But its improbability would be its best concealment, as had been the case earlier in history when, in 1789, Vietnamese patriots had used the same trick on the occupying Chinese in Hanoi. The offensive was planned in complete secrecy. The war in South Vietnam was to be taken from the countryside to the towns and cities, where, it was hoped, the people would rally to the NLF's side and rise up against the government of President Thieu. This was intended to bring about the collapse of the regime in Saigon and convince the American public in an election year that the war was futile and unwinnable.

The men and the weapons for the attacks in Saigon were assembled in the tunnels of Cu Chi and the Iron Triangle. They were systematically moved up to the edge of the city, and on the eve of the attack, to specially prepared safe houses inside it. The arms were transported in agricultural vehicles, fake funerals, and by other devious means. Four thousand guerrillas entered the city with the crowds anticipating the Tet holiday. The Americans were caught off-guard, and subsequent investigation would find a serious intelligence failure.

At the end of January, U.S. and South Vietnamese government installations were attacked at over one hundred cities, towns, and bases. Two long sieges—at remote Khe Sanh and the occupied citadel of Hue—prolonged the agony of Tet '68. But the attacks on offices in the heart of Saigon by F-100 had by far the greatest impact and psychological effect. These self-sacrificial Viet Cong raids turned the war in the Communists' favor. After Tet, many Americans began to doubt if they could achieve anything they might call victory in Vietnam.

The political commissar of the Viet Cong's Military Region IV, Mai Chi Tho, planned the attacks at a tunnel base near Ben Cat in the Iron Triangle. There is a photograph of him taken with a group of earnest young Viet Cong officers, some of them girls, grouped round a table of maps and plans. "During the Tet offensive," he said, "I was in the Iron Triangle. We were working day and night. It was a time of very secret and intensive activity. Many of our officers had to secretly reconnoiter the enemy targets. They moved around in Saigon on forged identity papers. Our fifth columnists, soldiers and officers working inside enemy military installations, came to report. They could come and return to their posts within a few hours. That would not have been possible if the headquarters were too far away; that's why Cu Chi was important. The tunnels were where preparations were made for the offensive, a place for stocking weapons and supplies and assembling troops. They were especially valuable after the offensive failed to achieve its objectives, because they provided a base for preparing subsequent attacks."

All over South Vietnam, towns and cities were hit by the Viet Cong. In Saigon itself, squads of commandos seized the radio station, the Philippine embassy, and other quarters of the city, and assaulted the presidential palace, the headquarters of MACV at Tan Son Nhut air base, and the U.S. embassy, then a newly built defensible structure in concrete on the city's main boulevard. South Vietnamese police fled when the two Viet Cong vehicles drove up in the early hours. A hole was blown in the wall, and the defense was left to U.S. marines and military police on duty. Of the attacking squad, all but one were soon killed, and the raid was dismissed by an American officer on the spot as a "piddling platoon action." But the incident shocked the whole world. Far greater damage was being done elsewhere in Vietnam, where ten provincial capitals fell under temporary Viet Cong control and key American supply bases and airstrips were bombarded. But the handful of guerrillas who got inside the embassy's wall attracted the attention of the entire Saigon-based press corps, and destroyed years of optimistic public relations efforts by the Joint U.S. Public Affairs Office, the Americans' information operation.

In purely military terms, most of the Viet Cong's Tet operations were failures. But that was irrelevant. It was the moment at which American casualties surpassed those in the Korean War. It was a moment of painful truth—always a rare commodity in Vietnam. Public and political opinion in America never recovered from the impact; within two months President Johnson announced that he would not run for reelection.

Ironically, it was an experience from which the Viet Cong would never recover either. In theory, North Vietnamese infantry battalions were to follow up the initial attacks by the Viet Cong sappers, but the advantage of surprise could not be exploited. Despite the near-perfect coordination of attacks across the country, their impact was dissipated by being so scattered. The attacks were driven off—destructively—everywhere except Hue and Saigon, and the capital was pacified within a week. Over forty thousand Viet Cong guerrillas died in the fighting, crippling the movement beyond repair. There had been no popular uprising in their support; their chances of victory were too uncertain for the pragmatic Vietnamese city-dwellers. Nonetheless, there had been no betrayal of the complex preparations for the offensive. General Tran Van Tra himself conceded that the offensive hurt the attackers as much as the defenders. The Communist military commander in South Vietnam was to publish his memoirs after the war; in Hanoi they were banned immediately and he disappeared, probably purged. In them, he wrote:

> One should not fear speaking about mistakes. During Tet of 1968 we did not correctly evaluate the specific balance of forces between ourselves and the enemy, did not fully realize that the enemy still had considerable capabilities and that our capabilities were limited. Although there was excellent coordination on all battlefields, everyone acted very bravely, sacrificed their lives, we suffered large sacrifices and losses with regard to manpower and matériel, especially cadres at the various echelons, which clearly weakened us. Afterward, we were unable not only to retain the gains we had made but to overcome a myriad of difficulties in 1969 and 1970 so that the revolution could stand firm in the storm.

But a month after Tet 1968, Tran Van Tra ordered further attacks, and yet more throughout 1968, to try to sustain the momentum of the war and dispel the disillusionment on the Communist side engendered by Tet's failure to live up to its idealistic promises. The Viet Cong had to be persuaded that victory was somehow within their grasp, and so the attacks—and the attrition—went on. The American response was a mailed fist. For the remainder of the 1968 dry season, and in the following winter's, waves of helicopters and APCs ferried in the troops for huge search-and-destroy operations that swept through Viet Cong base areas. (It was on one such operation that the massacre of villagers at My Lai occurred.)

The depleted guerrillas crept back to their tunnel hideouts, most of their fighting spirit exhausted. "There were only four of us fighters left at Nhuan Duc, next to Cu Chi base," said Captain Nguyen Thanh Linh, their local commander. "We were fighting for a few days in the towns, and left the countryside empty. We poured all our forces out to fight and lost our key cadres. When the Americans counterattacked, we had no good men left. We were nearly out of ammunition. Our food reserve was being used up day by day. Between four men we had just fifty grams of rice a day. We ate fish from the Saigon River and plenty of rats. Some people were worried that Cu Chi might be lost. You could say that the Americans were winning tactically, if not strategically."

The Tet attacks on Saigon had originated in the old hornets' nests of Viet Cong in Cu Chi district and the Iron Triangle.

This time, the American high command decided to obliterate the tunnel-riddled sanctuaries once and for all by the complete destruction of the ecology. Chemical defoliants had proved only temporarily effective. The Fil Hol plantation, the Ho Bo and Boi Loi woods, and the Iron Triangle were to be systematically flattened by Rome plows. "American grass" was planted from Chinook helicopters and periodically set on fire. This was a specially developed strain of coarse grass that burned easily and quickly. Colonel Thomas A. Ware commanded a battalion of the 25th Infantry on sweep operations. "We spent our time in the Ho Bo woods, and Fil Hol and the Iron Triangle. I think we cut something like 14,000 acres of trees. We'd run into tunnels every day. Sometimes our heavy bulldozers or tanks would collapse them. Sometimes we'd just blow the entrance."

Recalled Mai Chi Tho: "Yes, the Americans bulldozed the whole area; there was not a house or a tree left. One could stand on the bank of the Saigon River and see to Route 1 about seven miles away without any obstruction. We had to stay in short sections of tunnel. Our fighting was limited. There were no activities in the daytime, only at night."

The population of villagers had largely vanished already. On average, since 1965, over a million of South Vietnam's villagers a year had been displaced or fled the bombs, bullets, and defoliants and become refugees in government-controlled cities. This took away the Viet Cong's tax base, and its life support. And in a free strike zone, no one would survive for long above ground anyway.

"The trees were stripped of foliage," Captain Linh recalled. "It was very hot in the tunnels. If we failed to conceal our footsteps on a path, the helicopters would have spotted them. The Americans' greatest success at that time was two armed helicopters from the 25th Aviation Battalion—Cobras—on the front of which were painted the pointed teeth and red mouth of a magical beast; we called them the red-headed beasts. They had two gunners—blacks—who were excellent sharp-shooters. Just a glimpse of us and they swiveled their gun pods to shoot and kill instantly; many of our soldiers died. They flew low and fast and were deadly accurate. We made dummies holding rifles up so that we could attract them and shoot at them, and one crashed at Cu Chi base camp. We buried the victims of the red-headed beasts all in the same place as a warning to everyone. There were fifty or sixty graves, one added every two or three days. The cemetery no longer exists now."

The writer Vien Phuong returned to Cu Chi district from the safety of Cambodia in 1971. "The whole of the Cu Chi area was covered with American grass and bamboo. There were only about four guerrillas left in each village; there were no other people. . . . The guerrillas ate leaves to survive and washed their wounds in salted water. I had to live in a bomb crater, a hole at the bottom of the crater underneath a nylon sheet."

This was the darkest hour. Ironically, as the last American units pulled out in the early seventies, the Viet Cong was admitting defeat. Their hardships were so severe that even the resolute Captain Linh admitted that in 1969 and 1970 morale collapsed and there were many deserters from the Viet Cong, Hoi Chanhs. "There was just too much hardship at that time; the slightest mistake could have been fatal."

In February 1970 he was living with the remnants of his squad in a tunnel a few hundred yards from the perimeter of Cu Chi base camp. It was the same tunnel from which the Dac Cong had emerged for the attack on 26 February 1969 that destroyed so many helicopters on the base. Linh recalled: "Every day American troops passed over my head. They had no idea we were there, so did not look for us. We heard the metal tracks of patrolling tanks screeching all night long. We heard the Americans joking and laughing. We lived there a whole month, but after I left that place I was caught." Captain Linh's war was over; he was a prisoner after five years in the tunnels.

As a result of the growing number of Hoi Chanhs, the Viet Cong suffered yet another setback that hastened their collapse. Outside the free strike zones the Viet Cong still had a political and community infrastructure in the villages. Using intelligence derived from Hoi Chanhs, the Americans proposed to expose the tunnel hideouts of the cadres and root out the NLF infrastructure completely.

Phoenix, as this program was called, was devised by Robert Komer, a former CIA man and General Westmoreland's deputy for pacification. He was nicknamed Blowtorch, and created in 1967 a scheme called CORDS (Civil Operations and Revolutionary Development Support), which he foisted upon President

Thieu's government. Phoenix was its key element, to be implemented by South Vietnamese police, troops, and irregulars under CIA direction, in accordance with President Nixon's policy of Vietnamization, applied from 1969 onward. The object of the Phoenix program was to identify and root out the secret Communist apparatus in South Vietnam. In the early sixties the Vieg Cong had crippled the administration of the Saigon government by the systematic murder of appointed village chiefs and other officials. If the NLF's local organization of cadres, activists, and helpers could be wiped out, then, it was hoped, a recurrent pattern could be broken: the cycle in which guerrilla units, ground down by American military action, were rebuilt time after time by the NLF working among the population. In the event, the Phoenix program produced a tangle of graft, inefficiency, brutality, and murder. But combined with the depopulation of the countryside, it succeeded in gravely damaging the Viet Cong's organization, compromising the tunnels, and forcing General Tran Van Tra to rely instead upon the regular divisions of the North Vietnamese army.

The first phase of the Phoenix program was the collection and coordination of intelligence about the Viet Cong, chiefly from prisoners and Hoi Chanhs. Where possible, spies were placed inside the Viet Cong. Pham Van Nhanh, the former guerrilla commander at Trung Lap village in Cu Chi district, said that during Phoenix "one tactic of the enemy was to train pretty girls to infiltrate our organization. They seduced a number of our cadres and collected information about our organization and activities." Families in strategic hamlets were pressured by the police to persuade their younger members to betray the guerrillas, enjoying Chieu Hoi privileges if they did. The veteran Viet Cong leader Mrs. Nguyen Thi Dinh told American reporter Stanley Karnow, "We never feared a division of troops, but the infiltration of a couple of guys into our ranks created tremendous difficulties for us."

The second phase, exploitation, was carried out by specially trained squads of South Vietnamese national police and the ARVN. Equipped with names and addresses collected from the district Phoenix center, they slunk into the villages to deal with supposed Viet Cong officials or sympathizers. This usually meant assassination or arbitrary arrest. William Colby, the Saigon station chief of the U.S. Central Intelligence Agency, who masterminded the program, was to admit that "Phoenix became a shorthand for all the negative aspects of the war." But it succeeded. He estimated that over 60,000 authentic Viet Cong agents were killed, captured, or neutralized by the Phoenix program—a figure including Chieu Ho defectors. Of the 20,000 he admitted killed, Colby insisted to a congressional hearing in 1971 that most died in combat. But other witnesses testified as to the murderous and vengeful nature of the campaign and the prevalence of assassination and torture. At all events, the Viet Cong's rural structure was gravely disrupted. Since the end of the war, many top Communist figures in Vietnam have conceded that the period of Phoenix was the worst for them. One senior officer, Colonel Bui Tin, was quoted as calling it a "devious and cruel" operation that cost "the loss of thousands of our cadres." The betrayal of their tunnel bases compelled the remaining guerrillas and the North Vietnamese army to withdraw increasingly to sanctuaries over the border in Cambodia to await the U.S. Army's departure. In the spring of 1970, American and ARVN troops made a short but disruptive incursion into Communist base areas in neutral Cambodia, forcing the NVA back farther for a while.

By late 1971 Phoenix was doing serious damage. A particularly valuable Hoi Chanh was Nguyen Van Tung, the Communist village secretary at An Tinh, in the district adjoining Cu Chi. He had ordered the execution for rape of a young guerrilla who turned out to be the nephew of a high-ranking Communist official. Fearful of revenge, he turned himself in to the ARVN. His debriefings led to the arrest of over three hundred Communist sympathizers, and the compromising of numerous tunnel bases. Among them was the secret headquarters at An Tinh of the F-100 commandos. This was overrun in an ARVN operation following an artillery barrage. A Hoi Chanh guided the ARVN through the mines to the tunnels. All the guerrillas found there were either killed or captured. Among the captured documents were scrapbooks of press cuttings on F-100 "victories"—bombings in Saigon—and a notebook listing more than sixty agents in Saigon with their cover names, addresses, and instructions for secret meetings or message drops; all the agents were leading legal lives. These names were passed to the Special Branch in Saigon, who arrested fifty, but failed to find the battalion's chief of operations, a twenty-year-old girl called Nguyen Thi Kieu. She survived and was later acclaimed a revolutionary heroine. But the sapper team was finished. For the remainder of the war, there were no more major acts of sabotage in Saigon—largely because it was no longer possible to maintain guerrilla bases in the tunnels.

But the most decisive blow against the tunnels came from the air. On 31 October 1968, President Johnson had ordered an end to the bombing of North Vietnam as a gesture to hasten the convening of peace talks in Paris. Strategic Boeing B-52s, adapted to carry over a hundred "iron" bombs each, had long been flying missions from their bases at Andersen Air Force Base on Guam and U-Tapao, Thailand. These huge, high-flying aircraft never saw their targets; they were guided in and their bombing was directed by ground radar up to two hundred miles away. They were not allowed to bomb within a three-kilometer radius of error next to friendly forces. After the bombing halt in the North, they were more available to ground commanders in South Vietnam. The generals decided to use the bombers to saturate the free strike zones with 750- and 500-pound high-explosive bombs.

The bombs were dropped in sticks that left a mile-long swath of total devastation. The landscape erupted with a string of explosions. Tons of earth—along with trees, buildings, and human bodies—cascaded into the air. A B-52 strike could be seen, heard, and felt for twenty miles: a thunderous symphony of destruction that shook the face of the earth and left it permanently scarred. In Cu Chi and the Iron Triangle there was, by 1969, little vegetation left and few people; only a handful of guerrillas hung on in conditions of extreme privation in the tunnels. For them, the most destructive of the B-52s' bombs were those fused to explode, not in the air on impact, but after they had penetrated several feet into the ground. The explosion from one of these created a local earthquake that collapsed the sturdiest of tunnel walls. The resulting craters, which still deface the landscape, were up to thirty feet deep—huge pits that sliced into the tunnel system, making it unusable and irreparable. "A five-meter hole could be sufficient to destroy a tunnel," said Major Nguyen Quot. "B-52 bombs made holes twelve meters deep." Air holes were blocked by debris. When the tunnel system was blocked in several places, air could no longer circulate and the inmates suffocated. Carpet bombing by B-52s gradually succeeded where the CS gas and demolition charges of the tunnel rats had failed—denying the use of the tunnels to the Viet Cong.

But this military success came too late to affect the outcome of the conflict. The long, indecisive war of attrition, the shock of Tet 1968, and the war's deep unpopularity at home had already undone America's resolve in Vietnam.

The Viet Cong guerrillas were decimated in the unequal battle, but the huge regular army of North Vietnam was in place to carry the war forward. In December 1970 the Lao Dong party central committee in Hanoi formally decided to abandon the insurgency and resort only to large formation warfare. The guerrilla war had effectively been lost. Asian scholar Chalmers Johnson wrote in 1973: "Vo Nguyen Giap himself has admitted a loss of 600,000 men in fighting between 1965 and 1968 . . . Moreover, by about 1970 at least 80 percent of the day-to-day combat in South Vietnam was being carried on by regular People's Army of Vietnam (NVA) troops . . . Genuine black-pajama Southern guerrillas . . . amounted to no more than 20 percent of the Communist fighting force." The spring invasion of 1972 was by North Vietnamese troops with tanks and artillery; compared with Tet 1968, four years earlier, there was practically no guerrilla activity.

But by 1972, U.S. ground forces had been withdrawn, unit by unit, from Vietnam. President Nixon stepped up military aid to the South Vietnamese to compensate; it became the ARVN's war. By the end of 1970, most of the Tropic Lightning Division had returned to Hawaii and handed Cu Chi base over to the 25th ARVN Division, formerly based at nearby Duc Hoa. The ARVN's 25th had a poor reputation among American officers for avoiding combat at all costs and for doing deals with the Viet Cong. In 1967 more of its soldiers had died in traffic accidents than in combat; one U.S. general said the division had "turned its back on the war." For a year senior Americans lobbied for the removal of the 25th commander, General Phan Trong Chinh, who was eventually sent on "sick leave" in January 1968. His division was supposedly protecting Saigon's western flank during Tet 1968. In the succeeding years there was little improvement. General Tran Quoc Lich, appointed to command the 25th by President Thieu, was sacked in 1974 for selling rice to the Viet Cong. The selling of food, military equipment, and deferments from duty made the division combat-ineffective and unable to field a fighting force. By the war's climax in 1975, the 25th had been out of action for a year, its commander in jail on corruption charges.

The cease-fire agreement signed by Henry Kissinger and Le Duc Tho in Paris in January 1973 enabled the United States honorably to disengage from the war but left the Communists in complete control of large parts of South Vietnam. Three hundred thousand North Vietnamese troops were allowed to remain there. Following the Tet offensive, the ARVN had receded to defend the cities and a few outposts, abandoning the countryside. The NVA consolidated its military presence. When fighting began again in 1973—as it shortly did—the Communists made progressive territorial gains. There were periodic battles between the strengthened and rearmed NVA and a demoralized ARVN throughout 1974. The North Vietnamese began their final offensive that December. Moving from the highlands to the coastal plain, and then down to the piedmont, the North Vietnamese troops surrounded Saigon with a rapidity that surprised even themselves. In April 1975 they were poised to take the city.

The devastated Iron Triangle still had a role to play. Just before the final assault on Saigon, Generals Van Tien Dung (in overall command) and Tran Van Tra moved their forward headquarters from the security of long-"liberated" Loc Ninh to what remained of the tunnel base in Ben Cat district, where Mai Chi Tho had planned the Tet offensive on Saigon in 1967. It was, said Van Tien Dung in his account of the collapse of South Vietnam, "an old base of one of our special action units from Saigon, northwest of Ben Cat. From this base our special action forces had over the years organized many attacks into Saigon, causing heavy casualties to the Americans and their valets." Two days later two other senior North Vietnamese showed up there, unable to stay away from the action. They were COSVN secretary and politburo member Pham Hung, and Le Duc Tho, politburo member, signatory of the 1973 cease-fire agreement, and Mai Chi Tho's brother. When Vietnam's thirty-year war for independence came to its ignominious end, as the tanks converged on Saigon's presidential palace, the generals and politicians who commanded them received the good news, appropriately, at a former tunnel base in the most fought-over cockpit of the long struggle.

22

Hindsight

The Tunnels of Cu Chi have become for the Vietnamese Communists a symbol of their tenacity and endurance during the war against the Americans from 1965 to 1973. "Resistance," wrote von Clausewitz, the early-nineteenth-century military theorist, "is a form of action aimed at destroying enough of the enemy's power to force him to renounce his intentions." Such was the achievement of the Viet Cong. Colonel Harry Summers, a contemporary American analyst of his country's Vietnam failure, wrote that the Communists' objective in South Vietnam was "to wear us down"; he went on: "They were able to accomplish this with an economy of force effort—Viet Cong guerrillas supplied and augmented by selected North Vietnamese regular units." The American military was fought to a stalemate by an enemy who made up in psychology and cunning what he lacked in aircraft and tanks. In order to fight that enemy in his own redoubts, the Americans had to invent a military skill that was so—literally—down-to-earth that its successes were due not to advanced weapons or firepower, but to simple courage in the face of the most ancient and primeval fear, following the quarry into the unknown darkness of his lair.

G. K. Chesterton wrote that "courage is almost a contradiction in terms: it means a strong desire to live taking the form of a readiness to die." Few of the tunnel guerrillas survived the war. The Viet Cong can honestly claim the victory, but it was North Vietnam that took the glory, and the power. And when the American tunnel rats came marching home, their stories and courage, too, were ignored, and then swamped by the postwar trauma and recriminations that racked America.

It was the neutral earth itself that was lavishly honored, as the tunnels themselves began to yield to the forces of time and nature, finishing what the B-52s' bombs had begun. The entire district was formally awarded the title "The Iron Land of Cu Chi," Hanoi's echo of the grudging admiration in the original Western soubriquet for the Iron Triangle.

The former underground headquarters at Phu My Hung are being maintained as a memorial to the tunnel war. The old conference chambers and twisting communication tunnels have been carefully preserved. Today it is a quiet place. There is a caretaker who keeps things tidy. There is a visitors' book containing polite expressions of amazement from Communist delegations. Those who attempt to find out for themselves what it was like to exist in the tunnels, and make a short journey through, soon succumb to claustrophobia or the legions of ants and mosquitoes who have become the new guardians. In the hamlets of Cu Chi district, the remnants of the tunnels are dying of neglect. Entrances decay and holes crumble as the nation turns its attention to new campaigns against new enemies. The young cannot believe Vietnam will ever fight on its own soil again; the old are not so confident.

History, so often the propaganda of the victors, can now record the truth about those tunnels. The survivors on both sides speak with open respect about their former adversaries. As with most wars, hatred fades. What is remembered is how the weak outfaced the strong, and how both discovered new springs of courage and endurance—a lasting inspiration from a painful war.

SOURCES

Since almost every page of this book refers to one or other of the many sources used to assemble the story, we decided against numbered footnotes or annotations. Instead, we have listed below, first, the names of all those whom we interviewed personally, in the United States, Vietnam, and elsewhere. Transcripts or translations of all those interviews have been kept. Second, we have listed by chapter the most important and relevant documents we acquired and have on file. Many were declassified at our request and are quoted for the first time. And third, there is a list of the books that we found the most helpful and informative.

Personal interviews

In the United States:

Those who served in Vietnam with the 1st Infantry Division:
- Robert F. Batten
- Lieutenant General William E. Depuy
- Major Randy Ellis
- Jack R. Flowers
- Arnold Gutierrez
- Al Hylton
- Bernard Justen

Richard Keogh
Colonel Jim Leonard
Pedro A. Rejo-Ruiz
Lieutenant Colonel Jerry Sinn
Lieutenant Colonel David E. Sullivan
Rick Swofford
Herbert Thornton
Terry Valentine
Walter D. Wadsworth
William G. Wilson
Theodore Wood

Those who served in Vietnam with the 25th Infantry Division:
Lieutenant Colonel John Adams
Robert Baer
Lieutenant Colonel James Bushong
John C. Fairbank
Larry Larochelle
Gilbert Lindsay
Harley J. Mooney
Lieutenant Colonel James Muir
Major Jack Pryor
Harold Roper
Thomas A. Ware
General Fred C. Weyand
Major General Ellis W. Williamson

Those who served in Vietnam with the 196th Light Infantry Brigade
Lieutenant General Richard T. Knowles
William H. Pelfrey

Those who served in MACV intelligence roles:
Dr Bruce A. Mazat
Jan R. Shrader

Others:
Al Chang, journalist
Macdonald Valentine, former Vietnamese Ranger

In Australia:
Those who served in Vietnam with the Royal Australian Engineers:
Major Denis Ayoub
Christopher Carroll
Graeme Clarke
Les Colmer

Jim Duffield
Colonel Alex MacGregor MC
Bill Unmeopa

In the United Kingdom:
Colonel Robert Scott L/RAMC
Brigadier Sir Robert Thompson KCB CMG DSO MC

In France:
Wilfred Burchett

In Vietnam:

Military officers based in Ho Chi Minh City who fought in Cu Chi district during the war:
Colonel Do Tan Phong, former F-100 guerrilla
Lieutenant Colonel Duong Long Sang
Colonel Huynh Cong Cuoc, former Dac Cong
Major Nguyen Duc Y, former Dac Cong
Lieutenant Colonel Nguyen Phuong Nam
Major Nguyen Quot
Captain Nguyen Thanh Linh, former commander of Cu Chi guerrillas
Lieutenant Colonel Phan Van Tan, former Dac Cong
Major Tran Duc Tho

Military officers based in Ho Chi Minh City who fought in the Iron Triangle during the war:
Lieutenant Colonel Do Chieu Hau
Colonel Nguyen Quang Minh, chief military historian
Colonel Dr Vo Hoang Le
Captain Vo Minh

Civilians living in Ho Chi Minh City:
Mai Chi Tho, Party Chairman
Mai Van Tho, writer
Pham Sang, former entertainer
Vien Phuong, writer

Officials of Cu Chi district:
Bay Lap, theater director
Dr Hoang Minh Duc, director of Cu Chi hospital
Lieutenant Colonel Pham Thanh Tan, district chief
Dr Vo Van Chuyen, Cu Chi hospital

Former guerrillas in Cu Chi district:
- Do Van Chot, Nhuan Duc village
- Duong Long Quan, Phuoc Hiep village
- Le Van Nong, An Nhon Tay village
- Luong Huu Thi, Phu My Hung village
- Major Nam Thuan, Phu My Hung village
- Nguyen Van Anh, Nhuan Duc village
- Nguyen Van Tho, Phuoc Hiep village
- Pham Van Nhanh, Trung Lap village
- Mrs Vo Thi Mo
- Vo Van Duc, Nhuan Duc village

Villagers in Cu Chi district:
- Mrs Dang Th Lanh
- Ho Van Nien, Tan Thong Hoi village
- Mrs Huynh Thi Bia, sister of the late Huynh Van Co
- Mrs Le Thi Tieu, Tan Thong Hoi village
- Mrs Nguyen Thi Yen Chau, Phuoc Hiep village
- Mrs Tran Thi Day, Tan Thong Hoi village
- Mrs Truong Thi Thuc, Phu My Hung village

Officials of Song Be Province (which covers the Iron Triangle):
- Ho Trung Hieu
- Huynh Van Thu
- Captain Nguyen Huu Tan
- Colonel Tran Van Chau
- Tran Van Kha

Former guerrillas of the Iron Triangle:
- Huynh Van Minh, Phu An village
- Huynh Van Moi, An Dien village
- Nguyen Minh Chanh, Ben Suc village
- Pham Van Chinh, Ben Suc village

Villagers of the Iron Triangle:
- Mrs Nguyen Tha Trang, Ben Suc village
- Mrs Tran Thi Quit, Ben Suc village

Documents listed by chapters:

Most of the MACV and U.S. Army records of the Vietnam War fron which we have quoted are at the Washington National Records Center Suitland, Maryland. Others are held in the archives of military or ganizations, such as the Office of the Chief of Engineers, Fort Belvoir

Virginia, and other individual divisional headquarters. Some are held privately by people interviewed for this book.

Chapter 3: Operation Crimp

Combat Operations After-Action Reports (MACV/RCS/J3/32):
3rd Brigade, 1st Infantry Div., dated 15 February 1966 (Crimp) and 3 March 1966 (Buckskin);
HQ 173rd Airborne Brigade, dated 23 February 1966.
173rd Airborne Brigade: Commander's Combat Note No. 91—Operation Crimp, dated 22 January 1966.
173rd Airborne Brigade: Operations Report Lessons Learned 1–66, Operation Crimp, dated 22 March 1966.
After-Action Report of Royal Australian Engineers.

Chapter 5: The Tunnels

Captured Viet Cong documents translated by the Combined Document Exploitation Center:
Tunnels Manual, captured 28 September 1967 (Log no. 09–2421–67); "Techniques of Constructing and Camouflaging Underground Tunnels" (Log no. 01–1749–68); and many other captured VC documents.
Prisoner interrogation reports form the Combined Military Interrogation Center:

Captive Nguyen Truong Nghi (alias Tam Nghi and Nguyen Viet), CMIC No. 1389, dated 17 August 1967;
Captive Ngo Van Giang (alias Ba Van), CMIC No. 1890, dated 12 March 1968;
Captive Do Xuan Pho, CMIC No. A-917, dated 25 March 1967;
Captive Nguyen Van Binh, CMIC No. A-963, dated 1 April 1968.

Chapter 8: The Tunnel Rats

ARVN briefing on "Experiences Gained from Operations against Viet Cong Subterranean Warfare," given at the Gia Long Palace on 20 September 1963 (translation is MACV doc. no. 01290).
MACV: Lessons Learned No. 56: "Operations Against Tunnel Complexes," dated 18 April 1966.
U.S. Army Weekly Combat Intelligence & Security Review, 6 February 1968, pp. 20–31, "The Enemy Below."

Chapter 9: Not Worth a Rat's Ass

Army Concept Team in Vietnam: Evaluation of Tunnel Exploration Kit, dated 6 January 1967.
Army Concept Team in Vietnam: Final Report—Tunnel Weapon, dated 12 January 1970.

Chapter 10: Stop the Americans!

ARVN booklet (7610–66–024–0789): English edition, "Mines and Booby Traps Used by the Viet Cong in South Vietnam," dated November, 1965.
Combat After-Action Report of the 196th Light Infantry Brigade, dated 5 October 1966.
Secret communication from COMUSMACV to Dept. of the Army (No. 09903): Subject, VC use of rats, dated 24 March 1967.
Handbook for US Forces in Vietnam, December 1968.

Chapter 12: Cu Chi Base

Extensive references to the files of the *Tropic Lightning News*.

Chapter 14: Operation Cedar Falls

Oplan 58–66 (Operational Plan for Cedar Falls), HQ II Field Force Vietnam, Long Binh, dated 12 December 1966.
Combat Operation After-Action Reports (RCS: MACV-J3-32):
II Field Force Vietnam (undated);
3rd Brigade, 1st Infantry Division, dated 10 February 1967;
2nd Brigade, 25th Infantry Division, dated 16 February 1967;
173rd Airborne Brigade, dated 25 February 1967;
1st Engineer Battalion, dated 2 March 1967;
25th Infantry Division Quarterly Operational Report (RCS CSFOR-65) ending 31 January 1967, dated 20 February 1967.

Chapter 15: Dr Vo Hoang Le—Tunnel Surgeon

Col. Robert Scott of the British Royal Army Medical Corps advised on this chapter.

"Report on the Medical Services in MR IV," by Dr Vo Hoang Le, dated 1 October 1967, captured on 14 October 1967 and translated by the Combined Document Exploitation Center (Log no. 10–1708–67).
"Medical Causes of Non-effectiveness among VC/NVA Troops," is-

sued by the Combined Intelligence Center, Vietnam: ST 67–084 (17 November 1967) and ST 69–11 (31 July 1969).
Combat After-Action Report of the 3rd Brigade, 1st Infantry Division, dated 10 February 1967.

Chapter 16: Psychological Operations

After-Action Report of the 248th Psychological Operations Company, dated 23 January 1967.
PSYOP Policy, booklet issued by JUSPAO on 18 December 1968.

Chapter 17: Fighting Science

Joint Thai-U.S. Combat Development Test Center: Evaluation of Tunnel Detection Probe, dated July 1963.
USMACV Operations Report, Lessons Learned 9–66, dated 22 November 1965: "Employment of the Mity [sic] Mite Portable Blower."
U.S. Army Report, 1966: "The Employment of Acetylene in the Destruction of Viet Cong Tunnels."
Army Concept Team in Vietnam: Evaluation Report of Large Capacity Tunnel Flushers, dated 25 November 1966.
Telex from the Pentagon to U.S. Army HQ Tan Son Nhut about CS gas, dated 13 January 1967.
Telex from U.S. Army HQ Tan Son Nhut to the Pentagon requesting Large Capacity Tunnel Flushers, dated 6 February 1967.
HQ U.S. Army Vietnam: Combat Lessons Bulletin No. 5, dated 8 February 1967: "Engineer Operations in the Iron Triangle."
White House Fact Sheet on Tunnel Denial, dated 30 March 1967.
Telex from the Pentagon to U.S. Army HQ Long Binh requesting the testing of Seismic Tunnel Detectors, dated 14 March 1968.
Army Concept Team in Vietnam: Field Evaluation of Seismic Tunnel Detector, dated 14 June 1968.
Debriefing Report of Major General Charles M. Duke, commander of U.S. Army Engineer Command Vietnam, to the Chief of Engineers, dated 20 June 1968.
1st Engineer Battalion Tunnel Rat After-Action Report, dated 11 October 1968, describing liquid explosive test.
MACV brochure: "Hole Huntin'—Techniques to Detect, Neutralize and Destroy Enemy Tunnels in Vietnam," by Major Ben G. Crosby, dated 20 December 1968.
Army Concept Team in Vietnam: Evaluation of Tunnel/Cache Detector—Portable Differential Magnetometer, dated 21 August 1970.

Chapter 18: Rat Six and Batman

Citation for award of Army Commendation Medal for action on 8 February 1969 to 1st Lt Jack R. Flowers, dated 7 April 1969.
Citation for award of Bronze Star for action on 26 March 1969 to 1st Lt Jack R. Flowers, dated 1 June 1969.
1st Engineer Battalion: Unit Historical Reports for 1967 (24 March 1968) and 1968 (4 January 1969); Quarterly Evaluation Reports, 31 March & 20 June 1969.
Tunnel Rat After-Action Reports: 26 July, 27 July, 9 November 1968; 10 April, 20 April, 21 July, 22 July, 1 August, 17 August 1969.

Chapter 20: Rat Squad

1st Engineer Battalion: Quarterly Evaluation Report, 15 December 1969; Tunnel Rat After-Action Reports: 20 September, 14 October, 15 October, 20 October, 18 December 1969; 2 February 1970.

Books consulted:

Allen, George N. *Ri*. Englewood Cliffs, N.J.: Prentice-Hall, 1978.
Baker, Mark. *Nam*. New York: William Morrow, 1981.
Bonds, Ray, ed. *The Vietnam War*. New York: Crown, 1979.
Burchett, Wilfred. *Vietnam—Inside Story of a Guerrilla War*. New York: International Publishers, 1965.
——. *Vietnam Will Win!* New York: Guardian Books, 1968.
——. *Grasshoppers & Elephants*. New York: Urizen Books, 1977.
——. *Catapult to Freedom*. London: Quartet, 1978.
Cincinattus. *Self-Destruction*. New York: W. W. Norton, 1981.
Dawson, Alan. *55 Days—the Fall of South Vietnam*. Bangkok: Phimphilai Press, 1977.
Ewell, Lt Gen Julian J., and Hunt, Maj Gen Ira A. *Sharpening the Combat Edge*. Washington, D.C.: Dept. of the Army, 1974.
First Infantry Division in Vietnam: Yearbooks. Vol. I (July 1965–April 1967); Vol. II (May 1967–December 1968).
FitzGerald, Frances. *Fire in the Lake*. Boston: Little, Brown, 1972.
Garland, Albert N., ed. *Infantry in Vietnam*. Nashville: Battery Press, 1967.
Hay, Lt Gen John H. *Tactical and Matériel Innovations*. Washington, D.C.: Dept. of the Army, 1974.
Henderson, William Darryl. *Why the Vietcong Fought*. Westport, Conn.: Greenwood Press, 1979.
Herrington, Stuart A. *Silence was a Weapon*. Novato, Calif.: Presidio Press. 1982.

Hodgkin, Thomas. *Vietnam—the Revolutionary Path*. London: Macmillan, 1981.
Hope, Bob. *The Last Christmas Show*. Garden City, N.Y.: Doubleday, 1974.
Infantry Magazine, ed. *A Distant Challenge—the US Infantryman in Vietnam*. Nashville: Battery Press, 1983.
Johnson, Chalmers. *Autopsy on People's War*. Berkeley: Univ. of California Press, 1972.
Karnow, Stanley. *Vietnam—a History*. New York: Viking Press, 1983.
Klare, Michael T. *War Without End*. New York: Random House, 1970.
Le Gro, Col William E. *Vietnam from Cease-fire to Capitulation*. Washington, D.C.: U.S. Army Center for Military History, 1981.
Lulling, Darrel R. *Communist Militaria of the Vietnam War*. Tulsa, Okla: MCN Press, 1980.
McChristian, Maj Gen Joseph A. *The Role of Military Intelligence 1965–1967*. Washington, D.C.: Dept. of the Army, 1974.
Mackay, Ian. *Australians in Vietnam*. Adelaide: Rigby, 1968.
Maclear, Michael. *The Ten Thousand Day War*. New York: St Martin's Press, 1981.
Marshall, S. L. A. *Ambush*. Nashville: Battery Press, 1969.
Neel, Maj Gen Spurgeon. *Medical Support of the U.S. Army in Vietnam*. Washington, D.C.: Dept. of the Army, 1974.
Nguyen Khac Vien, ed. *Face to Face with U.S. Armed Forces*. Hanoi: Vietnamese Studies.
Nguyen Khac Vien, ed. *Sud Vietnam du FNL au Gouvernement Révolutionnaire Provisoire* (South Vietnam from the National Liberation Front to the Provisional Revolutionary Government). Hanoi: Vietnamese Studies.
Nguyen Khac Vien, ed. *L'Année 1968* (The Year 1968). Hanoi: Vietnamese Studies.
O'Ballance, Edgar. *The Wars in Vietnam 1954–1980*. New York: Hippocrene Books, 1975.
Oberdorfer, Don. *Tet!* Garden City, N.Y.: Doubleday, 1971.
173rd Airborne Brigade Vietnam Yearbook
196th Light Infantry Brigade Vietnam Yearbook
Palmer, Dave Richard. *Summons of the Trumpet*. San Rafael, Calif.: Presidio Press, 1978.
Pham Cuong. *Cu Chi—Terre de Feu* (Cu Chi, Land of Fire). Hanoi: Foreign Languages Publishing House, 1982.
Pike, Douglas. *Viet Cong*. Boston: M.I.T. Press, 1966.
Ploger, Maj Gen Robert R. *U.S. Army Engineers 1965–1970*. Washington, D.C.: Dept. of the Army, 1974.
Porter, Gareth, ed. *Vietnam—a History in Documents*. New York: New American Library, 1979.

Race, Jeffrey. *War Comes to Long An*. Berkeley: Univ. of California Press, 1972.

Rogers, General Bernard. *Cedar Falls—Junction City: a Turning Point*. Washington, D.C.: Dept. of the Army, 1974.

Santoli, Al. *Everything We Had*. New York: Random House, 1981.

Schell, Jonathan. *The Village of Ben Suc*. New York: Alfred A. Knopf, 1967.

Snepp, Frank. *Decent Interval*. New York: Random House, 1977.

Stanton, Shelby L. *Vietnam Order of Battle*. Washington, D.C.: U.S. News Books, 1981.

Summers, Harry G. *On Strategy*. Novato, Calif.: Presidio Press, 1982.

Taber, Robert. *The War of the Flea*. London: Paladin, 1965.

Tran Van Tra, General. *Concluding the Thirty-Year War*. Ho Chi Minh City, 1982.

25th Infantry Division Vietnam Yearbook.

Van Tien Dung, General. *Our Great Spring Victory*. New York: Monthly Review Press, 1977.

Vien Phuong, *To Van Duc the Inventor of Twig-triggered Mines*. South Vietnam: Liberation Publishing House, 1970.

Von Clausewitz, Carl. *On War*. 1832.

Walthall, Melvin C. *Lightning Forward—a History of the 25th Infantry Division*. 25th Infantry Division Association, 1978.

Westmoreland, General William C. *A Soldier Reports*. Garden City, N.Y.: Doubleday, 1976.

CHRONOLOGY OF MAIN EVENTS IN THE VIETNAM WARS

1945	2 Sept	Communist-led Viet Minh under Ho Chi Minh seize power in Hanoi and proclaim independent Vietnam.
	22 Sept	Return of French forces to Vietnam.
1946	19 Dec	Viet Minh initiate 8-year Indochina war against the French.
1950	26 June	Start of the Korean War.
1953	27 July	Armistice in Korea.
1954	7 May	French surrender to Viet Minh army at Dien Bien Phu.
	20 July	Geneva Accords divide Vietnam into North and South, with capitals in Hanoi and Saigon.
1955	26 Oct	Ngo Dinh Diem becomes president of South Vietnam, and cancels the elections agreed at Geneva.
1959	May	North Vietnam begins infiltration of personnel and weapons to the South via the Ho Chi Minh trail through Laos and Cambodia.
		Arrival of first U.S. military advisers in South Vietnam.
	Oct	President Diem promulgates the law suppressing Communists and former Viet Minh.
1960	8 Nov	John F. Kennedy elected President of the United States, pledges support for Diem.

	20 Dec	Formation of the National Liberation Front of South Vietnam (the Viet Cong) and resumption of guerrilla war; tunnel construction restarted in Cu Chi district and elsewhere.
1962	8 Feb	U.S. Military Assistance Command Vietnam (MACV) set up in Saigon.
	30 Feb	Start of strategic hamlet program in South Vietnam.
1963	2 Jan	Defeat of South Vietnamese army (ARVN) by Viet Cong at Ap Bac.
	April	Inception of Chieu Hoi amnesty program for Viet Cong.
	1 Nov	President Diem murdered in a military coup in Saigon.
	22 Nov	President Kennedy assassinated; Lyndon Johnson takes over.
1964	20 June	General William Westmoreland assumes command of MACV.
	Nov	Abortive ARVN operation in the Iron Triangle.
1965	25 Feb	Start of U.S. bombing of North Vietnam.
	8 Mar	Arrival of first U.S. combat troops at Da Nang.
	5 May	Arrival of U.S. 173rd Airborne Brigade and first Australian troops.
	27 June	173rd Airborne sweeps the Iron Triangle.
	Oct–Nov	Battle of the Ia Drang valley in the central highlands.
	Oct	Arrival of the U.S. 1st Infantry Division (Big Red One) at Bien Hoa Air Base.
1966	Jan	Operation Crimp in Cu Chi district, followed by Operation Buckskin in the same area.
	12 Jan	Lt. Col. George S. Eyster mortally wounded.
	Feb	1st Infantry Division moves to Di An base camp.
	March	U.S. 25th Infantry Division (Tropic Lightning) arrives at Cu Chi
	Sept	Operation Attleboro in War Zone C, Tay Ninh province.
1967	7–26 Jan	Operation Cedar Falls in the Iron Triangle and Cu Chi district.
	Feb	1st Infantry Division establishes Lai Khe base camp.
	Feb–Apr	Operation Junction City in War Zone C.
	6 July	Death in Hanoi of General Nguyen Chi Thanh, Communist commander in the South.
	3 Sept	General Nguyen Van Thieu elected president of South Vietnam.

1968	31 Jan	Nationwide Tet offensive by Viet Cong in Saigon and other towns, followed by sieges at Hue and Khe Sanh.
	16 Mar	My Lai massacre.
	31 Mar	President Johnson announces partial bombing halt, and says he will not run for reelection.
	4 May	More Viet Cong attacks—"mini-Tet."
	May	Preliminary peace talks begin in Paris.
	June	General Creighton Abrams takes over from Westmoreland.
	30 Sept	U.S. strength in Vietnam 537,800—the highest level.
	31 Oct	President Johnson halts the bombing of North Vietnam.
	5 Nov	Richard Nixon elected President and promises U.S. troop withdrawal and the Vietnamization of the war.
1969	26 Feb	Viet Cong raid on Cu Chi base camp destroys Chinook helicopters.
	10 June	Formation of Viet Cong Provisional Revolutionary Government.
	3 Sept	Ho Chi Minh dies in Hanoi.
1970	27 Mar	U.S. incursion into Cambodia.
	15 April	U.S. 1st Infantry Division leaves Vietnam.
	Dec	U.S. 25th Infantry Division leaves Vietnam; Cu Chi base taken over by the ARVN 25th Division.
1971	18 Aug	Pull-out of last Australian and New Zealand troops.
1972	21 Feb	President Nixon visits China.
	30 Mar	North Vietnamese Easter offensive on the South.
	12 Aug	Last U.S. ground troops leave.
1973	27 Jan	Cease-fire agreement signed in Paris by Henry Kissinger and Le Duc Tho.
1974	9 Aug	President Nixon resigns.
1975	30 April	Fall of Saigon to North Vietnamese troops.
1976	2 July	Proclamation of unified Socialist Republic of Vietnam; Saigon renamed Ho Chi Minh City.

GLOSSARY

AAR	After-action report
ADSID	Air-delivered seismic intruder-detection device; microphone and transmitter dropped into suspect areas
AK-47	Russian-designed Kalashnikov 7.62 mm automatic rifle used by Communist troops
APC	Armored personnel carrier
ARVN (Arvin)	The South Vietnamese army (Army of the Republic of Vietnam)
B-52	Strategic high-altitude bomber converted for conventional bombing over Vietnam
Big Red One	The U.S. 1st Infantry Division
C-rations	Combat rations
Cedar Falls	Search-and-destroy operation mounted in the Iron Triangle and Cu Chi district in January 1967
Charlie	Short for "Victor Charlie," meaning VC or Viet Cong
Chieu Hoi	Amnesty program enabling VC to defect with safety to the South Vietnamese government side
Chinook	CH-47 cargo helicopter
Chopper	Helicopter
CIA	U.S. Central Intelligence Agency

Claymore	Antipersonnel mine that propels shrapnel in a fan-shaped pattern
Cobra	AH-1G attack helicopter
Commo wire	Communications wire
COSVN	Central Office for South Vietnam: Communist HQ in the South
Crimp	Search-and-destroy operation mounted in Cu Chi district in January 1966, followed immediately by Operation Buckskin
CS	A riot-control gas
Dac Cong	Viet Cong special forces
DEROS	Date eligible for return from overseas: the end of a GI's tour in Vietnam
Det-cord	Detonating cord used with explosives
DH-5, DH-10	Viet Cong claymore (q.v.) mines
DMZ	The demilitarized zone between North and South Vietnam
Dust-off	Medical evacuation by helicopter
Fire base	Remote artillery base
Frag	Murder of officers or NCOs by enlisted men; derived from the use of fragmentation grenades
Free strike zone	Area where everybody was deemed hostile and a legitimate target by U.S. forces
Green Berets	U.S. Special Forces
Grunt	A U.S. infantryman
Gung ho	Enthusiastic
Gunship	Armed helicopter
GVN	The government of South Vietnam
H&I	Harassment and interdiction, meaning random artillery fire
Hoi Chanh	Defector under the Chieu Hoi program
Iron Triangle	VC-dominated area between the Thi Tinh and Saigon rivers, next to Cu Chi district
Kit Carson scouts	Former Viet Cong acting as guides for U.S. units
Lao Dong party	The Vietnamese Workers' (i.e., Communist) party
M-16	U.S. 5.56 mm infantry rifle
M-60	U.S. 7.62 mm machine gun
MACV (Macvee)	U.S. Military Assistance Command in Vietnam
MEDCAP	Medical civil action program—free treatment for villagers by U.S. and ARVN medics
Medevac	Medical evacuation by helicopter
Mighty mite	Commercial air blower used for injecting gas into tunnels

MR IV	Viet Cong military region surrounding and including Saigon
NCO	Noncommissioned officer
NLF	The National Liberation Front of South Vietnam
NVA	The North Vietnamese army
OJT	On-the-job training
Phoenix	Intelligence-based campaign to eliminate the Viet Cong infrastructure
Point	The leading man on a patrol or tunnel exploration mission
PSYOPS	Psychological operations
Punji stake	Sharpened bamboo used in primitive booby trap
R&R	Rest and recreation
Rallier	Defector from the Viet Cong
Rome plow	Specially designed bulldozer blade for landclearing
Slick	Helicopter
SOP	Standard operating procedure
SP4, SP5, etc.	U.S. Army noncommissioned ranks
Spider hole	VC firing position at tunnel opening
Tet	Vietnamese lunar new year festival, celebrated as a national holiday
III Corps Tactical Zone	ARVN military region: the land between the Mekong Delta and the central highlands of South Vietnam
Tropic Lightning	The U.S. 25th Infantry Division

INDEX